M000304833

Novels in the Time of Democratic Writing

The American Example

Nancy Armstrong and
Leonard Tennenhouse

PENN

UNIVERSITY OF PENNSYLVANIA PRESS

PHILADELPHIA

Haney Foundation Series

A volume in the Haney Foundation Series, established in
1961 with the generous support of Dr. John Louis Haney

Copyright © 2018 University of Pennsylvania Press

All rights reserved. Except for brief quotations used for
purposes of review or scholarly citation, none of this book
may be reproduced in any form by any means without
written permission from the publisher.

Published by
University of Pennsylvania Press
Philadelphia, Pennsylvania 19104-4112
www.upenn.edu/pennpress

Printed in the United States of America on acid-free paper
10 9 8 7 6 5 4 3 2 1

Library of Congress Cataloging-in-Publication Data
Names: Armstrong, Nancy, 1938– author. | Tennenhouse, Leonard,
1942– author.
Title: Novels in the time of democratic writing : the American example /
Nancy Armstrong and Leonard Tennenhouse.
Other titles: Haney Foundation series.
Description: 1st edition. | Philadelphia : University of Pennsylvania
Press, [2018] | Series: Haney Foundation series | Includes
bibliographical references and index.
Identifiers: LCCN 2017032703 | ISBN 9780812249767 (hardcover : alk.
paper)
Subjects: LCSH: American fiction—18th century—History and
criticism. | American fiction—19th century—History and criticism. |
Democracy in literature. | Comparative literature—American and
English. | Comparative literature—English and American. |
Nationalism and literature—United States—History—18th century. |
Nationalism and literature—United States—History—19th century.
Classification: LCC PS375 .A76 2018 | DDC 813/.209—dc23
LC record available at https://lccn.loc.gov/2017032703

For Ellen Rooney and Khachig Tölölyan

Contents

Introduction

Argumentum ad Populum

We are in the epoch of simultaneity: we are in the epoch of juxta-
position, the epoch of the near and far, the epoch of the side-by-side.
We are at a moment, I believe, when our experience of the world is
less that of a long life developing through time than that of a network that connects points and intersects with its own skein.

—Michel Foucault, 1967

Foucault's reading of the cultural environment in which he found himself in
1967 anticipates the very system of social relations in which the most interesting twenty-first-century novels invite a global readership to take part. If this
passage did not exactly leap off the page on our first reading, it has certainly
captured our attention now, at a time when traditional households and national governments are conspicuously failing to distribute natural resources,
goods, services, and information to the populations they are meant to serve.
Where Foucault's shift in perspective registers a definitive break from the past,
we have come to understand that his sense that something unprecedented has
happened is not a new one, even though the infrastructure in which our lives
are now caught up is of greater magnitude than ever before. We are convinced
that so long as there have been novels, there have also been readers who can
imagine human experience from either near or far, either "as a long life developing in time" or as "a network that connects points and intersects with its
own skein." As novel readers, we have always been both local and global, because we can only be either in relation to the other.

The very break from the past that Foucault experienced in 1967 was in the
making as early as the late eighteenth century when the colonies in British

North America asserted their sovereignty and seized control from Britain of the circulation of resources, people, goods, and information through their segments of the North Atlantic trade routes. We find it fascinating that although the former colonies managed to establish a government through Articles of Confederation, the government so established, for all its remarkable characteristics, failed to develop a single set of rules enabling the various state governments to conduct trade, share a form of currency, mete out justice, and educate their respective populations. Nor could any of the novels born of this paradox imagine anything like a single bounded community to which members of a national readership might belong. Quite the opposite was true. The novels written by and for Americans during the first thirty years of the new republic carved out systems of social relationships from the same international networks that once linked the colonies to Europe in a subordinate relationship. These novels reworked the novel form to establish protocols that regulated not only who and what came in and went out of their respective sectors of that network but also the forms of social interaction that took place in between these comings and goings.

Our reason for focusing on this peculiar body of fiction is twofold. To the degree that one thinks of the novel as a media technology and the printing and marketing of books as infrastructure, early American novels demonstrate that to see themselves as a national community in the modern sense, novel readers had to feel that they were subject to international forces capable of disrupting the established practices of daily life by setting their people, resources, goods, and information into circulation. In thus suggesting that modern nationhood was primarily a defensive maneuver, we do not presume to describe what actually happened to the geopolitical contours of the Atlantic world as modern nation-states began to establish themselves. Rather, we want to explain how, in this case, novels made it possible for the literate populations of various local communities and regions to think of themselves as belonging to the same national community. But if, as the substantial body of fiction that emerged in North America after 1789 seems to indicate, an international flow of people, goods, and information preceded and probably provoked the need to feel part of a community beyond one's household, village, or region, then would it not follow that imagining a national community—at once limited and sovereign—might in any case presuppose a system of international networks, just as those networks in turn presupposed nations as the sites of international exchange?

Though obviously in tension with each other, nation and network can thus be seen in this sense as mutually dependent components of a single political formation. That is indeed how novels that accompanied the rise of modern nations sized up their position in the Atlantic world. Another reason followed from the first and prompted us to focus on this particular moment in the history of the novel. To put it simply, we have always been perplexed by unwillingness on the part of literary scholars and critics to factor this first chapter in its history into accounts of the tradition of the American novel. In our view, these early novels offer privileged access to the novel's double role in nation making: how novels in general subjected what they take to be the prevailing system of social interaction to the force of the networks in which novels traveled but how, at the same time, novels made it possible for the formal variations that result to be recognized as novels in new places and appeal to the sense of belonging on the part of different groups. Hence the book you have in hand.

This book emerged over several years from a rather heated argument in which the two of us addressed the same problem from the fields of critical theory and early American literary studies, respectively. Given that the one field contained so many elements of the other—novels, writing, and democracy among them—how could the perspective from which each of us approached that problem make so little sense from the other? The answer came from our primary material, whose uniform resistance to what novels do according to theories of the novel, as well as to what form novels took from one moment of history to the next, suggested that ours were not two independent ways of thinking about a largely ignored body of early American fiction but quite the contrary. Each of us had been carrying on half of the same argument responsible for the disconnection between European political theory and the novels written in the decades following ratification of the U.S. Constitution. In itself, neither way of thinking could explain why a body of fiction that obviously spoke to that readership had been virtually expunged from the literary tradition: what was it about the American novel's contribution to the early United States that made it convenient, if not necessary, for literary critics to ignore? Armed with theory that defined novels as a literary form and trained us to read them accordingly, we were at a complete loss when it came to accounting for the novels produced in the early national period.

We first took up this problem about the time that Benedict Anderson's *Imagined Communities* (1983) appeared in print. In an excerpt from his memoir published in an issue of the *London Review of Books* (*LRB* 2016), Anderson called attention to the radically nonlinear process of reasoning he had pursued in what quickly became a classic study of modern nationalism. He had evidently come to understand his unorthodox approach to the relationship between novels and nationalism as a way to circumvent the intellectual divide within the discipline of political science at Cornell University, which had trained him in "the grand tradition of European political theory," while relegating the study of American government to a separate department. To avoid the Eurocentrism of the one and the exceptionalism of the other, Anderson decided to look at the co-emergence of novels and modern nationalism from a postcolonial perspective. "My first target," he writes of his method, "was the Eurocentrism I saw in the assumption that nationalism was born in Europe and then spread as it was emulated in other parts of the world. It was plain to me that nationalist movements had their historical origins in North and South America, and that these movements could not be explained on any 'ethnic' or 'linguistic' basis" (*LRB* 6). Convinced that previous accounts of the rise and spread of modern nationalism hewed to the genealogical thinking of European political theory, Anderson lifted Hugh Seton-Watson's claim to the effect that "nations have no consistent scientific definition but nevertheless exist" as the basis for his own definition of the nation as "an imagined political community—both limited and sovereign" (*Imagined Communities* 3). He was convinced at the time, as were we, that in making this move, he had untethered his theoretical argument along with his subject matter from the traditional European origin story.

Transplanting the central insight of Raymond Williams's *The Long Revolution* to an account of how colonies across Southeast Asia became postcolonial nations, Anderson made it possible for us to abandon genealogical accounts of novels and nations and assume that both emerged wherever authors and readers of the reigning print vernacular were so positioned as to imagine belonging to the same bounded and self-sovereign community.[1] But as we tried out Anderson's explanation of why the rise of novels coincided with modern nations in eighteenth-century Britain and her North American colonies, we confronted an additional set of questions key to understanding our material, which he had not addressed: How did novels persuade the diverse readerships of the former colonies, themselves internally fraught, to imagine belonging to a single community within but not coextensive with a print vernacular? Assuming the nation did exercise some form of sovereignty over its citizens, what form of government would those affiliations have authorized? How open to change was the form of community that produced such feelings of belonging? Did those novels inspire devotion to an already constituted nation, or was it more important to imagine such a community as something to wish for, believe in, strive toward, or even dread?[2] Finally, Anderson's exclusive focus on novels then considered "foundational fictions" left us wondering why—by contrast to preboom Latin American novels—those written in the early United States never acquired the same status.[3]

Looking back on the study that made him a household name well beyond the field of political science, Anderson came to see why the recent rise of nationalism across Southeast Asia had taken the form of a story that, by his own admission, reads "more like a novel serialized in a newspaper than the ordinary type of scholarly historical work," a story that forced his reader to "hop back and forth" from one major location to another, wherever novels had materialized along with nations (*LRB* 7). To detach his investigation of the relationship between novels and nations from the genealogical thinking in which he had been trained, Anderson devised what he considered a process more suited to tracking the metonymic spread of a pop cultural movement or a rash of sit-ins or political assassinations. But when he came to write his memoir three decades after *Imagined Communities*, he could see that the nations now yielding to the globalizing forces of late capitalism had not been all that independent or self-contained thirty years earlier. By his own admission, Anderson had to acknowledge that by designating "nations and the nation states as the basic units of analysis," he had "completely ignored the obvious fact that in reality these units were tied together and crosscut by global political-intellectual currents such as liberalism, fascism, communism and socialism, as well as by vast religious networks and economic and technical forces" (*LRB* 6). When he decided to focus on "nations and the nation states," Anderson had, in other words, inadvertently allowed his "units of analysis" to obscure the "global political-intellectual currents" that coursed through and connected them. Of equal importance to our own argument was the implication that if "nations and nation states" had to be rethought in relation to global "currents," then novels had to be rethought in those terms as well. Since historical research had confirmed that novels had indeed traveled along international political-intellectual trade routes with the rise of nationalism during the late eighteenth century, how could we ignore the strong possibility that novels provided a vehicle for spreading nationalism then as they later would in the time of postcolonialism?

Convinced that the recent production of novels for global circulation that imagine life beyond the nation would actually provide a more appropriate way of approaching the sudden outburst of American fiction during the period of the early republic, we abandoned the explanatory logic of traditional origin stories—a decision that brought the questions raised by Anderson's *Imagined Communities* into much sharper focus. It took only passing familiarity with the novels of the new republic to see that they'd done very little to persuade a diverse and scattered but highly literate population to imagine belonging to a limited and sovereign nation. Moreover, they had done nothing to persuade readers to affiliate with one another on the basis of their common relationship to the new central government. But neither did these novels offer any way for readers to see themselves as so many points of exchange in one or more of the trade routes circulating goods, people, and information throughout the Atlantic world. At the time, these routes were cutting across state lines and overwhelming the boundaries established by the Northwest Ordinances with the Indian nations. Despite their extraordinary range of subject matter, the sheer number and formal consistency of these novels indicated that they offered readers something else instead. To make sense to multiple readerships convinced that their identities, along with their existence, depended on unfettered movement, these novels had offered another basis of affiliation. Anderson had imported his "units of analysis" not only from European political theory but also from his education in classical and European literature. These novels told us that we, like Anderson, had imported our "units of analysis" not only from European theory but from an education in classical and British literature as well.

Armed with this awareness, we could see how conspicuously the novels of the new republic disregarded the conventional signs confirming principles of modern nationhood. Across the board, these novels failed to specify what relationships their households could tolerate, the boundaries that had to be maintained, or the rules its members must observe, much less the form of security they hoped to earn in exchange. From 1789 to the 1820s, so many novels displayed their antagonism to these same principles by launching a deliberate assault on the form perfected by Jane Austen that it was easy to see what American novelists thought they were supposed to do. But what could American novels have offered instead to readers who had not only been brought up on British fiction but also maintained their appetite for reading it during the very period when American novels first appeared in print?[4] We were at a loss to explain the obvious: somehow this disruptive rhetorical behavior struck a chord of recognition, if not affiliation, among readers thrown together by the same forces that had detached them from their respective homelands and divided them from one another. Though scattered and wary of any form of central government, a significant number were, at least for a thirty-year period, evidently willing and able to acknowledge that in reading these anomalous narratives, what they were reading was indeed a novel. We turned to novel theory for help.

Mikhail Bakhtin usefully describes the novel as a form of engagement with the congested field of vernacular writing he labels "heteroglossia" ("Discourse in the Novel"). To write a novel, an author had to engage the tangled skein that encircled a conceptual object as various writers vied to define it. To distinguish his or her writing as that of a novel, according to Bakhtin's definition of the form, that author used recognizable formal maneuvers that simultaneously engaged other writing in dialogue and removed that dialogue from the field of other writing. This "dialogic" maneuver restaged the novelist's disagreement with that writing on cultural turf that gave his or her novel revisionary power over other writing. As soon as we began to think of the novel form as such an engagement with other writing, we noticed the remarkable consistency with which early American novelists took issue with narrative fiction that imagined the nation as late seventeenth- and eighteenth-century Europe had once described North America, namely, as a world waiting to become private property. It stood to reason, then, that the first American novelists were restaging this fantasy to show that it had failed to provide the means of distributing food, labor, wealth, and information to the population. As they dismantled anything that resembled the English country house writ large or small, these early novelists went right to the heart of a political debate that surfaced with the formulation and ratification of the U.S. Constitution and raged unabated during the period that saw the publication of the first American novels. To write about property during this period was to produce fractures rather than connections among potentially antagonist groups.

Property, as Alan Taylor describes this turbulent period, was the source of often violent conflict: "Radicals insisted that a public good trumped private property rights; indeed property was illegitimate if it derived from exploiting others." Northern merchants and southern landowners felt entitled to use their property, which included slaves, as they saw fit. As late as the 1780s, the nation's leaders "worried that great property needed a king's protection," and those who "possessed great property" considered themselves entitled to a greater share of political authority than those destitute of it (*American Revolutions* 370–71). This was the conflict that three years of wrangling by a Constitutional Convention had attempted to resolve. Add to this the waves of would-be settlers that poured over the Appalachians heedless of national boundaries and treaties with the Indian nations, believing land was theirs to seize, as well as speculators who did "land office business" in that territory, and you have a debate over the nature and use of property that could easily erupt into unspeakable violence. This was not a conflict that could be politically resolved. As one European traveler said of the United States, "Here, all is circulation, motion, and boiling agitation" (Taylor 438).

Bakhtin's account of "the discourse in the novel" took us a ways toward explaining why an author with the literary ambitions of a Charles Brockden Brown went to such lengths to dismantle the novel as established by his British counterparts ("Discourse in the Novel"). But Bakhtin's explanation of the novel's dialogic engagement with the field of vernacular writing could not tell us what someone like Brockden Brown offered in place of the community based on a landed estate that took shape in such novels as Henry Fielding's *Tom Jones*, Samuel Richardson's *Pamela*, or Austen's *Pride and Prejudice*. Nor could Bakhtin help us figure out why the modern literary institution either ignored or simply failed to recognize the form of community that early American novels formulated instead. Jacques Rancière's essay on "The Politics of Literature" provided the next piece of the puzzle. Here, Rancière defines "literature" as a recent phenomenon and offers a rationale for its establishment in nineteenth-century France, one that holds true, give or take a few decades, for the emergence of national literatures in England and the United States as well. He provides a stunning reading to show that Flaubert carried out new "rules of appropriateness" that distinguished his work as "literature" from the heteroglossia of written speech that Rancière suggestively names "democratic writing."

Resembling Friedrich Kittler's "discourse network of 1800" in this respect, the metastatic spread of such writing in France and England during the very period that saw publication of the first U.S. novels made it possible for anyone who could read to address virtually anyone else in the vernacular. As authors developed the formal maneuvers, or what is conventionally meant by "style," to remove their work from the field of vernacular writing, sophisticated readers began to recognize "rules of appropriateness" that distinguished literary works from writing that anyone could use to address anyone else. These rules put a literary experience outside the purview of common reading competence. Rancière makes this point by explaining, as he puts it in the title of his essay, "Why Emma Bovary Had to Be Killed." When Flaubert condemned his heroine to death for fetishizing beauty and attempting to install it in her daily life, he not only cordoned off the proto-Proustian sensations in his work for those willing to observe literary protocols but also saw to it that the common reader would understand Emma's effort to beautify her life as a cautionary tale of seduction. But when Rancière then distinguished such literary writing from its readerly counterpart, he made the task of determining the politics of early American fiction far more complicated than we have just made it sound.

If a literary experience is indeed the product and means of restricting the redistribution of sensibility that exponentially expanded the reading public during the late eighteenth and nineteenth centuries, then there can be no basis for attributing the considerable appeal of early American novels to their literary quality. Nor can we blame their lack of literary quality for the fact that only specialists read these novels now. These novels simply must have observed a different formal standard than their British counterparts. An explanation as to how novels written during the early republic had engaged what we can assume was a much more diverse and scattered readership than Flaubert's would require us to adjust Rancière's concept of "democratic writing," just as we had used that concept to supplement Bakhtin's model of "heteroglossia."

It was easy to see that early American novels had indeed developed a rather consistent set of rhetorical moves to challenge the assumption that "property" could provide a stable basis of society. It was also pretty clear that by challenging the form of British fiction and the political philosophical tradition that underwrote it, novels of the early republic had challenged *avant la lettre* the "rules of appropriateness" that later on prompted critics and readers to establish James Fenimore Cooper as the inaugurator of a national tradition of the novel. But knowing that these rules restricted literature to a small and self-contained subset of vernacular writing answered one question only to raise another: on what basis had early American readers recognized fiction that consistently violated those rules as novels? The clear and consistent disagreement these novels carried on with their British counterparts did not strike us as, in itself, sufficient to identify this body of writing as novels in their own right. Indeed, it would have taken an alternative means of managing the field of information, including people, their property, and ways of life bound to property, to do that.

For those, like ourselves, trained to read novels for plot, character, point of view, and an authorial perspective and the kind of story it oversees, the habit is deeply engrained to read those novels so classified in these terms, just as it is second nature to approach them as self-contained texts—if not as worlds unto themselves and the property of an author, then as an example of an equally discrete subgenre, say, a historical novel, a sensation novel, a city novel, a colonial adventure novel, or a detective novel. To read any novel in such terms is to read it as a world made of property, no matter how subtly that particular novel may coax and nudge the reader to assume that world is potentially sufficient to support the full roster of its characters. This way of reading presupposes a formal standard based on the means by which particular novelists, individual novels, or entire subgenres dispose us to imagine managing such a world, and no one, not even Flaubert, does this with more proficiency than Jane Austen. Over the course of the twentieth century, this fantasy served as both the foundation of a national tradition of the novel and a staple of literary education. Anticipating the traditions proposed by Ian Watt, F. R. Leavis, Richard Chase, Leslie Fiedler, F. O. Matthiessen, and their counterparts in other countries, E. M. Forster's *Aspects of the Novel* explained how to read any novel that belonged to such a tradition in terms of formal machinery that at once detached it from the larger field of prose and set it in relation to other novels that redistributed property to provide the basis of a restored or reformed community. There was no question that this theory of the novel—in the guise of common sense and great erudition—obscured the very side of the political argument that classic novels countered by formulating seemingly self-sufficient communities. This gerrymandered concept of the novel helped us to identify the noncompliant aspects of the early American novel that had been ruled out by the literary institution.

The result is bound to strike our readers as an unusually eclectic critical vocabulary. The first three chapters sketch out the conditions that made it possible for novelists to come out independently but in force against the idea that a contractual agreement among men of property provided a basis for imagining a national community. We show how, in doing so, those novelists developed a set of countermoves, tropes, protocols, or what E. M. Forster dubbed "aspects of the novel" to formulate a basis of affiliation capable of addressing readerships of semiautonomous states who consequently understood the nation through the lens of regional, if not local, interests. Insofar as property removed such people, goods, and information from circulation and limited the extent of such circulation itself, property failed to provide the foundation of a social system that could expand and diversify and still cohere. Once we understood exactly how property failed, we could identify the components of a reading method that demonstrated how novelists produced a social system that succeeded in recruiting early American readers.

Our next five chapters bear out the fruits of this considerable labor in a sequence of five formal moves, or tropes, so consistently at work in those early novels that a reader, in picking up a book or reading a story serialized in a newspaper or magazine and noting that it performed some of these moves, must have known on the spot that he or she had picked up a novel. Each chapter develops a definition of one such trope that shows how a range of American novels use it to reverse a comparable move on the part of British novels of the period—an imperiled household, a protagonist who sets out on his or her own, an authorial perspective that assesses the hero's progress, a love object chosen for purposes of stabilizing an unstable community, and the personal style that we identified with the authorial source of this perspective.

Mounting an argument to the effect that property—whether inherited or acquired—was incorrigibly antisocial, the American novels we have in mind engineer a form of dispersal that puts persons and property that had cohered as a household back into circulation within a rapidly expanding and diversifying field of characters. Once so dispersed, the parts—both personal and material—of what had been self-contained individuals are released into new and seemingly random social relationships to become what appear, by literary standards, to be quite another field of characters. The result is a protagonist that can more accurately be called a population—a heterogeneous field of minor characters with an innate capacity, should their mobility be threatened, to feel and act as one. As its members independently and in various ways perform tactical maneuvers to detach themselves from a position within a world of property, the field of minor characters eventually reaches a tipping point where it begins to operate as something that could be construed as a community from a position within that field of information.

Along with dispersal, the narrative maneuvers responsible for forming this composite protagonist provided early American novelists with the means of scattering the component parts of a community based on property, thereby creating the demand, as well as the material, for something else. In order to mount a counterargument against the British novel, these novels had to challenge the tradition that figured nations as self-contained political bodies with a sovereign head and center. To produce what amounts to a popular political theory in their own right, however, these novels would have had to mine the affirmative potential of their argument and let it materialize; the onus was on them to do something more creative than simply oppose the British model, as if it were the only game in town. These novels took the turn from disruptive social behavior to community building by staging an impossible event—an event that converted the tactics for evading some form of captivity into a highly volatile network of horizontal affiliations that temporarily levels the regnant social hierarchy. We refer to this turn—without which no narrative would become a novel—as conversion. To put a political face on it, one might say that the machinery of conversion produces the infectious feeling of affiliation manifest in the forms of behavior characterized as popular democracy. While dangerous in its own right, this behavior opens up unlimited circulation and, with it, the freedom to associate.

The final two of five moves essential to becoming an American novel during the early republic install formal protocols designed to reduce the risks of just such freedom. The emergence of hubs would have told the early American reader that a narrative had begun to convert the bad behavior of its collective protagonist into a set of practices that reduced the risk of unfettered social circulation so as to ensure the mobility necessary to keep forming new connections. The emergence of hubs signaled the reader, in other words, that a prose narrative was well on its way to becoming a novel. To perform what is an essentially managerial task, the early novels replaced the household supported by private property with something like a relay station that made it possible for people to encounter one another and still continue on their ways somewhere else. Should a household curtail such mobility, it would fail in its responsibility to promote social interaction and soon vanish from a novel. To understand the basis on which such domestic hubs gained favor over households in these early novels, one needs to take a step back and rethink the notion of freedom that depends on the protection of person and property. Where the traditional British protagonist removed self and property, as Crusoe certainly does, from social circulation, the composite protagonist of early American fiction depended for its very existence on making preferential attachments.

In these novels, nothing coalesces the field of minor characters faster than a common threat of captivity. In that it shuts down the power of attraction that connects one character to many others and, by way of them, to the entire field of characters, this threat produces a version of the pleasure principle that compels the protagonist to make new connections as if life depended on it. Should property in whatever form deprive some group of that freedom, these novels contend, the entire network of social relations will be compromised and grow increasingly vulnerable to foreign interests. Given the heterogeneous field of characters, however, unlimited circulation proved a nonetheless risky proposition—as likely to take an individual out of social circulation as to destroy a hub that allowed just anyone to pass through. To transform the concept of the nation modeled on and composed of independent households into a sustainable system of hubs, the novels we discuss under that rubric proposed that writing itself was the means of managing the risks attached to the pleasure of unrestricted socializing.

There is no clearer example of just how writing managed this risk than the American seduction novel. Once she could no longer circulate and make new attachments, the letters, journals, or secondhand accounts of the ruined woman circulating in her place provided readers with a cautionary tale. If you want to pursue preferential attachments, such novels told the reader in no uncertain terms, then you must avoid strangers who want to remove you from circulation and hoard the pleasure with which you infuse the entire system of relationships by socializing. In this respect, seduction had the same effect that marriage does in a novel that aims to transform the pleasure of socializing into the exclusivity of reproductive love. The need for discretion, fostered by the pervasive dread of self-removal, was virtually the only control these novels were willing to place on the heroine's social impulse. As the pleasure of socializing subsumed sexual pleasure, the early American novel deprived reproductive sex of the erotic charge it tried and failed to monopolize in the European novel. And as their narration came to manage the pleasure of preferential attachments, the early American novel, as we read it, presented itself as a way of managing a rapidly expanding and diversifying readership.

Having come thus far, we have yet to explain the tactical maneuver by which these first American novelists—independently, but nevertheless in concert—recruited readers as participants in the community that emerged from within the field of characters itself. By means of formal protocols that openly defy E. M. Forster's anthropomorphized notion of "perspective," this community paradoxically expanded beyond the limits of the individual novel and engaged ways of seeing and forms of writing that novels designated as outside and fundamentally incompatible with theirs. Despite a number of admirable attempts, the novels of even so talented a writer as Charles Brockden Brown continue to defeat critical attempts to describe them as a coherent perspective traceable to a source in the individual author. As for a comprehensive American perspective on the new United States, on the other hand, the novels written during the time of democratic writing addressed too many local readerships within a national population for any one of them to lay claim to offering a representative view.

In our estimation, then, the novels of the early republic did not fail to produce a comprehensive perspective and the omniscience it implies so much as they succeeded in linking alternative and often incompatible perspectives in a composite view of the same phenomena. Guided by the principle of anamorphosis, the novels of the early republic walked a tightrope between one perspective and another without allowing either to dominate. To pull off this balancing act, these novels often included people, things, and behaviors that would seem perfectly ordinary from one perspective within the Atlantic world but resolutely unintelligible from another. Very much like the formless blotch that hovers above the carpet in the foreground of Hans Holbein's painting, *The Ambassadors*, these curious holes in the aesthetic surface of the text tell the viewer that an outside perspective has inserted itself within a picture that might otherwise appear to offer a comprehensive view. The intrusive perspective comes from elsewhere to expose the limitations of the framework that has organized the information within its parameters. Because it thus refuses to submit to intelligibility from any one perspective, the anamorphic object serves as a conjunction between such perspectives and makes the spectator hop back and forth in order to grasp the whole picture.

As it followed the protagonist across boundaries between country and city, North and South, black and white, Europe and America, the early American novel forged connections among a sequence of such perspectives. Rather than obscure "the figure in the carpet," Henry James's term for the concept now known as pattern recognition, anamorphosis endowed that pattern with spots of illegibility that concatenate the perspectives of the different and often incompatible groups and geographical regions, pulling form back into the process of formation. As they assembled a community that could simultaneously expand and diversify at these conjunctions, novels of the new republic indeed formed a recognizable pattern. Like the fundamentally unfinished process they assemble, their formal protocols posed what was at once a formal and a political challenge to the concept of community as bounded and self-contained: a decentered and open-ended social network that cut across and countered point for point the logic of a world of property.

Convinced that such a community required and deserves a critical vocabulary as eclectic as Forster's is consistently anthropomorphic, we drew our "aspects of the novel" from the social sciences, the biological sciences, cybernetics, and network theory, as well as from religious studies and art history. This struck us as somehow appropriate to the work of novelists who used the materials at hand, chiefly other novels, to assemble a community that was sufficiently open to new subject matter yet one to which a wide range of local readerships eventually imagined they belonged. Within a decade of their appearance in the 1790s, these novels were traveling between relatively self-contained local readerships within the new United States and inviting those readerships to imagine their nation from other points of view. Working on the premise that these novels are their best and only critical theory, we drew an explanation of each piece of our critical vocabulary from novels that used that particular trope to what we saw as the best rhetorical advantage—much as we did above with the seduction novel.

To explain how early American novels revised the form of the British novel, we have made a somewhat anachronistic and quite unfair example of Jane Austen, who—according to Ian Watt and F. R. Leavis, among others—performed the synthesis of preceding British novels and should therefore be considered the inaugurator of the British tradition.[5] During the twentieth century, the rhetoric of self-enclosure that she performed with peerless ingenuity fell into the hands of European modernism, where it became a means of detaching the community Austen had imagined, along with the novelist's imagination, from the turbulence that swept away national boundaries while leaving economic inequities intact. During this period, as Georg Lukács assessed the situation, literary modernism tightened the rules of appropriateness and shrank the domain of literary realism down to the parameters of the text and its author's imagination. As he explained it, "The decisive error is the misconception of perspective, its equation with reality. This fallacy, which produced the naturalist de-poeticization of reality in the first place, was now employed to turn back prose into poetry" (*Realism in Our Time* 125–26). From this, it would follow that to read the novels of the early republic, one must reverse the very turns in large part responsible for today's literary discipline and the procedures we use to read a novel as a work of literature.

With this aim in mind, we designed the body of this argument—Chapters 4 through 8—to show in some detail how a sequence of particular tropes mobilized a social network that replaced the traditional concept of property as the traditional means for a novel to organize its field of characters. Convinced that the novels of the Americas, as Anderson suggests, anticipated the rise of postcolonial fiction, we felt that it was up to us to show how each of the rhetorical moves we have identified persists in literary works of fiction by Nathaniel Hawthorne, Edgar Allan Poe, Herman Melville, Harriett Beecher Stowe, and Henry James, the very authors whose novels, when read as literature, constitute our national tradition. Extending the tropes of the early American novel into the later periods was our way of floating the suggestion that this early endeavor to imagine an alternative community did not simply vanish from the novel but, to the contrary, continued to argue on behalf of the idea of the nation as a set of hubs in an expanding social network over and against the nation as a bounded, self-centered form. What are the twin protagonists of *Huckleberry Finn*, after all, if not more companionable but no less incompatible actors in exactly this argument—Huck the errant principle of free circulation and preferential attachments and Tom the principle of a community limited to and supported by property?

Chapter 1

Style in the Time of Epidemic Writing

Despite the fact that well over a hundred American novels were published between the 1780s and the 1820s, neither increasing critical attention to this body of fiction nor its recent availability in classroom editions has made us rethink the canonical tradition, what is distinctively American about this body of fiction, and how it asks us to imagine a national community. To the degree that this is first of all a "literary" problem, we want to address the question of why the novels of the new republic have all but vanished from our national heritage, first, as a problem of style.

One could trace that problem back to an evening in the 1820s, when the American publisher Samuel Goodrich engaged his dinner companion, Sir Walter Scott, in a discussion of the relative merits of various novelists.[1] Though offering a rather spotty account of this conversation some years later, Goodrich did recall no less than four related points on which Scott had faulted the novels of Charles Brockden Brown. Scott objected to the American novelist's use of the tale of terror, first, on the grounds that "it is wholly ideal; it is not in nature" (Goodrich II: 203). By this, Scott meant that the American's writing style dealt in abstractions rather than attending to the actual details of ordinary life. Second, Scott found the characters of Brockden Brown's tales of terror unsatisfactory on grounds that they were "alien to common experience" and so failed to demand the sympathy that readers owed to members of their community. Third, Brockden Brown's narratives kept the reader "constantly on the rack of uncertainty," in Scott's opinion, because they violated the causal logic of individual intention and agency (Goodrich II: 203). Fourth, and for all these reasons, Scott declared that Brockden Brown had written in imitation of an outdated style of the British novel, by which Scott of course meant the gothic romance. Though granting that Brockden

Brown possessed many literary talents and especially excelled in the power of description, Scott concluded that the American had been "led astray by falling under the influence of bad examples" and had consequently sacrificed his own perspective to that of "others" (Goodrich II: 204). What Scott meant by the "bad examples" that had compromised his authorial perspective becomes clear in the light of Scott's earlier and highly favorable review of *Emma* as a contrastingly good example of what style a novelist should emulate.

Published nine years before his dinner conversation with Goodrich, this review equated the appearance of Jane Austen's *Emma* (1815) with the maturation of a form that had spent its "childhood" indulging in romance (*"Emma"* 227). Scott identified the qualities that made *Emma* superior to romance by way of contrast to the very deficiencies in previous novels that he also identified in Brockden Brown. Austen's characters do not seem "alien to common experience," Scott explains, because Austen draws them "from the common walks of life," which refers, throughout the critical reviews, to the experience of the middling classes (*"Emma"* 230). Her novels consequently offer the reader "a correct and striking representation of that which is daily taking place around him" instead of "the splendid scenes of an imaginary world" offered by her predecessors, presumably the "bad examples" that had influenced Brockden Brown (*"Emma"* 230). Trading in the "splendid" for the "common" could only enhance the novel's appeal for readers, Scott argued, because the "splendid" scenes of romance had "lost most of their poignancy by their repeated and injudicious use" (*"Emma"* 230). Austen, by contrast, had "produced sketches of such spirit and originality that we never miss the excitation which depends upon a narrative of uncommon events, arising from the consideration of minds, manners, and sentiments greatly above our own" (*"Emma"* 231).

To make the daily life of an eighteenth-century shire in the south of England seem so fresh and fascinating, Austen indeed took the customs "common" to the lower gentry with which she was intimately familiar and made those customs "common" by way of creating a new sense of class. To engage her readership, Scott reasoned, it was not necessary for Austen's novels to describe social relations her readers were seldom likely to experience themselves, so long as those relationships were the result of "the motives and principles which the readers *may* recognize as ruling their own and most of their acquaintances" (*"Emma"* 231, our italics). Thus, what Scott applauded as Austen's "art of copying from nature as she really exists in the common walks of life" was actually her ability to create a community of readers who felt they shared the protocols that regulated the feelings and behavior of her characters. In comparing their respective "styles" of writing, we are not suggesting that these novelists wanted to outdo each other. Quite the contrary, we want to understand how the protocols for making social relationships distinguished the first American novels from their British counterparts. Convinced that Brockden Brown succeeded with American readers for all the reasons that Scott found him wanting, we figured that his style should indicate how he differentiated his writing as American from hers as British. We consider the notion of style that served this purpose closer to the social scientific concept of "a style of relationship" than to the modernist concept of style as the highly individuated use of language that distinguishes a particular work or works of literature. As we adapted it, style consists of formal rules that writers must observe in order to engage prospective readers in a community that forms according to those rules. We think it was by means of their style of relationships, rather than their personal execution of such a style, that writers transformed a given field of characters into a system of relationships that identified their work as novels.

To perform this magic on the conflict-riddled population of the new United States, Brockden Brown saw fit to activate the same set of narrative moves, tropes, or aspects that, with commonsensical eloquence, E. M. Forster would describe more than a century later in the lectures he published as his classic work of novel criticism, *Aspects of the Novel*. No less self-conscious in making these moves than Austen was in crafting her famously self-enclosed communities, Brockden Brown's style departs decisively from hers as it drags those communities into the international field of vernacular writing from which she extricates them and puts the elements of her country houses back in play for purposes of telling other stories. Seen in these terms, it should seem rather obvious why Brocken Brown fell short of the British standard in Scott's estimation. What is not so clear is how the novels of the new republic successfully engaged an American readership by countering the very aspects of the novel that eventually defined both national traditions of the novel. The answer depends to a greater degree than literary criticism acknowledges on the measures those novels took to recruit a readership. We shall begin by showing how each novelist developed a style of relationships that proved the other's to be antisocial, indeed deleterious, to forming a community. Where Austen demonstrates that Brockden Brown's way of making relationships is dangerously indiscriminate and thus in need of containment and suppression, Brockden Brown returns the favor by mischaracterizing Austen's style as

virtual captivity. To escape the restrictions of any closed community, his protagonists break up and disperse the component parts of a traditional household, making those parts available for recombination.

We want to think of the codependence implied by the presence of one
style of relationship as a threat to the other as the dialogical engagement of
contrary ways of dealing with a common problem of economic instability.
England, as it happened, was feeling the impact of the crisis in currency
brought on by debts incurred during the war in North America, as well as the
conflicts in India, compounded by the waves of inflation accompanying the
French Revolution.[2] Not unrelated was the situation in the United States
during that same period, where the value of property was similarly at the
mercy of multiple currencies whose value was in turn calculated not in relation to that of gold or guaranteed by a national bank but in relation to various
forms of debt.[3] If by reattaching property to land and imagining a more liberal way of distributing it Austen provided her readers with protocols for social relationships that seemed to include them, then Brockden Brown
pronounced that solution to the problem of economic instability unworkable
to a substantial number of American readers. In order to explain what he
came up with instead, we have to consider how each of their respective styles
overturned the means of forming the social relationships that characterized
the other's style.

Two Worlds of Style

Written between 1794 and 1817, Austen's novels are today venerated and sometimes patronized for their minimalism. And who would not admire the economy of her style—just enough detail to get the job done and no more? Austen
pared down Samuel Richardson's epistolary excesses and stripped her English
manor house of Ann Radcliffe's oppressive atmospherics in order to expose
the process that organizes both, namely, a process by which the protagonist
secures for herself and her family a lasting relationship to property. The mem-
orable opening line of *Pride and Prejudice* says it all: "It is a truth universally
acknowledged, that a single man in possession of a good fortune, must be in
want of a wife" (5). Each of Austen's six major novels opens onto a situation
where inherited property is in danger of falling into the hands of strangers,
thereby threatening to leave the next generation—largely represented by
women—without a home or means of income. By novel's end, in keeping

with the Austen style, property and thus the very notion of home become extensions and expressions, respectively, of the man of fortune and the woman whom he "wants." As such a home, that property becomes a new compound substance: the foundation of an individual's social position, the source of wealth that frees him from labor, a reflection of his taste and discretion, the means of securing her private life, and the source of value that increases sufficiently over time and with improvement to sustain an expanding household.

All this is at stake in the marriage plots that unfold in a sequence of personal decisions that shifts the protagonist's position in society from one in peril to one that is comfortably secure. For all the attention paid to her minimalism, though, we have yet to consider what Austen achieves by sparing us all but the essential details of dress, landscape, and household appointments. Even in famously confining her protagonists' sphere of action to the radius of a one-day's carriage ride, Austen neglects to tell us what her heroine sees from this mobile viewpoint. In thus withholding such description, she sets her novels apart from those of Ann Radcliffe and Samuel Richardson. What, then, makes her sparsely furnished world nevertheless seem full? What, indeed, if not the merger of economic and affective value, can provide the sense of solidity, centrality, and normativity that stabilizes the economically unsustainable household in each of her novels. Austen brings about this merger by reconciling two distinct forms of property: (1) land and the resources that maintain it, including one's own labor, and (2) what Locke meant by "property in his own person," such as education, taste, and sensibility (*Two Treatises* II.28: 1–2). The detail is all in the preparation for this moment of closure—that is to say, in the process by which the Austen narrator transmutes what had been Elizabeth's dislike of Darcy's arrogance into her dawning appreciation of the way he exercises his responsibilities as a man of property. The process of falling in love includes Darcy's deepening appreciation of Elizabeth's personal qualities as well. This process sentimentalizes the mercenary negotiations that rescue her sister Lydia from a ruinous elopement, thus inoculating the Bennett family from a scandal that would have canceled out the value of Elizabeth's personal taste and intelligence in the marriage market. Were she deprived of this "property in herself," Darcy's alliance with Elizabeth would go down in the annals of local history as a dreadful mismatch.

The economic and social narratives attach themselves to the "flutter of spirits" that triggers this decisive moment in the heroine's gradual recognition of the kind of man Darcy really is beneath his mannered surface. Where a letter from her Aunt Gardiner discloses Darcy's role in engineering the marriage of Lydia Bennett to the infamous Wickham, Austen uses that revelation to disclose the complex interplay of reason and emotion that takes place in Elizabeth's mind. Within a paragraph, this information completely transforms the affective economy of characters that had included Wickham into one that connects her family to Darcy by way of her worthy aunt:

> The contents of this letter threw Elizabeth into a flutter of spirits, in which it was difficult to determine whether pleasure or pain bore the greatest share. The vague and unsettled suspicions which uncertainty had produced of what Mr. Darcy might have been doing to forward her sister's match, which she had feared to encourage, as an exertion of goodness too great to be probable, and at the same time dreaded to be just, from the pain of obligation, were proved beyond their greatest extent to be true! He had followed them purposely to town, he had taken on himself all the trouble and mortification attendant on such a research; in which supplication had been necessary to a woman whom he must abominate and despise, and where he was reduced to meet, frequently meet, reason with, persuade, and finally bribe, the man whom he always most wished to avoid. . . . Her heart did whisper that he had done it for her. But it was a hope shortly checked by other considerations, and she soon felt that even her vanity was insufficient, when required to depend on his affection for her—for a woman who had already refused him—as able to overcome a sentiment so natural as abhorrence against a relationship with Wickham. Brother-in-law of Wickham! Every kind of pride must revolt from the connection. . . . For herself she was humbled; but she was proud of him. Proud that in a cause of compassion and honour, he had been able to get the better of himself. She read over her aunt's commendation of him again and again. It was hardly enough; but it pleased her. (308–9)

The prose itself—or what D. A. Miller calls "Austen's style"—delivers a fine thread of affective glue that not only makes the entire community cohere around a pair of characters from slightly different levels of the traditional social hierarchy but also affixes that community to property.[4] As the pulse of Austen's prose, romantic love, is disciplined by judgment, it begins to transform property from the means of dividing the field of characters into a form of affiliation that coalesces them. To put it another way, as it fastens onto property, love itself becomes something akin to the affective intelligence or sensibility that informs the narrator's description of the protagonist's inner life.

No less distinctive than Austen's, Brockden Brown's style can be considered minimalism of another kind. His style, as we see it, pares down the descriptive excesses of William Hill Brown's *The Power of Sympathy* (1789) to a narrative process that incorporates a tale of mistaken identity, incestuous love, and the near impossibility of marrying both well and for love. In a novel like *Arthur Mervyn* (1799), Brockden Brown offers just enough and no more information than it takes to disperse and reconnect the virtually unlimited number and variety of characters with whom Mervyn makes contact, whether directly or by way of interpolated tales, during the year of the yellow fever epidemic. The principle that turns his account into the delivery system for a series of "incidents" is forthrightly described in the opening lines of the novel with an economy akin to Austen's but in a style that differs conspicuously from hers. Without saying who he is, his reason for writing, or the genre for which he is the spokesman, the narrator begins, "I was resident in this city during the year 1793. Many motives contributed to detain me, though departure was easy and commodious, and my friends were generally solicitous for me to go" (5). Without explaining whom he addresses in writing or why, this narrator then proceeds to adjust the expectations that his reader might bring to a novel: "It is not my purpose to enumerate these motives, or to dwell on my present concerns and transactions, but merely to compose a narrative of some incidents with which my situation made me acquainted" (5). Not until two chapters later do we learn that these are the words of Dr. Stevens, who took Mervyn, "disabled by sickness," into his home and found himself sufficiently distracted by his guest's aimless story to remain while he recuperated. Amounting to an elaboration that never reconnects with the marriage plot from which Mervyn flees to fever-ridden Philadelphia, his journey through that city suggests that exposure to other people rather than removal from such social contact is paradoxically the way to manage the threat of contagion.

In order to render a recent shift in the British economy as a shift in a young woman's feelings that paves the way for marriage between people of slightly different ranks, Austen recapitulates the marriage plot in miniature. Resolution of the problem posed by the differences in rank between herself and Mr. Darcy exacerbated by economic instability all hinges entirely on the process by which the heroine becomes aware of her admiration for a man whom she had more than once dismissed as arrogant. A close look at Mervyn's encounter with the Hadwin family shows Brockden Brown using the concept of property to dismantle the very synthesis achieved by marriage in *Pride and Prejudice*. Chapter VIII of *Arthur Mervyn* begins as the protagonist falls deliriously in love with the otherwise undistinguished Eliza Hadwin, the younger daughter of a Quaker family: "My days were little else than uninterrupted reveries, and night only called up new phantoms more vivid and equally enchanting" (96). A few sentences later, we learn that these reveries "gradually lead" Mervyn's thought "to rest on futurity." But let him imagine his attraction to Eliza as a possible future, and the pleasure of anticipated fulfillment turns sour: "My present labors were light and were sufficient for my subsistence in a single state; but wedlock was the parent of new wants and of new cares" (96). The instant he finds it unpleasant to contemplate marriage with Eliza, Mervin begins to cast about for "some means of controlling and beguiling my thoughts" (96), an attempt that leads to at least two lengthy digressions before his "thoughts were called away from pursuing these inquiries by a rumour which had gradually swelled to formidable dimensions, and which, at length, reached us in our quiet retreats" (99). As if the Hadwin episode were not sufficient to spell out the difficulties of imagining a traditional household as the model community, Brockden Brown follows up this abortive fantasy of romantic love with an even more devastating assault on the constellation of notions that make property the precondition for a life worth living; he dispatches Arthur Mervyn to a city ravaged by an epidemic.

Rumor works hand-in-glove with the yellow fever itself to erode the autonomy of mind and body.[5] This in turn exposes the hidden networks connecting the small worlds Mervyn previously encountered, including Wellbeck's town and the Hadwin farm, to the cosmopolitan city.[6] Having no discernible source, rumor circulates in an ever-widening sweep to spread fear and disrupt the practices of daily life, as fever follows close on its heels. Quarantine procedures prove helpless in stopping this two-pronged assault on the households of Philadelphia, which have failed to remove healthy individuals from its path. In direct contrast to quarantine, rumor works, much as inoculation does, to turn infection against itself. Rumor infects the population of Philadelphia with a lesser form of the disease. Circulating in advance of the fever, rumor infects all those exposed with a sense of dread that travels faster and farther than the disease itself as Mervyn, close on the heels of the rumor, pursues an erratic course from one house to another through the half-deserted city.

In becoming the agent of rumor, Mervyn transforms the internally differentiated society of Philadelphia into a single population in the throes of physical and emotional distress: "As often as the tale was embellished with new incidents, or inforced with new testimony, the hearer grew pale, his breath was stifled by inquietudes, his blood was chilled and his stomach was bereaved of its usual energy. A temporary indisposition was produced in many" (101). Mervyn himself suffers this "indisposition" with a frequency that makes his own condition one and the same as the information he distributes. An abiding sense that Wallace's "welfare was essential to the happiness of those, whose happiness had become essential to mine" (103), keeps Mervyn in motion. On first entering Wallace's deserted home, he recalls being "tormented with hunger" and then found that his "craving had given way to inquietude and loathing." The "roof over his head" promised to keep him from dying "in the public way," but what had provided a refuge from "the public way" soon became a prison (118), and on the basis of a rumor, he tracks Wallace to the house of the merchant Thetford, where Mervyn once again finds himself in a "vacant and silent" house (120). By repeating this pattern of flight and captivity, Mervyn's account of the yellow fever epidemic transforms a city parceled out as property into a population that grows stronger as its people begin to circulate and associate with others even at the risk of infection. Why?

As if his style were engineered to counter Austen's, Brockden Brown habitually thwarts any restriction on his protagonist's social encounters. The result is a sequence of temporary encounters that leaves any number of broken and partial households in its wake. Where Elizabeth Bennett's attachment to Darcy is hypermediated—through family, furniture, fashion, letters, and the irony of Austen's distinctive voice—Arthur Mervyn's relationships materialize instantaneously (Wellbeck) or not at all (Eliza Hadwin). Brockden Brown's style of writing prevents one from reading one of his novels as we would one of Austen's. Spending her genius in the emotional preserves of individuated subjectivity, she is reluctant to clutter her plots with secondary characters. The American novelist, by contrast, overstocks his narrative with minor characters.[7] As a result, Arthur Mervyn's experience of the world is, as Foucault says of the contemporary moment, "less that of a long life developing through time than that of a network that connects points and intersects with its own skein."[8] In our view, this style was not primarily a way for Brockden Brown to say that what made sense in England no longer made sense in North America, though it was certainly that as well.

What distinguishes his style from Austen's resides in its ability to mobilize the sheer force of narration in a manner that anticipates what is easily the most influential theory of narrative in the past fifty years, Deleuze and

Guattari's "rhizome" (*A Thousand Plateaus* 3–25).[9] Resembling the rhizome's metonymic expansion in its refusal to observe even ontological distinctions, this narrative style presents experience as a sequence of encounters unrestricted by the need to acquire or maintain an identity. These sequences displace a continuous identity with affective vectors that move and change shape, direction, and magnitude as they meet, conjoin, disrupt, and are disrupted by other sequences. Instead of forging relationships with familiar characters that affect a relatively narrow range of characters in relatively predictable ways, we might imagine those encounters taking place in rapid succession among characters who are rarely on a first-name basis. Coming from different stations in various places throughout the Atlantic world, such characters cannot expect to confront one another on a level playing field or under the same set of social rules. Those who try to predict the outcome soon discover that the rules on which they relied have changed with each encounter and can be inferred only after the fact of the encounters themselves.

While Austen's major characters learn to read each other with relative accuracy, diminishing the likelihood of negative encounters, Brockden Brown's characters observe the principle of the seduction story, which delivers its lesson of character retroactively—to wit, the heroine recognizes she was naïve and the gentleman irresistibly persuasive only after their encounter has redefined them as a ruined woman and a libertine. In a society where the options can't be boiled down to a Darcy or a Wickham—the one a good alliance, the other definitely not—readers who expected the kind of insight into human character that presupposed a knowable society were bound to be disappointed. How could a style of writing that prevented reader identification with the protagonist provide the basis for a style of writing that was distinctive to the new United States?

How to Recruit a Readership

As it follows the yellow fever epidemic, which seems to branch out arbitrarily and invade any household it has a mind to devastate, Arthur Mervyn's equally invasive journey through Philadelphia bears an uncanny resemblance to the contagious power of democratic writing as well. Rather than remove his protagonist from unregulated social contact, as Austen does, Brockden Brown uses his protagonist to make a virtue of that same lack of discrimination;

Mervyn establishes new connections wherever familiar ones have been severed or relocated by the spread of the disease. Rather than establish reader identification with this protagonist or, for that matter, any of the characters, Brockden Brown's style afforded his reader access to a process that connects one stranger to another and brings a dying city back to life as a new form of community. In that it was repeated in novel after novel during the early national period, the process of connecting dots to otherwise unconnected other dots constitutes a "style" in its own right, rather than the lack of one.

Mikhail Bakhtin's essay on "The Discourse in the Novel" dismisses, in passing, the notion that style pretends, much less could actually be the expression of an author's individuality. Any verbal utterance "directed toward its object," Bakhtin contends, "enters a dialogically agitated and tension-filled environment of alien words, value judgments and accents, weaves in and out of complex relationships, merges with some, recoils from others, intersects with yet a third group" ("Discourse" 276). For purposes of our own argument, then, "style" can be defined as the relationship in which a novel habitually engages with other writing and yet, as Bakhtin observes, even after centuries, can "break through to its own meaning across an environment full of alien words and variously evaluat[es] accents, harmonizing with some of the elements in this environment and striking a dissonance with others." It is by means of this dialogic process that the novel "shape[s] its own *stylistic* profile and tone" ("Discourse" 277, our italics). Thus conceived, a style of writing does not express the sensibility of the person who produced it so much as it produces the sense of the person to whom we attribute that style of writing.

If, as our reading of Brockden Brown suggests, style is a distinctive way of engaging a politically charged field of writing, then we can say that Austen addressed the problem of property by means of marriage plots that supplemented inherited property with commercial wealth, intelligence, a fine sensibility, and social benevolence, in this way proposing to expand a relatively exclusive system of relationships. It also makes sense to see Brockden Brown using his style to enter the same politically charged field by suggesting what social relationships would look like if they did not depend on any such form of property. To formulate a community of any kind at this moment in history, novelists on both sides of the Atlantic agreed that property, as presently understood and implemented, was the cause of social unrest rather than its solution, thus hardly providing the basis for a sustainable community. Working from this premise, however, British and American novelists devised diametrically opposed solutions to the question of how to reformulate the world of property as one that could in theory accommodate their respective populations.

Looking back on that moment from the position of a Hungarian exile in Russia during the 1930s, Georg Lukács could see this same question setting off "the inner process of differentiation which is to transform revolutionary democracy into compromising liberalism" (*Historical Novel* 171). By way of illustration, Lukács considers the contrary styles of Flaubert's *Madame Bovary* and *Salammbô* as testimony to the consistent "artistic fruitfulness of genuine hatred and love, however hidden and suppressed in the one case, the transformation of disinterestedness into sterile exoticism in the other" (*Historical Novel* 186). Thus, as Lukács suggests, what may appear as contrasting styles—the one novel depicting contemporary French provincial life and the other classical Carthage—both express Flaubert's uniform hatred for a capitalist present "that does not historically transcend its object" (*Historical Novel* 194). Lukács goes on to show that to understand any one of Flaubert's novels, we must understand what they share with one another, as well as with other novels that participated in the irreversible decline of the historical novel after 1848. He makes a politically informed appreciation of Flaubert's style contingent on recognizing the versatility with which that style consistently converted historical phenomena into the mere settings for purely subjective events. But even as he identifies this literary practice as symptomatic of a pervasive disinterest in the human struggle for a fuller life, Lukács nevertheless conceded that Flaubert's unforgettable description of the "accidental occasion for a love scene" in *Madame Bovary* was "essential to Flaubert's purpose—which was to elevate the lives of his characters" to the level "of an ironic symbol of philistinism" ("Narrate" 115). The nature of his investment in literary description indicates, in other words, that Flaubert's aesthetic disengagement from his subject matter was in fact a style of engagement. Thus, for Lukács, as for Jacques Rancière, the descriptive style of *Madame Bovary* serves as an antihero that saves the world from its diseased relationship to objects by punishing the heroine who used that style to sensationalize the banalities of bourgeois life.[10] For Rancière, the formal means by which Flaubert distanced his perspective from that of his protagonist was also a style of relationship that removed his novels from democratic writing.

In that they scrupulously avoided both the agrammaticality that marked dialect writing and rhetoric indicative of taste and erudition, the early American novelists adopted a polite style of writing that, in theory, any literate person should have been able to imagine writing, and perhaps they did. A glance at just one or two of the epistolary novels of the period published in America is enough to get a sense of how uniform a voice issued from a range of letter writers in contrast to the personalized voices characterizing the exchange of letters that Richardson stages in *Pamela* or *Clarissa*. In American novels of the period, the narrator lets the characters do the talking, which they tend to do in virtually the same transparent prose as he or she tells their stories. In that novels written in such a voice emerged from a nation composed of small and often sharply divided communities, many with a high degree of literacy and often speaking English with one of several dialects, the advantages of this way of establishing social contacts make a lot of sense.

By focusing on whether and how each such encounter intensified or diminished the capacities of those involved, the style of the early American novelists accomplished two things at once. In that they distributed a style of writing across a highly differentiated field of readers that made itself available to anyone for purposes of addressing anyone else, these novels gave voice in writing to a distinctively American vernacular English.[11] It was a style that strangers could use to address one another with an immediacy unavailable to Austen's characters.[12] This style not only made it possible to see how writing forms a comprehensive social network but also, as it did so, provided the technology for establishing such a network. The impacts of an impersonal rhetorical style and vernacular voice on British English were not in themselves sufficient to this task. More important, in our estimation, was the style of relationship that gave novels of the early republic the edge over other styles, dialects, and rhetorical forms competing for a readership. The apparent democracy of this style may have promised whole new groups of readers the means, as Rancière puts it, "to spin a life for themselves with the help of words stolen randomly from their reading" (*Politics* 27). But while the impersonal style that these novels shared with democratic writing might well explain why the later canonizers could not read them as literature, it fails to explain why the novels of the new republic were indeed read as novels.

Austen famously dealt with the problem of democratic writing with formal measures that anticipated the ironic distance from the language of life achieved no less conspicuously by the narrative styles of Flaubert, George Eliot, Marcel Proust, and Henry James. To punish those who would turn the polite style of relationships into the means of wish fulfillment, she disciplines the democratic tendencies of that style by restricting those tendencies, if not to the rigorously self-reflective subjectivities of her major characters, then to the wayward men and women whom her novels condemn to social death. In this way, her style of writing contains what might otherwise become infectious forms of social contact—capable, as Lydia Bennet's flirtatious behavior proves—of disrupting respectable households.[13] This style of relationship observes the procedures of a biopolitical fantasy being implemented in Europe at that time (see Foucault, *Birth* 61–70).

To Dream of Social Management

No one can lay bare the concept of government that responds to the fear of contagion better than Michel Foucault. His *Discipline and Punish* explains how accounts of the city under plague provided city officials with an opportunity to implement procedures choreographed by a specific dream of order: "This enclosed, segmented space, observed at every point, in which the individuals are inserted in a fixed place, in which the slightest movements are supervised, in which all events are recorded, in which an uninterrupted work of writing links the centre and periphery, in which power is exercised without division, according to a continuous hierarchical figure, in which each individual is constantly located, examined and distributed. . . . Against the plague, which is a mixture, discipline brings into play its power, which is one of analysis" (197). Where Foucault here predicates "the utopia of the perfectly governed city" on the illicit "mixture" of bodies produced by the excesses of festival as well as the plague, Austen's style transfers the libidinal energy intensified by her complicated courtship rituals onto the practice of disciplined writing, so that the reader can enjoy them. This inducement to discipline comes to the fore in the opening sentence of *Pride and Prejudice*, as the erotic meaning of her double entendres exceeds the heartless economy in which she has inscribed it. Indeed, two centuries have passed without producing a novelist nearly as capable of producing a heroine who seems so disciplined because her democratic tendencies are so strong.

The idea of removing oneself and family from the community may be as old as the concept of property, but it takes something like the threat of infectious disease, according to Foucault, to implement the dream of "the well-ordered city." Foucault holds this political fantasy responsible for the quarantine policies first developed during the Middle Ages for purposes of protecting the urban population from the recurring epidemics of bubonic plague. These regulations, as he describes them, "involve literally imposing a partitioning grid on the regions and towns struck by plague, with regulations indicating when people can go out, at what times, and what they must do at home, what type of food they may have, prohibiting certain types of contact, requiring them to present themselves to inspectors, and to open their homes to inspectors" (*Security* 10). Such procedures take as given that social contact was the means of infection and relied on supervised containment to remove individuals from circulation. This same dream of order lives on into the modern period to inspire the procedures of self-containment that Austen brought to bear on democratic writing.

During the eighteenth and early nineteenth centuries, as Foucault tells the story, this fantasy of government collided with a contrary dream of order that scripted modern methods of population management. The conflict between the two political fantasies prompted an uproar in France and England over the inoculation procedures developed to cope with the threat of smallpox epidemics. These procedures assumed that the disease was a condition not of individuals, who could be contained and supervised, but as "a multiplicity of individuals who . . . exist bound to the materiality within which they live" (*Security* 21). To deal with smallpox, Foucault explains, government did not think in terms of "fixing and demarcating the territory, but of allowing circulations to take place, of controlling them, sifting the good and the bad, ensuring that things are always in movement, constantly moving around, continually going from one point to another, but in such a way that the inherent dangers of this circulation are cancelled out" (*Security* 65). Variolation procedures did not try to prevent the disease so much as to introduce it into the population on the theory that an artificially inoculated form of smallpox could not only reduce the violence of the outbreak but also prevent possible future epidemics. Where quarantine enforced disciplinary procedures to combat the plague, inoculation took "security" measures to minimize the lethal effects of smallpox. Such measures, as Foucault describes them, are "simply a matter of maximizing the positive elements, for which one provides the best possible circulation, and of minimizing what is risky and inconvenient, like theft and disease, while knowing they will never be completely repressed" (*Security* 19). Lacking a utopian component, this way of governing aims at a state of homeostasis and generally works in countless small and nearly invisible ways. Thus, it takes a state of emergency to enforce these procedures with enough consistency to expose the "dream of order" choreographing them. To carry out the procedures of discipline and security, respectively, Austen and Brockden Brown relied on positive inducements to recruit a readership.

Two centuries have passed, and readers at all levels of critical acumen are still generally delighted to take part in the form of self-management Austen requires for admission to her modestly expanded world of property. Not so for the minimalism of Brockden Brown, who wrote in an American style that offered inducement of another kind. Countering her style move for move, his style put a distinctively American spin on the novel. As it undoes everything Austen accomplishes with her marriage plots, the ending of *Arthur Mervyn* transforms her dream of order into his political fantasy.[14] Here, Brockden Brown marries off the penniless protagonist to an "imprudent" widow, a Portuguese Jewess with property and an English name, to form a union that scrambles the elements of Austen's fortunate marriage of emotional attraction to economic value and recombines them with features that make a mockery of Austen's resolution. To marry into property not only removes Mervyn from social circulation but infantilizes him as well; he calls his new wife "mamma." Planning to resume his migratory practices in a year or two, Mervyn does not take the trouble to rehearse all the clichés signaling that both he and the novel have achieved domestic plentitude: "Our household, while we stayed in America,—in a year or two we hie to Europe,—should be *thus* composed. Fidelity, and skill, and pure morals, should be sought out, and enticed, by generous recompenses, into our domestic service. Duties which should be light and regular.—Such and such should be our amusements and employments abroad and at home: and would not this be true happiness?" (330). The novel's final clause questions the very possibility that, even were all its traditional elements in place, a life circumscribed by private property could add up to "true happiness." What were readers supposed to make of a style that unmakes its own conclusion in the act of formulating it?

If *Arthur Mervyn* is any indication, those who wrote in that style were positioned politically to think of novels as the means of clearing away the conceptual architecture of Europe, so that they could formulate a community that had yet to materialize. In moving, without apparent rhyme or reason, across a dispersed field of positively and negatively charged social elements, such writing consequently rewarded readers with flashes of counterintuition—moments when what appeared to be the turbulence of dispersed populations suddenly became a process of linking those so dispersed, even those not yet perceptible, to every other. This style could, in the manner of Brocken Brown's protagonists, offer any number of ways to connect those dots without designating any single pathway as representative or any one destination as the center and measure of the rest. This style invites us to participate in an open-ended experiment in social relations that affords glimpses of the affirmative potential in having no fixed identity, as well as the advantages of a government always in the process of reformulating itself.

Chapter 2

Refiguring the Social Contract

In this chapter, we consider how the attempt to formulate a national govern-ment in British America altered the European concept of the Social Contract. This term names the problematic wherein European intellectuals and men of letters rethought the story that modern government originated in an agree-ment among the people to be governed and derived its authority from them alone. The discussion of whether and how such agreement could be formu-lated in North America bears directly on how the first American novelists felt obliged to revise the British novel, which held to the assumption that having property was antecedent to belonging to a community. The previous chapter demonstrated that, for lack of the property to anchor his identity, a protago-nist like Arthur Mervyn achieved neither the consistency nor the sense of fullness that Austen's characters did. His unfinished character, like that of the community he forms, bears an uncanny resemblance to the unfinished quality of the framers' attempt to reformulate the Social Contract as they drafted the Constitution of the United States. The reason, as we understand it, has every-thing to do with the fact that, like the Constitution itself, the novels that ap-peared as soon as the Constitution was ratified similarly ruled out any principle of representation that could unify "the people" in favor of an open-ended system that could link an expanding and diversifying population in multiple ways.

Like the first American novelists, the framers of the Constitution were tasked with imagining a political order whose parts were free to interact in ways that neither reduced them to a common denominator nor positioned them in a core-periphery relation to a central government that resembled their former relation as colonial subjects of Britain. Any systematic attempt on their part to formulate an ideal contract between such a population and its government faltered on the same contradiction that Thomas Hobbes and John Locke covered up with a pseudo-anthropological origin story. It was by rethinking their before-and-after story that such intellectuals as Jean-Jacques Rousseau, Adam Smith, Cesare Bonesana-Beccaria, and Immanuel Kant attempted to revise the Social Contract so as to resolve inherent contradictions. They failed to come up with a workable model. Those who set out to formulate a new political society on the western shore of the Atlantic not only drew their inspiration from the Social Contract but also exploited the flaws in its conceptual architecture to insist on their right as British colonists in North America to overthrow British rule.[1]

Our task in this chapter is to show why the authors of a new government found it necessary to double Locke's concept of the citizen-subject and how this exposed the conflict resolved by his story of the original contract. What amounted to a conflict between two mutually exclusive origin stories of the new nation produced a model of government that could accommodate the political climate of the former colonies. We proceed on the assumption that to provide the means of organizing actual social relations, the Social Contract—and perhaps any political theory—had to be disseminated with its logic repackaged as a figure, image, character, or story of how the present government acquired the form of power it now exercises. Because it required the consent of the people to be governed and distributed the power of government to representative citizen-subjects, the story of the Social Contract made itself the only viable alternative to the violence of an unregulated commons. Yes, this relationship between the individual's subjection to and empowerment by government is definitely a chicken-egg affair, but simply knowing that cannot explain why Locke's "man of property" proved such a compelling iteration of the citizen-subject. As he described it, the man of property was not only the product of the Social Contract—by means of which the individual secured property "in his own person" in the form of individual rights—but also the precondition for enacting the contract. Only men of property, after all, would feel the need for government to guarantee such security in return for their support. This must have seemed like some powerful magic to pull off, unless of course one were already a person of considerable property. Locke's account of property makes men not only vulnerable to possible encroachments but also entitled to legal protection of their persons and property from those encroachments.

On recognizing their vulnerability in this respect, according to Locke, men entered into a contract with each other to prevent them from seizing one another's individual agency and goods (*Two Treatises* II.95–96). Rather than transfer their hostility toward one another to an external monarch, as Hobbes had proposed, Locke's contract converted a population riddled with inequities into an abstract unified citizenry that served as both the container of acquisitive energy and the protector of the property acquired. In that it produced an ideal unity out of disparate and isolated individuals, the Social Contract operated according to much the same cultural logic as religious conversion—part of an unruly mob one minute and a law-abiding individual the next. While both forms of conversion require a narrative that can spin straw into gold, so to speak, they differ profoundly on issues of cause and effect, where the magic comes from, and the nature of the transubstantiation that occurs. Where religious conversion implies an external agency that transforms the material substance of the man into his spiritual essence, political conversion allows no such external source of magic. To come into existence, the Social Contract requires an internal agent, usually characterized as collective "will" or "energy," to transform what is a fundamentally destructive force into individual productivity. In performing this magic, the figure of the Social Contract transfers the very basis of human identity from the domain of religion into that of politics. The Social Contract requires, this would imply, a veritable sea change in how men saw the natural world and could imagine it enhancing their ability to thrive and enjoy its resources. Where religious conversion transforms mortal human beings into members of a spiritual community, the Social Contract transforms the heterogeneous field of such attitudes and expectations into a form of political society that could act on the general will and for the general good. In purporting to transform the private man into the public man, however, neither religious nor political conversion claims to do this for everyone. Locke's man of property was a representative man.

The Man of Property

To create a representative individual by means of persuasion rather than force, a rhetorical supplement was necessary, which Locke identified as "property." For property to provide the magical additive that made it possible for the Social Contract to convert ordinary men into citizens of a political society, it was necessary that all potential citizens voluntarily subject themselves to a representative government. As a result, the man of property was at once the man who entered into the contract and the product of its enactment. It's not that difficult to imagine how thinking in terms of this figure would encourage potential settlers to entertain the possibility that land in North America was not only theirs for the taking, provided they made it productive, but would also entitle them to the privileges that came with owning property. One can also see where this belief that property could transform a common man into the representative man spelled trouble for the idea of an elite governing body. Those who were already men of considerable property generally thought themselves uniquely capable of representing everyone.[2]

In order to correct the origin story that Hobbes had devised as an argument for absolute sovereignty, Locke accepted the premise that their acquisition of "goods" forced men to form a government that secured their goods by appropriating their "force" or natural aggression, thereby transforming natural man into civilized man. To avoid the war of every man against all others on which Hobbes had predicated this transformation, Locke, too, went back to the moment when men first began to acquire property. Once there, however, Locke could imagine the conditions for an agreement among men of property that would yield an alternative to absolute sovereignty. He obviously had this possibility in mind when he enjoined his readers to imagine that "in the beginning all the World was *America*" (II.49).[3] America afforded a way of going back to the beginning when there was enough nature held in common to go around.

Under these conditions, man's "first" property—his body as the source of labor necessary to sustain its life—was all that Locke needed for purposes of reimagining man as an individual who could sustain and govern himself. This was the basis on which to claim that although God "hath given the World to Men in common" (II.26), each man nevertheless "has a *Property* in his own *Person*" (II.27). Thus, whatever "he hath mixed his *Labour* with, and joyned to it something that is his own," "[he] thereby makes it his *Property*" (II.27). Locke's *Second Treatise of Government* cannot say it often enough that once a man has annexed resources from the common as his property, he has canceled out his natural right to everything in common and, in its place, acquired an exclusive right to his property. With property, there should come a sense of security that quiets the need and, with that need, the desire for more. The conversion of ordinary men into a community of individual citizens accumulates religious residue in the form of the morality that disposes each such individual to act on behalf of the general good. Hand in glove with reason, virtue rises above self-interest, prompting men of property to form a civil society. At this point, Locke's origin story veers off sharply from that of Hobbes.

As Locke would have it, man's inherently social nature was sufficient to stop him—on becoming a man of property—from encroaching on the rights of others. In giving the world to men in common, he reasoned, God also saw to it that none of us can furnish ourselves with the full necessities of life. Having isolated individuals from one another by means of property, then, Locke proceeded to argue that an equally compelling need for sociability induced men to form social relations with one another. Given this need, he could conclude that mutual dependency rather than natural aggression was the true cause for men to form political societies (II.15). By resituating this origin story in North America, Locke took the contract down a distinctively modern road to nationhood. He proposed that, all men being equal in a state of nature, "no one can be put out of this Estate, without his own *Consent*. [This is done] by agreeing with other Men to joyn and unite into a community, for their comfortable, safe, and peaceable living one amongst another, in a secure Enjoyment of their Properties, and a greater Security against any that are not of it" (II.95). When "any number of Men" have so agreed "*to make one Community or Government* . . . they make one Body Politick, wherein the Majority have a Right to act and conclude the rest" (II.95). There can be no exceptions or outliers, for every person who enters into such an agreement "puts himself under an Obligation to everyone of that Society, to submit to the determination of the *majority*" (II.97). Once "the majority"—by which Locke meant the majority of men of property—had declared their consent to this agreement, each man would voluntarily subject himself to its laws.

That an individual's property was predicated on his voluntary subjection to the law and vice versa distinguished a "commonwealth" from every other form of "community," as well as from absolute sovereignty. Ultimately derived from the Latin *civitas*, Locke's idea of "commonwealth" assumes that the possession of property inspired man not only to seek protection from a higher authority but also, once so removed from the common, to seek the company of other men of property.[4] To become a "commonwealth," all that was necessary was for the community of men of property to become a de facto sovereign body. To this effect, Locke insists, in "a Constituted Commonwealth, standing upon its own Basis, and acting according to its own Nature, that is, acting for the preservation of the Community there can be but one *Supream Power*, which is the Legislative, to which all the rest are and must be subordinate" (II.149).

But Locke also saw to it that his model government had an escape clause—a way of delegitimating the sovereignty of any "commonwealth" so constituted: "there remains still *in the People a Supream Power* to remove or *alter the Legislative* [body] when they find the *Legislative* act contrary to the trust reposed in them" (II.149). The legislator who doesn't hold to this standard nullifies his status as a member of the legislative body and can be voted out. Should that body not come by its authority as a "representative" of the people but be appointed in perpetuity, the same principle obtains. The entire body and thus the government delegitimizes its authority were it to fail to act on behalf of the people as a whole. Even in this early formulation—before the man of property became the presumptive authority of Enlightenment letters—the figure was already enveloped in a paradox. Owning property identified one as *subject to* the body of law that regulated property. But owning property also—in Locke's view—identified one as free from want, free from the need to labor, and thus qualified to represent the general interest. By his reasoning, then, the man of property was not only *subject to* the law but also the *subject of* that law, an abstract citizen who in his very body becomes the government, embodying both its power and its limitations.[5]

To consider what happened to this figure in North America during the period just prior to and immediately after the War of Independence, we must also look briefly at another revision of Hobbes's account of the origin of political society, for Jean-Jacques Rousseau's ideas were unquestionably part of the mix.[6] Like Locke, Rousseau circumvented the Hobbesian dilemma of *bellum omnia contra alles* by refiguring the man of property as a subject in both senses—not only as subject to law but also as the embodiment of disinterested virtue informing the law that he lived by. As the symbolic resolution of this conceptual opposition, the figure of the man of property identified the lines of conflict along which the prevailing notion of sovereignty was about to split open, as colonial settlers had a mind to challenge the legitimacy of British rule over her North American colonies.

In writing *The Social Contract* (1762), Rousseau rewrote the exchange whereby Hobbes's multitude, out of fear for their very lives, agreed to hand over their natural power to a sovereign in an exchange that gave the people exclusive authority over themselves. Rousseau famously felt it went completely against a man's self-interest to abandon the power and freedom that were "the chief interests of his self-preservation."[7] For lack of a model of government that might serve as an adequate alternative to a sovereign positioned outside and above the law, Rousseau proceeded to dream one up. In doing so, his goal was to "find a form of association that will defend and protect the person and goods of each associate with the full common force, and by means of which each, uniting with all, nevertheless obey only himself, and remain as free as before" (I.6.4). To return the power to the people who have been alienated from their natural rights, Rousseau had to solve what amounts to a riddle: what "form of association" would make it possible for the individual not only to forsake his self-interest, thus "uniting with all," but also to "obey only himself"? To make sense of this riddle, as Louis Althusser explains, Rousseau used the story of the original contract to create the conditions under which his ideal notion of the contract could take place, so that "behind the juridical concept of the contract, we are dealing with an exceptional contract with a paradoxical structure" (Althusser 126). A clearer sense of how this paradox shaped the Enlightenment theories of government that would form the basis for nineteenth-century liberalism will also be essential to explaining the succession of failed attempts to formulate a viable American alternative to notions of sovereignty.

To form a government that did not in some way mirror the British concept of sovereignty, Americans soon found themselves in a situation very much like the one in which Rousseau's just-so story had placed the man of property. This situation required men to subject themselves voluntarily to the law of a community that did not yet exist. The juridical concept of the contract, not to mention common sense, required such a community to exist *before* men could agree to subject themselves to it. But as Rousseau imagined it, the Social Contract describes neither the process nor the principles by which to form a contractual government, according to Althusser, so much as "the constitution of the *a priori* condition of the possibility of any (real or empirical) exchange" (Althusser 135). While Rousseau could not make the story of the original contract any more logical than his predecessors had, he did succeed in establishing certain preconditions for such an exchange to take place.[8] These conditions included a governing body made of no one else but the man of property himself. Before the contract could be enacted, as Rousseau concluded, a body of proto-citizens must be already disposed to enter into such an agreement. In thus revising Hobbes's origin story, Rousseau also made a small but decisive correction to Locke's. He identified property itself, rather than human sociality, as the motivation for men to form a political society.

Rousseau conceded Locke's point that in giving up his force and goods, an individual would receive them back in the form of property in return for agreeing to obey the law. In his view, the individual clearly benefits from the exchange of his highly vulnerable force and goods for exclusive rights to property and the protection of his rights to property in himself, thereby ensuring his freedom. Even so, the shadow of class difference, of purchased or coerced votes, and thus of rule by faction necessarily intrudes into Rousseau's happy account of the birth of political society. The logic of that narrative was flawed to the extent that it relied on the magic of an original contract to convert common resources into the basis for private property. Rousseau was well aware that his representative political society presupposed the universal human willingness to give up both aggression and the social instinct that drew one man into combination with others who shared his interests. He knew only too well that once this transformation had occurred, nothing could prevent the formation of political factions or partial societies—the very problem he had hoped to counter.

In order to carry out the general will, Rousseau's origin story would require not only an ideal legislator but also an a priori man of property. "There is often," he admits, "a considerable difference between the will of all and the general will: the latter looks only to the common interest, the former looks to private interest" (II.3.2). In a final effort to imagine a workable Social Contract, Rousseau tried to figure out under what conditions his theory of government might avoid the problem of interest groups. "[When] an adequately informed people deliberates," he reasoned, "the Citizens [must have] no communication among themselves," in which case "the general will would always result from the large number of small differences" (II.3.3). Were it not for the information they receive and their power to sway one another, he concluded, people would have more or less the same interests. Thus, if government could forbid factions and require "every Citizen [to] state only his own opinion," these conditions would "ensure the general will is always enlightened"; the will of all and the general will would be the same (II.3.4). As he concluded his revision of the origin story, Rousseau admitted that an educational institution of some kind to establish these conditions was necessary before individuals would be willing to make such an agreement.[9] Without this a priori government, he was at a loss to say how his plan could materialize. The narrative of the contract—a magical exchange between an enlightened political community and a subject predisposed to join it—indeed produces the very parties necessary for such an exchange to be enacted. In that his ideal man was both a prospective convert to and already a member of an enlightened community, Rousseau's figure of the man of property embodied the same paradox of representative government that troubled the process of formulating a federal government for the United States.

With only the king of England to uphold their charters, the colonists fell back on the European theory of the Social Contract in order to object to British abuse of their charters. They put themselves at a disadvantage by using the traditional story of political origins to identify what they found unsatisfactory about their relation to the British sovereign. They justified their claims to independence in terms of the charters that guaranteed their rights inhering in their property. Insofar as the British king was bent on compromising those rights, however, the European model of the Social Contract expressed their disappointments and insecurities. This situation opened up the tautology concealed in Locke's origin story: were they citizens first and subjects only on the condition of being fully represented? We attempt to read the process of formulating a government for the United States as a conflict between these two origin stories.

What Happens in Boston Doesn't Stay in Boston

As historians routinely point out, the story of the original contract and the concepts attached to it not only persuaded any number of British subjects to immigrate to North America but also afforded a way of understanding who they were and what they were entitled to once they had arrived and settled. During the formative period from the colonial reaction to the Stamp Act in 1765 to the ratification of the Constitution in 1789, the figure of the Social Contract provided a conceptual framework within which a literate American could imagine himself or herself as to some degree part of a community apart and different from Great Britain, on the one hand, and from local communities, on the other. Though far from unanimous in what they wanted by way of a federal government, these people were quick to rally around the claim that Britain had violated her original charters with the colonies. The representatives to the First Continental Congress understood that a confederation of states was needed to maintain the strength that the colonies had exercised when united against the British.

Working within the theoretical framework of the Social Contract and with its figures of thought, for fourteen years the delegates repeatedly failed to overcome the contradiction that shaped the model they were using. Like Rousseau, they did succeed in identifying the a priori conditions required for a representative government to materialize in North America. In purely conceptual terms, the plan of government finally ratified by the states in 1789 distinguished itself from the models with which it had been thinking by virtue of the fact that the architects of the U.S. Constitution institutionalized some of problems that developed over years of debate. Defining government as the framework within which they could continue to challenge the extent and limitations of their authority as state representatives, the delegates to the Constitutional Convention in Philadelphia transformed the contract from a government already formed into an ongoing process of forming one and thus a work in progress.[10]

A glance at the Declaration of Independence will suggest what the delegates to the Continental Congress from the thirteen colonies were up against. They had no trouble using the language of the contract to identify the violations of their rights by Parliament and, on that basis, to characterize George III as "Tyrannical." This act of renaming British authority provided them—under Locke's escape clause—with the philosophical grounds for considering their contract as British subjects with the imperial government null and void; as Locke had put it, "There remains still *in the People a Supream Power* to remove or *alter the Legislative* [body] when they find the *Legislative* act contrary to the trust reposed in them" (II.149). A sequence of parliamentary acts following the French and Indian War strained the colonists' belief in their contract with the British government to the breaking point and yet confirmed their faith in the principle of the contract itself.[11] But when Parliament levied a special tax in 1765 to cover the debt incurred by fighting a war to protect the colonies against the French and their Indian allies, the colonists refused to pay. They did so on grounds that the tax had violated charters modeled on Locke's original contract. In chartering each of the thirteen colonies, they maintained, the king had agreed that his government would not tax its colonies without their explicit consent or that of their representatives.[12]

The colonists were not wrong in reading the contract this way, but then neither was Parliament wrong in levying taxes to help pay off the war debt. Locke's *Second Treatise* had explicitly introduced slippage into the term "representative government" that indicated that not all the people need be *directly* represented in Parliament in order that all the people be represented, because all the people were *virtually* represented in an idealized legislative body that acted in the general interest. As British subjects, the colonists may well have been part of the virtual "people" from a British perspective, but the colonial understanding of representation, as Jack Rakove argues, "was 'actual,' not virtual" (*Revolutionaries* 20). Because land was relatively available in the colonies, Rakove explains, local communities routinely sent delegates to colonial assemblies whom they considered their agents and *not* members of a separate governing elite. In their view, the state legislatures were not supposed to legislate on behalf of a unified people or the general interest; it was the people who legislated through representatives chosen to protect their particular interests. Lacking actual representation in Parliament, the colonists understandably felt that their interests had not been included under the general interests and so were not represented by Parliament.

During this same period, a decisive shift in Parliament's self-characterization contributed to the colonists' sense that they were not being treated as freeborn British subjects but as a subjected people like the Scots or, worse, a conquered people like the Irish. Turning his back on the consensual character of the Social Contract, jurist Sir William Blackstone said it all when, in 1766, he described Parliament's power in Hobbesian terms. "There is and must be a supreme, irresistible, absolute, uncontrolled authority in which the *jura summi imperii,* or the rights of sovereignty reside," he claimed, and in Britain that authority resided in Parliament (Rakove, *Revolutionaries* 21). In that the Stamp Act placed a direct tax on all paper traded within the colonies—wrappers, legal documents, stationery, newspapers, shipping ledgers, and even playing cards—it put a mark of British intervention on American commerce that was visible across regional, occupational, and class lines. In view of its widespread impact, one has to wonder why it took the colonial governments ten years and a series of localized acts of Parliament punishing the city of Boston to produce *the* event that justified their throwing off British rule.

To put it another way, why would the Coercive Acts of 1773, known in America as the "Intolerable Acts," have provided the occasion for open political dissent on the part of thirteen colonial governments? Quite simply, such events were perceived as acts of terror perpetrated by Parliament, and they produced a response on the part of colonists to seek from their colonial governments some form of protection. Take, for example, the Declaration of rights and League for their support by the inhabitants of Virginia. One of many such declarations drawn up in response to the Intolerable Acts, the document claims, "An act lately passed to take away the trade of the inhabitants of the town of Boston in the province of Massachusetts bay" poses a "[danger] to the rights of the British empire in general and should be considered as its common cause." Having sounded this alarm, Virginia's declaration calls for a form of preemption that promises to stand with Boston for the sake of the security of the colonies: "We will ever be ready to join with our fellow subjects in every part of the same in exerting all these rightful powers which god has given us for the re-establishing and guaranteeing such their constitutional rights, when, where, and by whom, soever invaded" (Mason). Though crafted in the European tradition, the rhetoric of property invaded, rights violated, and commerce disrupted refigured the story of the Social Contract as a broken contract. What happened in Boston did not stay in Boston.

What happened in Boston reverberated throughout the colonies as the fear of broken contracts. It was not fear of an actual breach of contract so much as fear of the dissolution of the original contract that protected Americans as British citizens that produced a disruption of government and a rash of declarations that the charters between Britain and her North American colonies had been violated. The fear of such a violation would seem at once to anticipate and to ward off the feared event itself. To see what has come down in history as the Boston Tea Party in these terms, we need only follow the Virginia declaration as it translates an empirical fact—that is, the sequence of acts visited by Parliament in 1773 on the city of Boston—into what was clearly "an affective fact."[13] When an event acquires an affect with the capacity to convert the empirical fact of the event into an affective fact, any reference to the event will generate affect. "Paradoxically," Brian Massumi contends, the "self-effecting [capacity of affect] produces certainty, even when the trigger is the opposite, the looming uncertainty of ill-defined threat. . . . As soon as there is any sign of threat, its most feared effects have already begun to materialize" (8). According to this principle, once the American response had established itself as an affective fact, the British didn't have to mount an invasion or pass other punitive laws in Parliament. On the recommendation of the First Continental Congress in 1774, colony after colony responded to the threat of the fear of disruption with a decisive act of preemption in the form of a string of state constitutions. The fear of a broken contract with Great Britain had both displaced and produced the feared event.

Just how such fear had rippled across the language of the contract and transformed both parties to the contract becomes especially clear in the Declaration of Rights issued by the New Hampshire state legislature.[14] The authors of the New Hampshire declaration open by "PROTESTING and DECLARING that we never sought to throw off our dependence upon Great Britain, but felt ourselves happy under her protection, while we could enjoy our constitutional rights and privileges" (1). Having no particular complaint of their own against their British protectors, the New Hampshire legislature nevertheless threw off that dependency on the grounds that they

> have taken into our serious consideration the unhappy circumstances, into which this colony is involved by means of many

grievous and oppressive acts of the British Parliament, depriving us
of our natural and constitutional rights and privileges; to enforce
obedience to which acts a powerful fleet and army have been sent to
this country by the ministry of Great Britain, who have exercised a
wanton and cruel abuse of their power, in destroying the lives and
properties of the colonists in many places with fire and sword, taking the ships and lading from many of the honest and industrious
inhabitants of this colony employed in commerce, agreeable to the
laws and customs a long time used here. (1)

Reading through this generic list of indictments, one can see here that the
specific punitive measures visited on Boston by Parliament have morphed
into the threat of an invasion, increasing the magnitude of that threat and the
intensity of fear in proportion to its vagueness.

By granting such causal status to the fear so generated, we are not suggesting that the Boston Tea Party itself set off political revolution. We are
chiefly interested in the impact of the Boston Tea Party at the level of affect—
not only how it generated fear capable of converting a diverse and scattered
population into a single community that considered itself subject to British
tyranny but also how that community of feeling gathered rhetorical force that
reshaped the pervasive understanding of British sovereignty. We assume it
took much more than any one local event to set off a rapid and pervasive metastasis of the fear of an invasion of the colonies or to create the security apparatus that sprang into action to preempt it. If anything, it was probably such
an apparatus that enabled fear to spread in the first place, for one was already
working to coordinate the various committees of correspondence that had
established themselves in almost all of the colonies during 1774 for purposes
of "remov[ing] the uneasiness and to quiet the minds of the people" (Middlekauff 221). In the words of the charge that created such a committee in
Virginia, their purpose was to share "early and authentic" information and
intelligence "with our sister colonies" concerning "Acts and resolutions of the
British Parliament, or proceedings of administration, as may relate to the British colonies in America" (Middlekauff 221). It could in fact be argued that
dissemination of politically charged information through and by a network of
these committees of correspondence was responsible for converting the independent colonies into a de facto union—though certainly not one that could
consolidate what were often contentious states and regions.[15]

It was apparently a small step from spreading emotionally charged information throughout the colonies to convening the First Continental Congress in 1774 to discuss the rights of the colonies and how to defend them. At its conclusion, the congress appointed three committees, respectively, to draft a declaration of independence, to negotiate with foreign countries, and to draw up articles of confederation of the thirteen colonies. As a preemptive security mechanism, in other words, a network constituted of corresponding societies not only disseminated and intensified fear but also strengthened the horizontal affiliation of quasi-sovereign colonial governments. Without this medium, it is difficult to imagine that the fear that grew out of Parliament's response to the Boston Tea Party could have reached a tipping point that congealed a host of local grievances, some of which went back ten years, into a pervasive, self-generating antagonism to the fact and form of British sovereignty. Composed of countless contributors speaking for their local interests and largely unknown to one another, this process of writing by committees of correspondence, the publication of proclamations and declarations, and the spread of rumors as news from city to city and town to town nullified the rhetorical power of the idealized representative body that both Locke and Rousseau had proposed as the second party to the original contract. Henceforth, it was impossible to imagine such a body expressing the general interest.

It was as if Rousseau had in mind the consequently disunited states of America when he argued that in a situation where the legislators had no means of imposing their general will, the customs and values of various local interests would naturally dominate political thinking. In 1774, we must again insist, the population of British America was a rapidly expanding demographic mix of people largely from the British Isles and Africa. Compared to the more homogeneous populations of France and Britain, the North American colonies were mostly small communities divided from one another on the issue of property, both in terms of what their relationship to property had been and what they thought it should do for them in North America. Compounding the difficulty of imagining themselves as one people was not only the porosity of borders to the north, west, and south but also the internal movement of various currents within the population that followed intricate trade and communication routes from north to south and east to west, as well as back and forth to Europe, the West Indies, and Africa.[16] Imagine how difficult it would have been for those charged with forming a national government to fashion a representative man from this tangle of overlapping and competing interests. Confronting the impossibility of doing so, they had to formulate an alternative basis on which to found a government.

Men of Interests

The delegates appointed by the Continental Congress to draft the Articles of Confederation were hardly starting from scratch but had to argue their way through different layers and various forms of government, some of which clung to the concept of an original contract in the form of colonial or city charters, while others were intent on remaining extremely fluid and free from any government restrictions. Where established landowners probably understood property as the basis of their rights and protections as British subjects,[17] the migratory sectors of the population looked to government to ensure the right to pursue property wherever and in whatever form it became available. Thus, no matter how the Continental Congress might try to divide, classify, and balance the opposing political camps, they found that in ever-increasing numbers, American colonists were aligning themselves with groups of citizen-subjects whose economic freedom, more so than their land or wealth, had to be protected from imperial, foreign, and domestic encroachment. Upon securing enough property to sustain a comfortable life, such men of interests would hardly be of a mind to consider their freedom from labor sufficient cause to put their particular interests aside and to act on behalf of the general interest. Men who wanted only their economic freedom were unlikely to think of "disinterest" as the virtue that Enlightenment discourse considered it to be, much less of economic restraint as a remedy for their often straitened circumstances.

Thus resistant to traditional republican virtue, such men were only too aware that their status was quite different from that of the representative individuals who entered into the agreement envisioned by Locke and Rousseau.[18] In that the Declaration of Independence redefined the colonies and the British government as "we, the people" and "Tyrannical," respectively, one can consider this document as the vanishing point of Locke's story of the origins of political society. The authors of the Declaration of Independence used the language of the Social Contract to declare that contract invalid on the grounds "that to secure these rights, Governments are instituted among Men, deriving their just powers from the consent of the governed, —That whenever any Form of Government becomes destructive of these ends, it is the Right of the People to alter or to abolish it, and to institute new Government, laying its foundation on such principles and organizing its powers in such form, as to them shall seem most likely to effect their Safety and Happiness." Until its last paragraph, the Declaration of Independence doesn't noticeably depart from a traditional origin story. Its adherence to that narrative thus makes it obvious that the Declaration of Independence is not only the vanishing point of Locke's origin story but also the point at which an alternative account emerges of how the nation first came into being.

Jefferson, like the members of the congress who revised his draft, did not presume to describe empirical fact so much as to produce a document that resembled *The Social Contract* in specifying the a priori conditions necessary for an ideal version of the contract to materialize. It becomes apparent that this iteration of the contract recognizes its limitations as soon we shift our attention from the boldness with which the Declaration of Independence catalogues the king's "abuses" of their rights as citizens to the uncertainty that infiltrates and overwhelms the statement finally spelling out what they intend to do about it. In this statement, the authors claim the right "to abolish [their charters with England], to institute new Government, laying its foundation on *such* principles and organizing its powers in *such* form, *as to them shall seem most likely* to effect their Safety and Happiness" (our italics). In contrast with the precise list of abuses compelling the colonists to separate themselves from a tyrannical government, these last dangling participles seem suddenly at a loss to say how they imagine establishing the principles of the contract on new political territory. In appealing to some members of the congress, a clearer statement of what form of government founded on which principles would be the one "most likely to effect their Safety and Happiness" would have alienated many others. Thus, the final draft of the Declaration of Independence concluded on the only possible note—a self-eviscerating appeal to the general interest.

Hannah Arendt famously considers Jefferson's "We hold," as in "We hold these truths to be self evident," as a speech performance that in and of itself "brings something into being which did not exist before" (*On Revolution* 130). Rather than depend for its authority on either God or the Social Contract, Jefferson's "We hold" authorizes itself by means of its display of what she calls "the world-making capacity of the human faculty of making and keeping promises" (175). While we would modify Arendt's own declaration to say that Jefferson's *Declaration* constituted its authority by means of the act of writing it without any reference to precedent or absolute authority, that does not alter the fact that by invoking "the people," Jefferson was inventing a unanimity that did not in fact exist and perhaps never would. That the concept lives in the performance "We hold" becomes abundantly clear in the course of the document that concludes on a contrary note:[19] "We, therefore, the Representatives of the united States of America, in General Congress, Assembled, . . . do, in the Name, and by Authority of the good People of these Colonies, solemnly publish and declare, That these United Colonies are, and of Right ought to be Free and Independent States; . . . and that as Free and Independent States, they have full Power to levy War, conclude Peace, contract Alliances, establish Commerce, and to do all other Acts and Things which Independent States may of right do." One paradox follows another— "Representatives of the united *States* of America," "the good *people* of *these* Colonies," "Free and Independent States"—each iteration of which tries to think either of the many in terms of the one or of the one as many. In sequence, they indicate the difficulty of transforming a polity so divided into a single nation. So long as the issue was a matter of protecting property from an external threat, everyone was on board, but when it came to managing the threat posed by conflicting interests among colonies, regions, or sources of wealth, anything that smacked of a unified or unifying policy was ruled out.

To understand how this riddle answered itself—how property provided not only the vanishing point of one origin story but also the point of emergence for another and in many ways an opposing one—we find it helpful to think of property as the point in the Möbius strip where the outside crosses over, without breaking continuity, and becomes the inside. In the American discourse on property, the outside of the European contract—the incompatible partial societies that Rousseau excluded—became the inside of an American contract that would have to manage such conflicts. So, too, the inside of the European contract (a sovereign legislative body) became the outside of an American version of the social contract hell bent on avoiding any solution that made recourse to sovereignty. The process that took the "united States" (as it was designated in lowercase by the title of the Declaration of Independence)—from the Articles of Confederation in 1776–77, through ratification in 1781, to the drafting and approval of the U.S. Constitution by the Constitutional Convention in 1787, as well as the Federalist/Anti-Federalist debates of 1787–88—thinks through the logic of the Social Contract in a process that resembles the built-in and continuous reversibility of the Möbius strip. In appropriating the paradox of the Social Contract, the Americans understood that interests took over at the point where securing property no longer represented the general interest and became one of a multitude of particular interests. This transformation redefined government as the means of regulating group interests, an avatar of what Rousseau called factions.

In *The Passions and the Interests*, Albert O. Hirschman offers a historical account of the concept of "interest" from Niccolò Machiavelli through Adam Smith that shows how the term changed sides in the stubborn opposition between passion and reason. During the eighteenth century, in Hirschman's account, interest migrated from the category of passion (as in "particular interests") to situate itself as a conceptual "wedge" between passion and reason. As such, "interest" transformed the idea of how a government should govern in a way that instructively resembles what went on during the period from independence to ratification of the U.S. Constitution in 1789. Coming out of Machiavelli, as Hirschman explains it, the concept of "interests" was initially opposed to the passions and, in this role, could be invoked to curb the sins of the body to the advantage of specific groups or factions—hence the maxim circulated during the English Civil War, "interests do not lie." When used in the singular, "interest" (*interesse*) referred to an individual's ability to reflect on his condition and perform a disciplined assessment of what was required to advance his wealth and power. Hirschman surveys a remarkable range of seventeenth- and eighteenth-century European sources to track what he calls a "drift" in this concept of "interest" from its status in Machiavelli as the lofty faculty of an untroubled rational will to the menial faculty that calculated how best to pursue the individual's particular material advantage. During the eighteenth century, "interest" in this materialistic sense broke free of the higher faculty that made it possible for Machiavelli's Prince to judge the interests of various groups for purposes of playing them off against one another. At the same time, the concept of "interest" nevertheless continued to operate counter to the essential aggressivity of the passions and eventually became the primary counter to antisocial behavior, tantamount to reason itself.

At this point, Hirschman makes what came to be known as his signature move in explaining the rhetorical means by which "interest" could operate not only as one of the passions but also as an enabling force that managed the other passions. In thus doubling its meaning, "interest" in the singular became the answer to the question of how to govern "interests" in the plural. As certain passions rose to prominence in eighteenth-century thought and assumed institutional authority over the rest, "interests" became the chief means to counter the passions and prevent men from returning to a state of nature. Its decisive shift in meaning aligned "interests" with "government." Writing during the early eighteenth century, Giambattista Vico gave this principle what Hirschman considers perhaps its most concise formulation: "Out of ferocity, avarice, and ambition, the three vices that lead all mankind astray, [society] makes national defense, commerce, and politics, and thereby causes the strength, the wealth, and the wisdom of the republic: Out of three great vices," Vico continues, "which would certainly destroy man on earth, society thus causes the civil happiness to emerge" (17). Hirschman sees the theory of countervailing passions as the principle that authorized the Social Contract in the first place and holds it responsible for the persuasive power of the contract as a way of accounting for the origins of political society (31). Men enter into such an agreement, he claims, only when they "are guided by their interests to avoid the calamitous [Hobbesian] state of affairs that prevails when men give free reign to their passions" (32). Here, the plural "interests" indicates one "interest" per man. In view of Hirschman's history of the term, we should not be surprised to discover "interests" eventually flexing its affective muscles to overturn the repressive figure of "the general interest." As it does so, however, the plural "interests" overwhelms the troublesome concept of "particular interests," as in those originating in individual citizens.

This shift in the subject of political discourse—from the man of property to men of interests—brought about a corresponding change in the modality of interest—from a state of being "interested" rather than "disinterested" to the perpetual pursuit of another state of being, so that one was always in between states, or in a state of *inter-esse*. In other words, the right to secure property consequently dropped into second place behind the right to pursue it. Interest acquired aggression in proportion to power to transform multiple "particular interests" into "interest groups." "Men of interests" was a different subject from either the "particular interests" or the "general interest," which had, for the framers of the new government, personified the two parties of the Social Contract. To the degree that this new subject could be understood as a shifting system of variable "interests" rather than demographic groups or class alliances, it proved resistant to the idea that any form of private property, much less land or a well-appointed household, could express what Americans pursued in the name of happiness.[20]

To give the Articles of Confederation a fair shot at ratification, the Continental Congress had to gut the draft that came back to them from the committee appointed for this purpose, leaving the states with the key powers of taxation, regulation of trade, and even the means of electing representatives to the congress. This, in turn, left the Articles of Confederation incapable of protecting states as well as sectional interests from one another, much less from British and Spanish control of trade in the West Indies and Mississippi delta. As the Constitutional Convention convened in 1787, the problem of representation must have seemed insoluble. Any policy that favored all the states equally would allow small states to gang up on the large states; any measure that favored expansion into Western territories favored the large states over the smaller ones; any policy that favored the plantation system in the South would unfairly restrict trade and limit the possibilities for future manufacturing in the North, and so forth.[21]

By the time the Constitutional Convention was called, there was a move afoot among the larger states "to unite in firmly refusing to the small states an equal vote" (Rakove, *Revolutionaries* 368). The plan proposed by the Virginia delegation featured a lower house elected by the people and an upper house elected by the lower house, as well as a national executive and judiciary. But if the larger states were afraid of equal representation on the part of smaller states overriding the interests of what were clearly a larger and more diverse proportion of the nation's land and population, the small states felt perhaps more threatened by the idea of the larger states consolidating their interests as those of virtually separate nations likely to annex the small states of each region. Cathy D. Matson and Peter S. Onuf explain the results of this open struggle among competing interests with remarkable clarity: "The brief flirtation of some frustrated reformers with the idea of separate unions can be seen as a crucial step toward conceptualizing an extended republic" (88). Heretofore dedicated to obstructing any form of legislative body whose laws would override those of the states, the state delegates were forced to acknowledge the need for a higher government that could prevent a large state from combining with smaller ones to form what would amount to a foreign nation. "By raising questions about the very existence of national interests," Matson and Onuf conclude, "sectionalism forced reformers to articulate a new, inclusive conception of interest that could justify a continuing national union" (90–91). The result was a form of government based on rules to make sure the struggle would continue. In just this way, the threat of sectarianism paved the way for precisely the turn, or "drift," in the term "interest" in American political discourse that Hirschman chronicles in Europe.

A new origin story was born: "Development-minded writers of the 1780's began their historical accounts with a dark age of natural barbarism. . . . Lacking objects toward which to direct their will, 'savages' were left enslaved by their animal natures" (Matson and Onuf 92). Early agricultural communities found it necessary to their survival to define virtue as a negation of self-interest, but once conditions improved, so the story went, men began to express their social nature through commerce. Taste and refinement in turn spurred industry and improvement. This narrative, as Hirschman suggests, not only collapsed the opposition between particular interests and the general interest but also recoded the conflict among particular interests as the engine of development—and a persistent engine it proved to be for the framers of the U.S. Constitution.

If anything, the debates leading up to ratification of the Constitution escalated the splintering process where a deal cut to resolve one conflict of interests would immediately produce another conflict between a different set of opponents. No sooner had the conflict between large and small states been settled by an agreement to form both a higher house in which states were equally represented and a lower house in which states were represented in proportion to their populations than an even more intense debate arose over the issue of how to count the population to be represented in the lower house. This issue pitted northern manufacturing and commercial states against southern slave-holding states on the question of whether to count slaves as property or as "persons," which found resolution in the infamous three-fifths rule. The debate's shrillest moments exposed contradictions that both generated the ongoing argument and restricted the possibilities it could imagine between poles defined by two unacceptable forms of sovereignty—the nightmare of a tyrannical elite, on the one hand, and the nightmare of popular sovereignty, on the other. Within these limits, no one interest group could overrule the rest.

By the time the congress called delegates to the Constitutional Convention in Philadelphia in 1787, James Madison had already formulated a position on the question of what powers should be shifted from the states to the federal government. Madison had come to the conclusion, in the words of Jack Rakove, "that the real problem of rights, was not to shield the people as a whole against the arbitrary act of government, but to shield minorities and even individuals from the democratic acts of popular majorities" (*Revolutionaries* 362). To argue this position on behalf of property rights later on in *Federalist* No. 10, Madison showed how the same flaw in the logic of the contract that Locke and Rousseau tried so hard to suppress—namely, the problem of factions—was actually the solution to that very problem.[22] Convinced that "interest" could neither be defined by way of reference to some overarching general principle nor understood as the specificities of its own mode of being, Madison saw that any plan of government would have to deal with the question of how to manage a multiplicity of impersonal and preindividual interests. His contributions to *The Federalist Papers* establish such "interests" and not some representative individual as the basic unit of a civil society. Here, "interests" is detached from property, which becomes but one of many interests.

Hirschman sees Madison's declaration that "ambition must be made to counteract ambition" as a strategy for selling the "comparatively novel thought of checks and balances" by presenting it as an application of "the widely accepted and thoroughly familiar principle of countervailing passion" (30). In *Federalist No. 10*, one can indeed follow Madison through the steps of an argument that agrees point by point with Hirschman's, which links interest to passion by way of what Madison calls "opinion." "Opinion" is so loaded a term in this context as to render whatever "interest" happens to be at stake utterly resistant to reason. Thus, as Madison explains, "As long as the reason of man continues fallible, and he is at liberty to exercise it, different opinions will be formed. As long as the connection subsists between his reason and his self-love, his opinions and his passions will have a reciprocal influence on each other; and the former will be objects to which the latter will attach themselves" (73). To formulate a government capable of securing property rights, modern nations had heretofore used the figure of the Social Contract to address the problem of the unequal distribution of property and tried to resolve that problem by a branch of government that operated in "the general interest." But in Madison's view, the conditions for even imagining such a solution had radically changed. If "from the protection of different and unequal faculties of acquiring property, the possession of different degrees and kinds of property immediately results," he reasoned, then "from the influence of these [inequities] on the sentiments and views of the respective proprietors, ensues a division of the society into different interests and parties" (73). Madison was careful to distinguish "parties" based on the division of interests from the factions based on the division of property on which Rousseau had run aground in attempting to imagine a workable contract.

His list of the factors that had stalled the process of forming a federal government indeed shows Madison translating the traditional concept of "factions" into the "interests" responsible for multiplying and exacerbating the divisions within and among the various state representatives. Topping the list is "zeal for different opinions concerning religion," followed by contending opinions on the form government should take and whether to restrict economic speculation (73). In terms that recall Hobbes's *Behemoth*, Madison also lists the public's attraction to "different leaders ambitiously contending for pre-eminence and power," as well as to "persons of other descriptions whose fortunes have been interesting to the human passions" (73). He thinks of these rhetorical forces as contributing factors in transforming traditional social divisions into an exponentially more heterogeneous field of men disposed more "to vex and oppress each other than to co-operate for their common good" (73). This field being the condition of possibility for formulating a federal government, according to Madison, any solution to the problem of party and faction would have to involve "party and faction in the necessary and ordinary operations of the government" (74). In both its details and its overarching plan, the ratification process demonstrated that Madison succeeded in reconceiving contractual government as an agreement to disagree.

Neither/Nor

More than a decade of disagreement over what that government should look like—who should be represented and how various partial societies might pursue their interests as such—had all but institutionalized the process of proposing laws that could then be countered, debated, corrected, and sometimes implemented. If institutionalized so as to prevent any one concept of sovereignty from taking over, "interests" had already begun to provide a conceptual basis for running an expansive and internally divided nation. It could certainly be said that the Federalists succeeded in shifting significant power to the federal government. But there was, as Isaac Kramnick contends, "no watershed victory of liberalism over republicanism," and each side used alternative paradigms for purposes of articulating political positions that made sense primarily in opposing each other (32). The government had in fact become a work in progress—that is to say, an agreement to disagree within parameters that excluded alternative models of sovereignty—that of a governing elite, on the one hand, and that of the masses, on the other. On the basis of these twin exclusions, Gordon Wood is among those who see the Constitution of 1787 as "designed in part to solve the problem created by the presence in the state legislatures of [so many] middling men" (*Empire* 31).

While we understand full well the inclination to see a unified nation where historical research shows there were only partial societies with conflicting interests, the novels that began to appear in the late 1780s tell a different story. Those who consumed this body of fiction could not mistake the operations of the intricate networks linking demonstrably diverse groups of people for the formation of a coherent middle-class ethos. Those men with some property but who were not especially secure in that property would have had the most to gain or to lose in the fluid economic situation that prevailed during this period. Yet it is still considered reasonable for historians to assume that, of the different groups in the society, it was "the middling sorts" "who launched the momentous social struggle that eventually turned them into the dominant 'middle class' of the nineteenth century" (*Empire* 30). According to this argument, the proto-middle class would include all those "who could not be classified either as gentlemen or as out-and-out commoners" (*Empire* 28). In advocating this view, Wood acknowledges that "there were immense differences among the middling sorts," but he goes on to claim that while artisans "ranged from the very wealthy to the marginally poor," weavers and shoemakers to clockmakers and goldsmiths, as well as other middling persons, nevertheless "tended to be united in a common antagonism to the would be aristocracy above them" (*Empire* 29). This version of the story sounds almost as reasonable as it does familiar, but the literary evidence forces us to side with those historians who argue that this formulation depends on an unworkable definition of class.

As Matson and Onuf explain in some detail, "The nationalists' idea of a dynamic, interdependent continental economy stood opposed to the realities of conflicting interests within and among the states" (100), which was perhaps most clearly revealed in the "controversy over *export* taxes" (114). The process of resolving the thorny issue of representation exposed "the fundamental rift between northern commercial interests and slave owning staple exporters of the southern states" (115). Matson and Onuf go on to show how this pattern continued unabated throughout the ratification debates, which required that a deal be cut to ensure that once the Constitution had been ratified, a process would be initiated to formulate a supplementary Bill of Rights. The recurring pattern of conflict that leads to a resolution that in turn creates another conflict shapes his explanation for the system of checks and balances proposed in the draft Constitution. *Federalist* No. 51 spells out his reasons for rejecting the tripartite class hierarchy that provides Wood's basis for arguing for the formation of a nascent middle class in the years following ratification. To the contrary, Madison contends, "Different interests necessarily exist in different classes of citizens" (320), from which he concludes, "Whilst all authority in [the federal republic] will be derived from and dependent on the society, the society itself will be broken into so many parts, interests, and classes of citizens, that the rights of individuals, or of the minority, will be in little danger

from interested combinations of the majority" (321). This statement acknowledges that nothing like a representative class, let alone a representative man,
could stand in for the entirety of diverse interests that Wood includes under
the rubric of "middling sorts."

The very thing that promises to unify competing groups is also the thing
that ensures their disunity—they are all men of interests. Moreover, as Charles
Sellers explains, by the 1820s, this group grew especially unstable. Workers
and farmers, "struggl[ing] for middle class status . . . managed only a precarious respectability while giving their all to capitalist production" (239). For this
reason, "as never before, young adults and nuclear households were forsaking
kin and neighborhood to wander from place to place . . . [in] two great migratory tides, one flowing from East to West and the other from country to
town or city" (239). Rather than develop from these unpropitious beginnings
into a coherent class ethnos and economic interest group, Sellers insists, the
so-called middling sort would have experienced "American history's sharpest
rise in 'the permanent inequality of conditions and [thus the rise of the] new
wage-exploiting aristocracy' feared by Alexis de Tocqueville" (238). To assign
these men of interest any one character would require a category that could
cut across a vast field of variants that were always on the way to becoming
something else again.

From our perspective as novel scholars, it makes more sense to characterize these men of interests as "in between," or *inter-esse*, in several senses. In
between geographical locations, they are between local communities and interest groups as well. Like Charles Brockden Brown's protagonists, then, they
are always between encounters and therefore on their way to becoming someone else in combination with another party—a contractual relationship between one character and another as established by an exchange that gives one
party, say, the protections of property, in exchange for her exclusive affection
and sexual attention. In the force field of competing interests, by contrast, one
character chases and replaces another in a process much like the encounters
that Gilles Deleuze, borrowing from Spinoza, makes his own: "We are, [Spi-
noza] says, very much spiritual automata, that is to say it is less we who have
the ideas than the ideas that are affirmed in us." In addition to this succession
of perceptions, Deleuze continues, "something else" besides the succession of
ideas "also operates in me." He provides his own example: "When the idea of
Paul [which pleases me] succeeds the idea of Pierre [which upsets me], it is
agreeable to me to say that my . . . power of acting is increased or improved;
when, on the contrary, the situation is reversed, when after seeing someone

who makes me joyful I then see someone who makes me sad, I say that my power of acting is inhibited or obstructed" ("Deleuze on Spinoza's Concept of Affect"). This idea of the human subject as something like a vector of affect that increases or diminishes in power with each encounter comes much closer than a model of contractual exchange to describing social interaction within a field of interests. In that the protagonist of what Deleuze calls his "stupid example" is neither the source nor the destination of ideas so much as their retroactive definition, that subject resembles the men of interests whose competitive interaction kept the framers of the U.S. Constitution from establishing a fixed system of political representation. But insofar as this subject operates as a moving and variable vector of affect, he is more like one of Brockden Brown's protagonists, namely, a conduit for information that can temporarily override scattered and variable interests to form a social network capable of becoming an affective fact.

From this perspective, those who see the production of novels as testimony to a modern nation and rising middle class see only what today's literary institution teaches us to find: a "representative" individual who—once defined by the personal and material property he or she acquires—can resolve the contradiction between negative and positive rights. Assuming their readers were more than willing to consider that conflict unresolved, the novels of the early national period broke up the form and dispersed the contents of one origin story in order to create a field of characters that gave rise to new interest groups lest any one interest group assume a position of dominance. Of necessity, such novels reject the well-rounded and continuous experience of an individual protagonist for one capable of interacting (or not) with several others without reducing any to another's stereotypes. To understand how the first American novels managed this volatile field of characters, we turn from the political arguments that rethought the subject of the Social Contract as a force field of "interests" and consider the theories of the novel that help us understand that field from within the vectors of affect that negotiated it.

Chapter 3

Novels as a Form of Democratic Writing

The year when the U.S. Constitution was ratified, 1789, was also the year when the first novels by, for, and about Americans saw publication. For the next three decades, a steadily increasing number of these "early" novels appeared in print, along with a rash of slave and Barbary captivity narratives, as well as reprints of Indian captivity narratives from the late seventeenth and eighteenth centuries. In working through the successive revisions of the European story of political society that produced a federal government for a collection of former colonies, we could not keep from wondering how the first American novelists managed the same plurality of interest groups. Convinced that these novelists had their own bone to pick with the British model, we assumed that such an argument must have shaped the novels appearing between the publication of William Hill Brown's *The Power of Sympathy* in 1789 and Cooper's *Precaution* in 1820, a domestic novel supposedly based on Jane Austen's *Persuasion* (1817) that preceded his Indian tales by not all that many years.[1] Having argued in Chapter 1 that the novels of this period did indeed engage in formal disagreement with their British counterparts, and after describing the climate of political debate in which they did so, we want to consider what it means to reopen what is, from both perspectives, the losing side of an argument with the British novel and the model of government it took for granted. We turn now to novel theory in an effort to explain how the first American novelists dealt with the problem of competing origin stories that had for a decade perplexed the framers of the U.S. Constitution before them.

There is comparatively little disagreement over which formal features characterize the epic, even when the term is used to describe a work so different from the classical examples as, say, Wordsworth's *Prelude*, and despite the fact that it is invoked in reference to half the stories featured on the evening

news, and the same can be said of tragedy. Or the sonnet—that most restrictive of literary forms—is still a sonnet, at least in theory, when its iambic
pentameter lines fall short or exceed fourteen in number. But there is no such
consensus on the form of the novel. Because the novel has tempted critics,
educators, and novelists themselves to propose formal definitions ever since
novels first began appearing in print, this particular form of writing presents
critical theory with a fascinating definitional dilemma: to what extent does
the form of the novel depend on the concept of property? In addition to challenging the reigning distribution of property, can a novel indicate an alternative basis of community?

Forget the Nation

Claude Lévi-Strauss is not likely to be the first name that the term "novel theory" calls to mind, but his structuralist study of myth nevertheless gave rise to
a school of narrative theory that accompanied the rise of French structuralism
during the 1950s. Those of us who came by that route to the reading method
associated with cultural studies during the 1980s and 1990s have enjoyed the
clarity and power of his thinking. Understanding myth as a cultural and ultimately political way of organizing culture around a foundational contradiction, Lévi-Strauss's brief description of the place of such myths in modern
novels simplifies the impossibility of an origin story for a population that
could not be considered a unified people or even the representative body essential to the Social Contract.

In *The Origin of Table Manners*, Lévi-Strauss offers a thumbnail sketch of
the novelist as a latter-day mythmaker "who drifts at random" among "the
floating fragments" of cultures that shamans and oral storytellers were supposedly able to capture whole (131). The novelist collects these "scattered elements
and reuses them as they come along, being at the same time dimly aware" that
his materials "originate in some other structure" while he is himself "carried
along by a current different from the one that was holding them together"
(131). The novelist repurposes these fragments of other cultural forms and, in
doing so, gets a sense of something immanent in this material that resists his
efforts to resolve the conflicts of his moment. Though removed by modern
history from the wholeness that Lévi-Strauss attributes to earlier cultures, the
novelist nevertheless depends for his material on fragments of that world. And
because the world to which those fragments once belonged has long since

vanished, reassembling them gives rise to the novelist's melancholic sense of being too late. Produced by the conflict between the process of history and the epic wholeness of former cultures, the novel is not so much a structure as an "exhausting pursuit of structure" (*Table Manners* 131). In keeping with the parable encapsulated in Lewis Carroll's Humpty Dumpty rhyme, Lévi-Strauss's novelist can no longer inhabit what have become mere fragments of a once viable whole. Only the artificial structure on the order of a child's rhyme ("Humpty Dumpty sat on a wall . . .") can do that.[2] Composed of such "fragments," the novel form is the process of patching together a belated form that lacks the "freshness" of a lived reality. That reality recedes into the past as the novelist follows "a current different from the one which was holding [those fragments] together" (131).

In "The Structural Study of Myth," Lévi-Strauss explains how the oldest origin stories nevertheless persist into the present. They live on in the problem-solving narratives, or "myths," that recombine pieces of a given classification system until they come up with symbolic resolutions to conflicts that cannot be resolved in real life. This study of myth reduces the question of origins to a flaw or tear in a culture's otherwise coherent map of human experience. The classical version of the Oedipus story, for example, offers a symbolic resolution to the problem of his double origins that makes the human hero at once human and divine. But as Lévi-Strauss suggests in *The Origin of Table Manners*, the novel is something more than a failed problem-solving narrative that tries to offer a sense of the whole that no longer exists. The novelist must also dismantle the order of the modern world as he tries to patch it together with fragments of cultures past. Georg Lukács reworked a similar opposition between narrative process and what he called "structure," as he came to terms with the novel as *the* form of modernity itself. Something of a mythmaker in his own right, Lukács periodically reformulated the conflict that novels strive to resolve into a political conflict that turned Western Marxism into a comprehensive interpretive system. He came to see the novel as the means of proposing the conflict shaping human experience under the conditions of industrial capitalism as one that could not be resolved so long as those conditions prevailed.

By the time he wrote "Narrate or Describe?" Lukács had already translated the dialectical relationship of subject (inner) and object (outer) worlds informing the Hegelian argument of his *Theory of the Novel* (1916–17) into a historically grounded relationship between two styles. The style that gains ascendancy during the nineteenth century recounts an event "as *described* from the standpoint of an observer." In *The Historical Novel*, Lukács shows how, around 1848, this style eclipsed the style he much prefers—as he puts it, the event "as *narrated* from the standpoint of a participant" ("Narrate" III). Here, he identifies the wasteland that supplies the subject matter for novels as the world of "things" related to each other by the operations of the capitalist marketplace that determines their relative value. By mirroring the order of such objects, the descriptive style collaborates with the dehumanizing mode of commodity production. Accordingly, Lukács condemns the modernism of James Joyce and John Dos Passos as a form of "extreme subjectivism" that "approximates the inert reification of pseudo-objectivism" ("Narrate" 144). He sees modernism pushing description to a point where the "inner life of characters" becomes "something static and reified," which puts the possibility of dynamic interaction between subject and object out of reach (144). What is a novelist to do?

To keep the promise of its unfinished form, in Lukács's view, the novelist must turn narration against its own tendency toward social entropy. He or she will "intercatenate" events so as to expose not only "what objects, what institutions . . . significantly influence men's lives" but also "how and when this influence is effected" (128). In a novel striving to fulfill its dialectical potential, the protagonist struggles against his or her incorporation in a world of meaningless objects, thereby affording readers "direct experience with the struggles to restore meaning to life" (147). Just imagine his disappointment when, midway through his discussion of Dickens and before he dissects Flaubert, Lukács finds that "narration" no longer uses objects to express human needs but has succumbed to description that puts them in control of the desires of their consumers. Thus, he concludes, novelists after Dickens could no longer "see the world in its contradictory dynamics" with the clarity that allowed Scott, Cooper, Balzac, or Tolstoy to show how it feels from the position of "a hero in whose life [those] major opposing forces converge" ("Narrate" 142). Living at a moment when there was no way of resolving this contradiction, the novelist, in contrast to Lévi-Strauss's mythmaker, is tasked with exposing the reasons why. The novel can still fulfill its promise as *the* modern narrative form so long as its protagonist struggles against a world bent on turning subjects into objects; the novel fulfills its promise by mobilizing narration against description. But insofar as this conflict requires a political resolution, the novel must remain an unfinished form.

Over the course of a career that rivals Lukács's in political turbulence, Mikhail Bakhtin sees an equally foundational relationship between the novel and human life. Because modern history is still in process, the genre designed to render the present moment in spatial form is necessarily an unfinished one. In "Epic and Novel," Bakhtin singles out "the novel [as] the sole genre that continues to develop and is as yet uncompleted. The forces that define it as a genre are at work before our very eyes" (3). Why is this activity the salient trait of the novel? In "Forms of Time and of the Chronotope in the Novel," Bakhtin describes the "chronotope" as the "constitutive category" of literature. In literature, "time, as it were, thickens, takes on flesh, becomes artistically visible" (84). By activating whatever it is that disposes things and people in familiar spatial relationships, the "chronotope" both "determines to a significant degree" key differences among literary genres and fleshes out the specific "image of man" that occupies each moment of time so spatialized (85). We might compare the "thickening of time" that defines all literary forms except the novel to Lukács's notion of "description." The novel itself, being not yet so thickened, not only provides an archive of such chronotopes but also makes them "responsive to the movements of time, plot and history" (84). In this respect, we can say that the novel does in Bakhtin's definition what "narration" does in Lukács's. Chronotopes provide the materials from which the novelist assembles a patched-together modern world, just as the debris of a previous culture does in Lévi-Strauss's scenario.[3]

The fact that Bakhtin devotes only nine pages of 174 to the chronotope of the novel suggests that the novel is not just another chronotope. Rather, the chronotope of the novel is its characteristic way of retemporalizing past chronotopes, which he compares "to the uninterrupted exchange of matter between living organisms and the environment that surrounds them. As long as the organism lives, it resists fusion with the environment, but if it is torn out of its environment, it dies" (254). By understanding the organism's interaction with its material environment as similar to the novel's interaction with its discursive environment, we can also see that "the work and the world represented in it enter the real world and enrich it, and the real world enters the work and its world as part of the process of its creation, as well as part of its subsequent life" (254). Simply put, its incompleteness is what makes the form of the novel comparable to that of a living thing.[4] In "Discourse in the Novel," Bakhtin rethinks the process of incorporating and reconfiguring chronotopes as the means by which the novel enters a field composed of "thousands of living dialogic threads, woven by socio-ideological consciousness around the given object of an utterance. Within this environment," he concludes, the novel "cannot fail to become a participant in social dialog" as it inscribes "its own meaning and its own expression across an environment full of alien words and variously evaluating accents" ("Discourse in the Novel" 276–77). The novel takes what it needs from the tangled skein of discourse and offsets those elements one against the other in relations of harmony or dissonance that display the novel's unique capacity to negotiate, if not comprehend the entire field of writing. Its unfinished form materializes the novel's ongoing participation in an inhospitable world of discourse outside itself.

For purposes of the argument at hand, Jacques Rancière's account of the "politics of literature" as a relationship between "the regime of literature" and "the word-at-large" recasts the same scenario of struggle as the novelist's struggle to differentiate his writing from a field of writing in which it is likely to get lost or stolen. "Literature," according to Rancière, "is the reign of writing, of speech circulating outside any determined relationship of address . . . without any specific addressee and without a master to accompany it—in the form of those printed booklets that trail around just about everywhere, from reading rooms to open-air stalls, making their situations, characters, and expressions freely available to anyone who feels like grabbing hold of them" (*Politics of Literature* 12–13). In comparing writing to "grabbing hold," Rancière has in mind the form of literacy distributed by journalism and popular fiction. Such literacy made it possible for virtually anyone to grab hold of such writing "either to appropriate the life led by the heroes or heroines of novels for themselves, or to turn themselves into writers, or to insert themselves into the discussion of common affairs" (13). By thus "grabbing hold," he maintains, the new literacy exercises political force in its own right. Rather than think of this force as an "irresistible social influence," however, the power of the new literacy manifests itself in "a new distribution of the perceptible, . . . a new relationship between the act of speech, the world that it configures, and the capacities of those who people that world" (13). Because it seemed to circulate indiscriminately, this writing called for "new rules of appropriateness between the significance of words and the visibility of things" (21).

As an account of the origins of modern literature, Rancière's essay on "The Politics of Literature" credits novelists themselves with distinguishing "rules of appropriateness" that required a more restricted literary literacy than common literacy. Like Lukács, he credits literary modernism with institutionalizing the techniques that transformed writing into a self-enclosed system of signs that invited one to read it as the product and expression of an author. In order to be so read, then, a novel would have to do exactly what Lukács and Bakhtin claim it cannot do. A novel would have to restage the very argument that it carries on with other forms of writing, revising the conditions for its resolution, closure, or completion. This sleight of hand, as Rancière describes it, transforms the prosaic relationship of words and things into "a relationship of sign to sign" that can symbolically resolve its argument with other writing (15). While his account of the rise of the literary institution goes a long way toward explaining Austen's influence on Scott, as well as Scott's on Cooper, it will nevertheless require some adjustments before it can explain how the first American novelists engaged their British counterparts, much less how that engagement changed the field of democratic writing.

The Novel as a Form of Property

To cease being a popular medium, the English novel made it all but impossible to see alternatives to European liberalism as other than disruptive, chaotic, or, in a word, antagonistic to the concepts of both government and literary form. Of all the attempts to define "the novel," E. M. Forster's brilliantly commonplace *Aspects of the Novel*, based on his Clark Lectures at Cambridge in 1927, is unquestionably one of the most successful in this respect. The influence of Forster's "aspects" extends well beyond the thousands of citations garnered in books and articles covering a broad range of topics related to the novel. But the most eloquent testimony to the enduring influence of *Aspects of the Novel* comes from all those novel readers for whom Forster's formal definition of the novel simply goes without saying. Such readers feel no obligation to mention the source—not that the rest of us feel we have to do so either. And why should we? Given their ubiquity in literary criticism and classroom teaching, can anyone say that "story," "plot," "character," "point of view," "form," and "style" belong to anyone in particular? These aspects of the novel are simply the means by which a novel asks to be read as a novel. In coming up with these terms, Forster—ever the novelist himself—set a deliberately chatty tone and arrived at such reasonable judgments that his entire audience doubtless felt they were hearing a good deal of common sense.

The lectures themselves slide easily back and forth between registers—between critical models of plot, character, and narrative form that go back to Aristotle and the terms in which the popular reader presumably made sense of his or her own experience and discussed it with other people. The strategy succeeded. "Casual Critic[isms]," a 1928 review of *Aspects of the Novel*, describes the engaging quality of Forster's book as that of a "conversational monologue" (Frierson 376), and forty years later, we find this initial reception remarkably unchanged. On the occasion of yet another reissue, a reviewer characterized *Aspects of the Novel* as "light and pleasant reading." Although he found Forster's judgments about novels, as this reviewer put it, "brilliantly penetrating at times," they nevertheless "give the impression that common sense is always in control" (Gallagher 214). But the most powerful by far of all Forster's rhetorical moves has to be the one that got rid of the literary ideal of epic totality and allowed the novel to establish its own exclusive standard. His formalist method serves much the same purpose Flaubert achieved in killing off his heroine. By demanding to be read as works of literature, these novelists removed themselves from the field of democratic writing.

To begin with, Forster proposes that the novel is neither interested in nor capable of providing a view of the social landscape as a whole. He describes the novel "as a formidable mass and it is so amorphous—[there is] no mountain in it to climb, no Parnassus or Helicon, not even a Pisgah" (5). Sticking with geographical metaphors, Forster goes on to spell out the dilemma that such a "formidable mass" poses for the novelist who wants to manage it. Where Lévi-Strauss's figure of the novelist pictures this dilemma as the difficulty of making a habitable world from the fragments of past epochs that drift by on the river of time, Forster removes selected novelists from that very flow of information. History provides an irrigation system that enriches the novel's cultural chronotopic ecosystem, but too much hydration of this kind is definitely a bad thing. The novel, he claims, "is most distinctly one of the moister areas of literature—irrigated by a hundred rills and occasionally degenerating into a swamp" (5). Forster consequently requires that readers "visualize the English novelists *not as floating down that stream which bears all its sons away* unless they are careful, but as seated together in a room, a circular room, a sort of British Museum reading-room—all writing their novels simultaneously" (9, our italics). Could he be any more explicit about the reader's obligation to remove the novel from the world of historical flux and confine it to a category that no particular reading could challenge?

Forster knew full well that the novel wouldn't limit its purview to that of a claustrophobic reading room without some help, which he recruits from readers who can appreciate the "aspects of the English novel" spelled out in the lectures that follow. Before they can proceed, however, Forster requires that these readers "visualize the novelists as sitting in one room" and "force them, by our very ignorance, from the limitations of date and place" (9). To cut the many ties between the novelist and the field of writing that he or she engages, Forster cautions, readers cannot subject the novel to "the principles and systems [that] may suit other forms of art" (23). To the contrary, he wants his reading room for novelists to contain "that spongy tract, those fictions in prose of a certain length which extend so indeterminately." Once detached from the "formidable mass" of writing, on the one hand, and from "other forms of art," on the other, that "spongy tract" provides a buffer zone or "borderland lying between history and literature" (22). Once confined to writing in this intermediary position, novelists can determine which other novelists should keep them company. Gone is novel's scrappy dialogic form and dialectical potential.

Forster's reading room indeed suggests that something like the process that distinguished literature from democratic writing had done its work in England. The figure of the reading room indeed corresponds to certain strains of Anglo formalism that transformed what and how literature was taught in British and American classrooms throughout the twentieth century. Teach readers how to read a novel as a self-enclosed text, Forster proposes, and they will select fiction accordingly. Trained to focus on the aspects of the novel he elaborates, readers will be unlikely to consider why so many novels, indeed, most of the novels published in English, openly resist that way of reading. In this respect, Forster's reading room did for novelists in general much the same thing that Virginia Woolf's "room of one's own" did for women novelists in particular. Forster gave the novel its own cultural category with an origin and a genealogy and, on this basis, established a generic standard and a national tradition. Forster makes it clear that although he admires Tolstoy and Dostoyevsky and views Proust as the most successful novelist to have analyzed modern consciousness, his aspects of the novel define the *English* novel (7).

When he sought to define the English novel, one might say, Forster sought to define Englishness itself. To the exclusion of whole domains of experience shared by English people, domains of experience that Englishmen and Englishwomen shared with literate populations elsewhere, Forster's reading room deliberately severed the connections between the English novel and the vast majority of people who read and wrote in a vernacular English across the English-speaking world. Ahistorical though it appears, the island mentality cultivated by such formalism was itself overdetermined by historical conditions in England during the decade following the Great War—an effort, that is, to remove the English novel from the conflict at the near and far borders of empire. As a well-known novelist writing during the period of high modernism, Forster was acutely conscious of his position at the center of the greatest empire in history as it appeared to be heading into a precipitous decline.[5] His insularity—in stark contrast to the internationalism of the novel as defined by both Lukács and Bakhtin—caricatures the liberal response to the Great War in Europe. To grasp the theory of the novel that shapes Forster's reading room, we have to understand the self-containment of the "reading room" as a way of maintaining the continuity of human experience during a period of wide-reaching economic change. Nor was he the first to do so.

Two centuries before Forster came on the scene as both novelist and critic, authors were busy developing narratives around a Robinson Crusoe, a Moll Flanders, and countless other hypothetical individuals, most of them soon forgotten. Such writing immediately gave rise to a clamor of criticism. Moralists came out in print to claim that novels would inflame the imagination and produce in readers the same desires that drove male protagonists to go off to sea or to the city and send any number of female protagonists to perdition in the arms of unscrupulous men. Novelists not only instigated the clamor, which they discovered good for business, but also incorporated and managed it. Thus, Henry Fielding and Samuel Richardson used the novel to combat what each saw as the other's abuse of the form. Though published posthumously in 1818, *Northanger Abbey* poked fun at the novels of Ann Radcliffe in particular and the system of lending libraries in general for inciting young women to make themselves ridiculous in their pursuit of eligible men. As they guided the behavior of her characters through the rigors of courtship, Austen's six major novels did a compelling job of anthropomorphizing the rules of appropriateness for both novel writers and respectable young women. We could go on. Historical evidence suggests that if anything, the criticism aroused by the eighteenth-century British novel only enhanced the popularity of the new medium; novels did not take off slowly but rapidly infiltrated the daily practices of certain sectors of the literate population and spilled over national boundaries to occupy the leisure time of an international readership who might otherwise not feel they had time for reading. Amid the clamor of criticism, certain British novelists established those rules by means of procedures that were no more stable than the form of the novel itself.[6]

In his influential *The Rise of the English Novel* (1957), Ian Watt attributes both the popularity of the novel and its maturation as a genre to the fact that eighteenth-century English novel readers saw their interests mirrored in the household that forms at the end of Samuel Richardson's *Pamela* (1740). The gratification of basking in this reflection explains why, in Watt's view, "the great majority of novels written since *Pamela* have continued its basic pattern,

and concentrated their main interest upon a courtship leading to marriage"
(148–49). In order to follow in Forster's footsteps, it would seem, and define
the form of "the novel" as a pattern that both spoke to the aspirations of a
particular readership and reproduced itself in future work, Watt chose to ignore the countless failed relationships that litter the social landscapes of other
novels—including, of course, the sensational rape and subsequent abandon-
ment of Richardson's Clarissa. In this respect, too, Watt was among the first
literary critics after Sir Walter Scott to offer what amounted to a novelistic
account of the English novel, one in which the novel matured according to
much the same principles as its protagonist—as it acquired self-discipline.

In writing *The Great Tradition* (1948), less than a decade before Watt, F. R.
Leavis had already looked to the English novel as a distinctive form of Englishness. Before Watt extended the tradition of the English novel back to its
origins in Defoe, Leavis had seen it originating with Austen and continuing in
novels that featured individuals no less perplexed and yet just as self-contained
as her fictional households. In thus claiming that Austen "follows Richardson
in basing her novels on marriage," Watt had hitched his tradition of the English novel to Leavis's (298). On the basis of admittedly slim and even contrary evidence to suggest that Austen's novels engaged the burgeoning world
of writing in a quite different way than those of Richardson and Fielding,[7]
Watt placed his tradition of the novel squarely in line with Leavis's and joined
him in equating Austen's novels with the form of the genre itself, which was
"to form a morally and emotionally refurbished household" (298). No doubt
the postwar climate in which he wrote disposed Watt to assume that an
eighteenth-century readership would have seen their own rapidly changing
world much as he saw his own, as sorely in need of a cohesive and self-
contained model of community within which a diversity of readers could
imagine self-fulfillment. By so aligning his definition of the English novel
with Leavis's, Watt's *The Rise of the English Novel* established a national tradition that stretched from Daniel Defoe to Jane Austen and from Austen to
Henry James and Joseph Conrad.

During the same postwar period, R. W. S. Lewis's *American Adam* (1955),
Richard Chase's *The American Novel and Its Traditions* (1957), Leslie Fiedler's
Love and Death in the American Novel (1960), and Daniel Hoffman's *Form and
Fable in American Fiction* (1961), among others, set about to create a tradition
of the novel that was as American as Leavis's and Watt's were English. Their
search for a novelist who did for the United States what Austen had done for
England, however, made it necessary for the American tradition makers

apparently to bypass most of the fiction written by and about Americans during the early republic. Lacking anything like the formal cohesiveness of Austen's country shires or a prose style with half the grace of her irony, how could these "early" novels be said to launch a comparable tradition? Accordingly, those histories of the American novel still considered influential neglect to account for the number and wide variety of novels written during the early republic. If they mention Charles Brockden Brown at all, it is to pay him an obligatory visit before settling in earnest on Cooper as the novelist "who first fully exemplified and formulated the situation of the novelist in the New World" (Chase 14).

Novel Networks

Thanks to the recent scholarship in early American letters, we feel we are on solid ground in assuming that, during the early national period, most novelists wrote for local readerships, most of whom also read English fiction.[8] Steeped in English taste and well aware of what they had to do in order to write a novel, these novelists appropriated certain aspects of the English novel—the very aspects that Forster identifies—and deliberately altered them to show how a community might take shape in the fluid demographic situation of the new United States. These early American novelists were no more reluctant than Charles Brockden Brown to target the English novel as the prose form to engage in dialogue. They consequently provide a rather clear idea of how they adapted the novel form to address American readerships who could understand and well appreciate those adjustments. Whether set in the teeming city of Philadelphia or in a small village like Sleepy Hollow, this fiction encouraged readers to do exactly what Forster's reading method would ask his readers to avoid; they invited readers to imagine a community that crossed local as well as national boundaries and redistributed the field of characters along potentially unlimited chains of unanticipated relationships.

Given that it was designed to keep incorporating new demographic information, such a community could not by definition begin whole or hope to remain the same over time. In place of individuals or clusters of individuals that might be boiled down to a recognizable type or placed in a stable social category, readers of the early American novel experienced a succession of strange encounters between one-of-a-kind characters that combined, broke up, and recombined along narrative pathways that formed as they did so. In other words, these novels indulged the very tendencies that would get them ushered out of Forster's reading room. These are the very tendencies or formal moves that make the novels of the early republic interesting to us. We consider these moves as elements of a style of argument essential to the formation of American political culture. We also see these moves, tellingly, as the means by which any novel eluded the "rules of appropriateness" that compelled British novelists to work within the limits of a world made of property.

Roberto Esposito's analysis of property as an "immunization paradigm" affords a way of rethinking Forster's model of the novel as a self-contained reading room. In his haste to build a fortress of a home on an uninhabited island, Robinson Crusoe reveals the defensive character of the move to detach oneself and one's experience from the life in common of which one is necessarily part. On arrival, he quickly discovers that nature has stocked his island with most of the resources necessary to sustain individual life indefinitely. With that issue off the table, however, Crusoe quickly discovers that what appeared to be a deserted island is actually teeming with potential threats that oblige him to protect himself and his property. This double move perfectly encapsulates John Locke's origin story. The defense of property that motivates men to form a government is also, in Esposito's view, a profoundly antisocial move (41–77). Esposito contends that the very self-sovereignty that supposedly frees us to act, move in the world, and think for ourselves without fear of reprisal is based on a foundational negation of community. If we consider *communitas* as "that relation, which in binding its members to an obligation of reciprocal donation, jeopardizes individual identity," he reasons, then we must see *immunitas* as the condition of "dispensation" from that obligation, thus as "the defense against the expropriating features of *communitas*" (50). Immunity protects one's person and property from "risky contact" with elements of the population who are not so protected and, in this way, "restores [one's] own borders that were jeopardized by the common" (50). To tell the story of the modern individual, Defoe had to negotiate two paradoxes.

In creating the individual, first of all, Defoe knew that he had to define his protagonist in terms of the property Crusoe accumulates and that to do so, he had to dislodge his protagonist from the identity he was assigned at birth. The novel begins, then, with repeated attempts to cut Crusoe off from virtually all human contact—father, wife, ship captains, and the like—and it takes repeated attempts at such self-removal to make him master of his labor, not to mention any number of defensive maneuvers to retain that self-command. After the appearance of a single human footprint on the shore puts him in a panic, his geographical detachment ultimately proves insufficient to the task, as an assortment of intruders wash up on his shore. From the paradox of a self that is defined by its self-removal, a second paradox follows. Crusoe's island situation exposes this paradox as it nullifies the value of gold. Finding himself in a situation where all that matters is what it takes to stay alive, gold loses all value, and Crusoe puts it on a shelf until he leaves for England. Did Defoe arrange the shipwreck in order to return Crusoe to the world before men found it convenient to substitute a quantity of gold for the goods that guaranteed them a quality of life? It seems likely. Thanks to the increasing frequency of such transactions, trade had become a way of life by the time the novel appeared in print, and the value of money was already displacing that of the land and human labor as the means for a man to sustain a household. In the process, money loosened the bond between the man as desiring subject and the man objectified as property. Once so detached from the laboring body, property displaced the owner's wishes and intentions, and its worth in money put his identity at the mercy of impersonal laws of exchange. The inversion of person and property—whereby property becomes the essence rather than the extension and expression of the man—redefines the individual as nothing other than noncommon property or what we now call real estate.

When limited to the personal or private sphere, as Hannah Arendt explains, liberty can only be the basis of negative rights. Even "the power of locomotion, without imprisonment or restraint, unless by due course of law," which Sir William Blackstone considered "the most important of all civil rights," is, in Arendt's view, nothing but freedom from unjust imprisonment or restraint and thus a negative right or liberty. To enjoy freedom in a positive sense would require a revolutionary demand for the public freedoms of assembly and direct access to the political process of decision making, she contends, which is what we mean by "the pursuit of happiness" (Arendt 22). From this perspective, the master in his own house is not free but simply protected from possible encroachments on his person and property. Esposito looks at Locke's story of the individual from much the same perspective. According to this retelling, "liberty" initially refers to a social instinct or "connective power that grows and develops according to its own internal law." This connective power undergoes "expansion" until it "unites its members in a shared dimension" (Esposito 70). Locke needs this "shared dimension" in order to imagine men spontaneously agreeing to a binding contract that will protect them from one another.

At the moment the individual submitted to the sovereign body of law that would protect his person and property, however, his liberty is embedded in society and his desires restricted to private life. This frees him to play host to others and to move in the world without fear of harm to person or property. But when it comes to the social relations he might enter into and the selves he might become in so doing, property rights show their negative face and operate restrictively. As Esposito puts it, property guarantees one only the freedom "not to be other than himself" (71). A terrible confinement—but nevertheless one that Robinson Crusoe finds necessary to self-preservation and thus to life itself.[9] As a form of freedom that does not entail any affirmative rights, modern liberty comes into being according to the negative logic of Hobbes's fable—as "that which insures the individual against the interference of others through the voluntary subordination to a more powerful order that guarantees it" (Esposito 72). In the most reductive terms possible, this is what is now generally meant by liberalism. In order to protect the life of the individual, this form of government removes speech, actions, associations, enactments of desire, the pursuit of happiness, call it what you will, from collective experience and limits it to the domain of private property. To challenge the idea that a community could be based on self-removal, it was incumbent on early American novelists to overturn the fabled origin of modern society itself.

In Chapter 19 of Volume I of *Capital*, Karl Marx proposed that the phrase "the value of labour-power" inverts the concept of "value." This is the point where his argument turns the corner from critiquing the practice of wage labor and begins to formulate an alternative to that dehumanizing exchange. According to this well-known argument, the phrase "the value of labour-power" substitutes an abstraction in the form of the amount of money a man can demand in exchange for the quality of labor it takes to keep him alive. This substitution does no end of harm when it encourages people to imagine the cost of a given product without regard for the extraction of vital energy required to put it in their hands. It is instructive to recall that in trying to unveil the mystery of surplus value, Marx traces the inversion of the relation of vital human energy to inanimate objects back to the inversion of the relation of land to property. Substituting an abstract quantity for the quality of skill and ingenuity extracted in calculating "the value of labour" performs the same inversion as substituting "the value of land" for "the land" on which people live in common. "The value of labor" was therefore, as he put it, "an expression as imaginary as the value of the earth" (677). In order to formulate a community on some basis other than property, a novel would have to expose the inversion of land and human skill and ingenuity that took place when land was first imagined as a world of property. Once it had exposed the fiction of property as such, however, the novelists of the early national period faced the challenge of imagining an alternative with half a chance of materializing at a time and place where property was generally considered the origin of modern society and the only ground on which its idea of government could materialize. [10]

In a revealing critique of the concept of "possessive individualism" that C. B. Macpherson drew from Locke's *Second Treatise of Government*, Étienne Balibar shows how Macpherson's concept of property eliminates one of the two contrary definitions of property that inform Locke's claim that "every Man has a Property in his own Person." If we accept Macpherson's definition of property as "constituted" property, or property one already owns, as the sole basis of political rights, we will necessarily overlook an equally valid but conflicting definition. [11] Balibar reads this other meaning of the claim "every Man has a Property in his own Person" from the vantage point of Locke's *An Essay Concerning Human Understanding*. Finding that this second meaning of property occasionally surfaces in the *Second Treatise*, Balibar insists that the claim "every Man has a Property in his own Person" can also indicate that "every man comes into existence already in possession of a bundle of 'constitutive' rights." [12] Such rights belong to the persons one could become if not tethered to an original identity. Were men to exercise those rights, they would transform their "property" as something that they already had into the basis for becoming someone else. We have a reason for pointing out the parallels between the argument in which Balibar engages Macpherson and the argument that early American novelists mounted against their British counterparts. Defining "property" with qualities immanent in the person, much as Balibar does in his reading of *An Essay Concerning Human Understanding*, these novelists formulated a basis for social relationships that directly challenged Locke's. [13]

Formalizing Democratic Writing

Clearly intent on being read as novels, prose fiction during the early national period characteristically began by offering readers material for a world of experience that observed a process of formation on the order of Locke's little commonwealth. Rather than unfold an American version of the English country house, however, these novels break up that basically linear progressive narrative into multiple plots that prove incapable of producing an adequately coherent and comprehensive whole. We can imagine no other reason for making such moves than that these novels considered it impossible to formulate a community based on property that would make sense to American readers.[14] In countering the formal protocols of their British counterparts move for move, these novelists generated narratives that were received as novels in their own right.

The redactions of English novels popular in colonial America and throughout the early republic would have shown novelists exactly what had to be done to the British novel to tailor it for an American readership.[15] A glance at a few of these redactions is all it takes to see how, for example, the redactors stripped Richardson's novels of the frantic rhetoric that evidently blunted what was, for American readers, the point of such a novel. By doing so, they purged the British novel of the overwrought emotional life that became the basis of its "literary" value. Thus, while British editions of *Pamela* and *Clarissa* ran to 250,000 words and 1,000,000 words, respectively, the edition of *Pamela* published in Philadelphia in 1792 totaled 27,000 words and *Clarissa* only 41,000, about the same length as Susannah Rowson's *Charlotte Temple*. Cutting back these novels to approximately one-tenth the number of pages of the British original was so much more than a practical measure that allowed Americans to slip *Clarissa* into a pocket or that made redacted *Pamela* appeal to a lower level of literacy. Based on the 1756 British edition, the redaction first appeared in North America in 1764 and many more times thereafter. Let us consider what it was about these redacted editions that Americans seemed to prefer in novels.

By switching from first- to third-person narration, the redaction boiled down the discursive prolixity of Richardson's letter-writing heroines to physical actions and oral communication that advance the plot. Rather than a sequence of agonistic decisions, the redacted editions brought one body into immediate contact with another, a difference that becomes perhaps most conspicuous in the fabled rape of *Clarissa*. The British edition skewed and scattered the lines of print of Letter 262, Paper X to create a damaged text that bonded the inner life of the woman to the print that registers the condition of her soul. By contrast, the third-person narration of the redaction offered no more of the heroine's direct testimony than necessary for readers to know that she suffered "the most vile and inhuman acts of violence." As we see it, the redaction made a power play when it denied Clarissa's rape the status of an affective event. Stripped of the means of heightened emotional expression, the heroine is denied the power her writing requires to put her at the sympathetic center of a field of characters and attract an adoring readership. By this means, the redacted editions transformed Richardson's plots from a succession of highly mediated emotional negotiations into a succession of immediate confrontations between one character and another—the very style we saw at work in Brockden Brown's *Arthur Mervyn*.

To challenge what English novels asked their readers to take for granted— namely, that belonging to a community depends on having property of some kind—American novelists had to insist on another basis for belonging. Resembling the early American committees of correspondence in a number of key respects, the novels of the early national period themselves also persuaded a population of diverse and semiautonomous states that they could momentarily feel and act as one—and do so without losing their local identities. If, as we argue, each time a novelist addressed one such readership in a style of writing whose formal moves resembled those of other novelists, eventually a familiar pattern of relationships within the field of characters would reproduce itself outside the novel as an expanding network of novel readers. Historical evidence supports our speculation that, with the spread of these novels, such imaginary networks supplemented and eventually displaced the networks binding colonial American communities to European homelands.

In a spirit contrary to the argument of Benedict Anderson and the followers of Jürgen Habermas, Trish Loughran offers this important observation: "There was no 'nationalized' print sphere in the years just before and just after the Revolution, but rather a proliferating variety of local and regional reading publics scattered across a vast and diverse geographical space" (xix). Loughran sees this scattered and acentric disposition of communities as a network failure: "the absence of roads and canals to carry goods into the western interior, up to the Canadian border, and throughout most of the South" meant, she says, that the "newspapers, novels, plays, and pamphlets" had very limited domestic circulation until the 1830s; they were more likely to make it to England from Philadelphia than to the west or south (20). Having attributed to insufficient networks of communication the novel's inability to address a national readership, a situation we take entirely to heart, however, Loughran seems to undervalue her own observation when it came to explaining the emergence of distinctively American novels. She attributes their ability to gain traction in speaking to the collective imagination much as she claims the U.S. Constitution did, "rhetorically, as one seemingly univocal, unified thing in the 1770s and 1780s" (26). The Constitution's ability to fabricate a national unity is owing, she contends, to its "dispersion of parts, their generative dislocation out of actual face-to-face ties into the elusive realism of the (early) national" (26). Though pursuing a different line of reasoning, we have learned a great deal from Loughran's carefully researched portrait of the American readership as a patchwork affair, a composite of various local readerships that each enjoyed its own works of fiction. Her demographic picture of the early United States supports our own hypothesis that novels that emerged during the decades immediately following ratification of the U.S. Constitution were written with full awareness of what Loughran calls "the dispersion of parts," many of which were incompatible.

As we see it, the early novels succeeded, as the U.S. Constitution did, precisely because they rejected anything like a unified model of community in favor of a form that could link its countless dispersed and heterogeneous parts. Like the U.S. Constitution, the first American novelists were tasked with establishing a way of connecting these "parts" that neither reduced them to a unified form nor organized them according to a core-periphery model that characterized their relationship to the European homeland. With this double avoidance ever in mind, American novelists turned Britain into the "other" world that readers would see as a form of government they didn't much like. Rather than a model to emulate, as we have shown, American novels reconfigured Britain as one location with its own perspective within an expansive and diversified field of social possibilities. The internal organization of the community that took shape in these early novels consequently veered away not only from the liberal pattern of "representative" government but also from the republic of semiautonomous states imagined by the framers of the U.S. Constitution who spent the two decades after ratification trying both to limit and to guarantee the right to participate in the new body politic.

As they circulated throughout the former colonies, these novels would have provided readers with the protocols for strangers to encounter one another. By virtue of the fact that such writing qualified virtually anyone to address and be addressed by anyone else in writing, no writing in this style could in itself be considered the property of a particular individual. One acquired that style by reading novels and, by so doing, increased the number of people doing the same and so on. In stark contrast to the cloistered exchange of letters staged by Richardson, then, novels of the new republic generated chains of letters, and the power of an American vernacular increased exponentially each time readers heard its variation of British English and then put that voice into writing. Where there is no property, there can be no theft, and the attempt to contain and possess writing that nobody owns will render it valueless within such a semiotic system.[16] What may appear to be the theft of one character's speech by another—as happens on more than one occasion in the novels of Charles Brockden Brown—established a social network rather than the author's property.

Fixed on explaining the similarly metastatic tendencies of this relationship between writing and reading in nineteenth-century Germany, Friedrich Kittler's work also sheds revealing light on the process by which the novel might well have produced a mass readership in the United States and wherever novels happen to circulate in the vernacular. Kittler describes the "discourse network of 1800" as "a culture in which reading and writing were coupled and automatized." The purpose of their coupling was a universal education, prerequisite to which was an alphabetization that "connected reading and writing by linking both back to the singular kind of listening." He characterizes this relationship of writing as listening to a voice one loves as "pure" and "non-alienated" (108). Children learned to read by listening to the sounds of the alphabet, Kittler explains. Reading easily became a form of writing when, in learning to listen, one also learned to "speak" with the pure and non-alienated voice of writing. As he puts it, "The continuous transition from authors to readers was a kind of mobilization." It dispensed with layers of aesthetic displacement that mediated between the common reader and writing and placed both "love" and "danger" squarely in the realm of the senses, where they were defined not by what one thought but by how they made one feel. By exploiting the potential to produce subjects susceptible to the affective force of the new medium, new forms rose to the challenge of making love and danger operate "as so many promises of happiness" (109). It is to this susceptibility, Kittler argues, "that writing, a cold, age-old technology owed its sudden universalization. What technically would be signified without references became psychologically endogenous voices or images that created pleasure," along with the sense one had entered into a relationship with the author who "had come to dwell among the pages of the book" (109).

In practice, one local readership would not read exactly the same novels that other readerships did. If they shared a willingness and ability to listen to the human voice of someone speaking to someone else in dialect-free writing, these novels would belong to virtually the same readership. Thus, any number of such novels could address their respective readerships and disseminate the same form of literacy. Where her historical description of U.S. print culture shows the early republic to be a series of local and regional reading publics with distinct political and geographic identities, Loughran's picture is arguably incomplete until we factor in the operation of the novel as a medium capable of spreading a form of literacy that situated local readers within a common network where information could pass through a different network from that established by the market in print. Kittler's definition of the discourse of 1800 explains why the readership exceeded the distribution of novels themselves. Indeed, it is safe to say that novels depended on a form of literacy vaguely compatible with Rancière's concept of democratic writing, a relationship where each prepared the way for the other to expand. Different variants of novels worked through local markets to distribute the same literacy and fuel an appetite for more, and those who read one novel were disposed to read others to understand their own experience in similar terms.

Though no experts in contemporary network theory, we know enough to recognize that the novels of the early republic, for all their indications of rebellion against the British novel and the literary institution that was to come, did more than challenge the liberal mode of political society. They equated the freedom to participate with the freedom to write and to circulate freely what one wrote. To guarantee the freedom of democratic writing, they developed an alternative set of rules to those designed to define writing as if it were the property of an author. In order to do so, these novelists could not simply allow democratic writing to take its course. To distinguish their writing as novels, novelists writing during the early national period formalized the procedures, tropes, or "aspects," if you will, of "democratic writing." By observing what we will demonstrate was actually a precise and yet elaborate set of formal rules, these novels made their plots multiply and intersect until they had not only decentralized the supervisory perspective formulated by their British counterparts but also broken up, sometimes violently, any cluster of characters that began to turn in on itself and keep others out. To become a novel during the period of the early republic, we concluded, a narrative had to remain open to new connections, acknowledge the multiplicity of partial perspectives it afforded, and distribute agency throughout the network to whomever was likely to make connections. Before it could be considered inappropriate for any individual or group of individuals to represent others, we will insist, the rules of democratic writing had to observe protocols no less rigorous than those associated with literary discipline. The novels of the early republic established such rules.

This form is virtually indistinguishable from the concept of style described in Chapter 1: a voice that could narrate many different stories while observing a deceptively simple set of procedures to push and pull the reader from one position to another without any of the internal machinery of motivation and decision making that maintains a fuller inner life with which the reader could identify. Finding its way around the Atlantic within the social network it maps out, these novels spoke as someone within that field to virtually everyone else. With not all that much doctoring, as a result, what Hardt and Negri say about the political discourse of the early republic actually comes closer, in our view, to describing what the novels of that same period achieved: "What opens is the basis of consensus, and thus, through the constitutive network of [voices] and counter [voices], the entire sovereign body [of a readership] is continually reformed" (166). The aspects of the novel to which we devote the next five chapters lay out the set of rules that developed as the first American novels linked networks of people to networks of information by way of the printed word.

Chapter 4

Dispersal

Why dispersal? As in *Arthur Mervyn*, so across the wide variety of early novels that we shall now attempt to read as their own best theory, otherwise unimpressive characters break up households and fly in the face of their own economic gain by doing so. Nor do these protagonists leave one household in order to form another more gratifying version of the same, as is the habit of their British counterparts. Quite the contrary, by so dismantling a sequence of small communities that threaten to arrest his or her mobility, the protagonist forms a system of social relations capable of surviving and even thriving on periodic dispersals. In this respect, the system of social contacts thus formed bears striking similarity to the way people, goods, and information circulate throughout the world with ever increasing speed and efficiency, and it was indeed tempting to describe the moving parts of those early American networks as "flows" in today's lingua franca. But when it came to naming the encounters that simultaneously scatter and connect small communities in novels of the early national period, we considered that term misleading and opted for "dispersal." Why misleading? "Flow" encourages us to overlook the importance of ruptures, collisions, and awkward conjunctions produced when strangers encounter one another and thus not to ask what propels the narrative through and across such obstacles. The metaphoric resonances of "flow" also encourage us to leap to an allegory that glosses the system of relationships developed in these early novels as a relatively smooth and gradual process of nation making as the confluences of different migrant groups.[1]

By contrast, the term "dispersal" is meant to call attention to the erratic movement and uneven distribution of demographic groups within the new United States. "Dispersal" should also serve to remind us as well that for most of recorded history, most of the world's population, including the people of the new United States, was relatively sedentary.[2] To mistake the immigration of eighteenth-century populations for the twenty-first-century "society of control" would be to ignore the very problem these novels set about to solve—most immediately, that of diverse and scattered readerships. As they redistributed information that might have otherwise become a representative experience and way of life across many small communities, these novels also established new connections between those communities. In settling on "dispersal" as the narrative mechanism that releases the elements of human character to form a network, we were also aware of using a term that came to us loaded with resonances of "diaspora" and the considerable work in the field of diaspora studies.[3]

In key respects, "dispersal" works against "diaspora." As we understand it, "diaspora" refers to a group of people who see themselves bound to a vanishing origin and cling to some "inalienable possession," in Annette Weiner's phrase, that connects them directly to the homeland and indirectly to one another. This self-defining trait differentiates members of the group from the rest of the population in whom they are embedded, no matter how often or how widely that group is dispersed.[4] By contrast, the novels we are considering here put their protagonists through encounters that strip away and scatter any possessions, personal or material, that might attach them to a point of origin. Despite their publication in small editions that spoke to local readerships, these American novels, across the board, rejected the self-enclosed models of society offered in British novels.[5] To put the members of those societies into circulation, American novelists developed forms of dispersal that were at once innovative and predictable: innovative, in that these dispersals worked counter to the circuits of internal trade, and predictable, because in doing so, they disrupted the very form of community their European counterparts had sanctified. To explain just how central "dispersal" is to forming the novels of the new republic, we will consider the affirmative as well as the negative operations of the trope as it displaces constituted property with the constitutive property enabling one character to become many others.

The Besieged Enclosure

By the end of the eighteenth century, a Europe under threat of social instability inspired measures that would control the redistribution of people and property.[6] Writing in the wake of the French and American revolutions and at the moment of England's industrial takeoff, neither Immanuel Kant nor Thomas Malthus could contemplate the erosion of national boundaries without reference to the former settler colonies in North America and the experiment in nationhood under way there. At the moment in history characterized as the greatest growth spurt of European nationalism, these two influential thinkers imagined the Western European nation as an endangered species. In view of their conflicting causal explanations for the increasing porosity of territorial boundaries, we consider their points of convergence especially significant. Both men thought of the nation as a bounded territory and proposed defensive strategies for preserving those boundaries in the face of encroachments by commercial interests, speculation, and debt. At the same time, both conceded the inevitability of international trade and tried to figure out a means of protecting persons, property, and local practices while allowing the movement of people, goods, and information essential to a modern national economy. Despite the imperial expansion of European nations into other regions of the globe, and although Kant and Malthus approached the problem from quite different theoretical orientations, both wrote from the position of a man of property in a world dominated by men of interests.

In "To Perpetual Peace: A Philosophical Sketch" (1795), Kant attempted to resolve the conflict between the sanctity of a man's property in himself, his labor, his household and land, and his way of life. At a time when Europe was becoming increasingly dependent on international commerce, Kant proposed an international federation to guarantee the integrity of peoples represented by such men. Given that "the natural state is one of war," no nation could put an end to international war by guaranteeing the security of its people. But requiring the members of each nation to "tolerate" the ethnic and religious differences between various nations might go a long way, he argued, to mitigate the warfare that erupted when people did business in other countries. With the model of the Social Contract in mind, Kant proposed a universal "law of hospitality" to guarantee "the right of an alien not to be treated as an enemy when he arrives in another's country" (118).

While "hospitality" comes from the Latin *hospes*, meaning "host," "guest," or "stranger," *hospes* comes in turn from *hostis*, which links the term "stranger" to "enemy." Thus, like the "uncanny," Kant's term is one of those concepts that always carries two antithetical meanings, and he exploited this potential. Detaching the concept from the relationship of host to guest within a nation engaged in international commerce, Kant transformed "hospitality" from a concept that promoted a local identity—the trading of women and exchange of gifts—into a concept aimed at consolidating a cosmopolitan elite of property owners. Rather than see the nation either "(like the ground on which it is located) a possession" or as "a society of men whom no one other than the nation itself can command or dispose of," Kant thought about it as a living being that "like a tree" has "its own roots." For one nation to appropriate "another nation as a graft, denies its existence as a moral person," consequently "turn[ing] it into a thing, and thus contradicts the concept of the original contract, without which a people . . . has no rights" (108). The Social Contract that protects the man of property is not a sufficient umbrella once persons or property become subject to commercial speculation in foreign lands.

To revise the Social Contract so that it could accommodate the forms of property that circulated throughout the Atlantic world, Kant returned to Hobbes's origin story and pondered that moment before men had to wage war with one another in order to survive. So long as there was sufficient land, he contends, men had no reason to engage in a struggle with one another for resources. In order to found civil society, the original contract had ensured their separation from one another by defending every man's right to property. But the peace that resulted was not perpetual: "By virtue of their common ownership of the earth's surface," men "cannot *scatter* themselves infinitely, but must, finally tolerate living in close proximity" (118, our italics). If their proximity to one another once motivated individuals to form national governments, then one nation's encroachment on another's territory and resources requires an international law of hospitality to guarantee people of all nations "the right of association."

As his concern shifted from the negative rights accruing to the property owner to the affirmative right to travel unmolested throughout the world, Kant's plan ground to a temporary halt on the aggressive behavior of Europeans engaged in international commerce and the imperialistic behavior that inevitably accompanied it. He abandoned his affirmative argument on behalf of "the right of association" and recast his law of hospitality in negative terms, namely, a law to counter "the inhospitable conduct of the civilized nations in *our* part of the world, especially the commercial ones" (119, our italics). This behavior has reduced Europeans to "the inhospitableness that [Barbary] coastal dwellers . . . show by robbing ships in neighboring seas and by making slaves of stranded seafarers, or of desert dwellers (the Arabic Bedouins) who regard their proximity to nomadic peoples as giving them a right to plunder" (118). Primitive as piracy and plunder are, however, they are nothing compared to European imperialism. Kant finds "the injustice [they] display towards foreign lands and peoples (which is the same as *conquering* them) terrifying." He reserves his harshest condemnation for the violent appropriation of whole nations following the discoveries of the Americas, when "the lands occupied by the negro, the Spice Islands, the Cape, etc., were regarded as lands belonging to no one because their inhabitants were counted as nothing" (119). Those lands were in fact held in common by the Indian nations, but because they had not been parceled up and declared property, Europeans considered them theirs for the taking. Once in territory whose indigenous peoples lacked what Europeans would consider a legal right to property, settlers and adventurers reverted to a state of savagery. This restaging of the European origin story suggests that property created the very problem of encroachment on the rights of others that it claimed to have resolved in Europe. Once Kant thought in terms of North America, his "law of hospitality" ceased to provide a way of guaranteeing the right of association and became the means of extending the negative rights of property to areas in the world where no such laws exist.

Published in 1798, only three years after Kant's proposal for achieving "perpetual peace," Thomas Malthus's *An Essay on The Principle of Population* offered a different angle on the problem of perpetual war that exposed the inadequacy of imagining the world as property. Neither property rights nor human reason could induce people to live in peaceful proximity until they solved the problem of scarcity, which was, in his view, at the root of human hostility. Malthus boiled down the reason for recurring famine and disease as well as war to the relationship between two immutable principles: "First, That food is necessary to the existence of man. Secondly, that the passion between the two sexes is necessary" and cannot be effectively curtailed on a mass basis (19). The relationship between these two laws produced what he called "the principle of population," namely, the principle that "population, when unchecked, increases in a geometric ratio," while "subsistence increases only in arithmetical ratio," which leads to an exponential increase of population over the yield of a piece of land. For most of human history, Malthus argued, this ratio had played out in one of two ways. Population growth had either been checked by famine or disease or brought nations to war over the resources necessary for their survival and decreased the population that way (19). The disproportion between the number of mouths and the food to feed them inevitably made men cruel.[7]

Why neither property law nor individual reason were sufficient to curb population growth becomes especially clear, as Malthus compares population growth in the United States to that of England by way of debunking William Godwin's claim that man's reason would eventually transcend his animal passions. Demographic statistics indicated that the population of British America had grown from 21,200 in 1643 to an estimated three million before the American War of Independence, while England's numbers were still recovering from losses incurred through mass emigration and the London plague. That England had experienced nothing like the American surge in population was owing to a combination of factors: workers had not begun to amass in North American cities, while several states had abolished the inheritance of land, and one state passed a law granting uncultivated land to anyone willing to cultivate it. Assuming, as Kant did, that a nation was first and foremost the habitat for people who led a certain way of life, Malthus blamed the abundance of land available for food production in North America for the increase in its rate of population growth over England's.[8]

In a notably tortured simile, Malthus makes it clear why, contrary to common sense, he saw the abundance of food as the source of the problem of sustaining a population, paradoxically, and not as its solution. In order to grow an unnaturally large flower by adding "richer mould" to the soil, as the story goes, an "enterprising florist" runs the risk of "burst[ing] the calyx" or protective enclosure of the bud, thereby "destroy[ing] at once [the flower's] symmetry." By means of this simile, Malthus carries the figure of a self-enclosed organic structure disfigured by too much fertilizer into the domain of politics. "In a similar manner the forcing manure used to bring about the French revolution, and to give a greater freedom to the human mind, has burst . . . the restraining bond of all society. . . . And however large the separate petals have grown, however strangely or even beautifully marked, the whole is at present a loose, deformed, and disjointed mass, without union, symmetry, or harmony of colouring" (91). When we apply this simile to the potential productivity of North America, as Malthus encourages us to do, it yields two conclusions. First, the blasted flower implies that America's more democratic distribution of resources (through immigration, as well as the relaxation of property laws) would disrupt the proportionate distribution of resources according to class and lead to an even more uneven distribution of resources in the future. Second, the florist's botched experiment with natural growth, if applied to the human population, would not produce a harmonious political society but a "loose, deformed, and disjointed mass, without symmetry, or harmony of colouring" (91). This comes close to describing the way Malthus understood the situation in postrevolutionary France, as well as the new United States. Thus, despite the fact that he "considered chiefly the mass of mankind and not individual instances," Malthus nevertheless shared Kant's conviction that a reasonably stable social order would have to be bounded, relatively homogeneous, and legally engineered to maintain a balance between the owners of land and laborers. In that it eroded boundaries, encouraged heterogeneity, and disrupted the ratio of population growth to food production, Malthus thought, international commerce and trade would eventually resemble the "enterprising florist" and dismantle the body it overfed. Like Kant, he confronted a body politic whose sovereignty had once guaranteed his own identity as author but was now eroding the very boundaries on which that sovereignty was based. Like petals that had burst their calyx, a population that exceeded the limits of its property monstrously disfigured the nation's form.

Early American novelists understood—at least as well as any European—how the international circulation of persons and property violated the fantasy of self-enclosure that owning property seemed to guarantee. Their novels put "dispersal" to work on behalf of the affirmative right of association over and against the negative rights accruing to property. By so dismantling the fantasy of property, American novelists writing in response to the same historical conditions that so troubled Kant and Malthus made it clear that their purpose—by contrast to their European counterparts—was to formulate an alternative basis for social relationships.

Unsettling Form

To formulate such an alternative, the novels of the early republic require a protagonist with little or no interest in securing his or her person and property. This protagonist neither has a family whose members can be said to belong to one another nor, on the other hand, grants much autonomy to other individuals. Marrying well consequently makes no more sense to him or her than keeping an inheritance intact. Such freedom from the fear of encroachments on one's person and property will sometimes open the door for wayward passion to break up and scatter the community of origin, setting his or her story in motion. Thus, Mervyn's widowed father succumbs to the wiles of his milkmaid, and Mervyn must start from scratch to form a character. When a man swindles her father, Constantia, the protagonist of Brockden Brown's *Ormond* (1799), loses everything but her name, becoming vulnerable to the advances of the libertine Ormond. In *The Power of Sympathy*, Harrington Senior's seduction of Maria Fawcet drives his son to suicide on learning that the woman he loves is his half-sister. Let a libertine seduce someone's daughter, as they often succeed in doing, and her family disintegrates.

But these novels nevertheless reject discipline and self-containment as the means of mitigating the impact of sexual passion. Nary a one goes along with Malthus's claim that the natural passion between the sexes is responsible for dispersing the community, any more than these novels blame human beings for failing to live peacefully together, as Kant does, on man's natural impulse to exploit other men. Sheer curiosity is so often the only reason offered for the protagonist's inability to make himself or herself a home that sexual passion and competitive aggression lose their power to explain why his or her life so regularly gets derailed. Captain Farrago begins his travels in *Modern Chivalry* simply "to see how things were going on here and there and to observe human nature" (4). In just this way, by going "here and there," these novels systematically subordinate the age-old forces of love and war to a drive to circulate widely and combine freely. This, as we have argued, is the distinctive style of early American novels.

The community of origin need not be European, so long as it enforces homogeneity—witness the occasional appearance of Algerian narrators during this period. Peter Markoe's *The Algerine Spy in Pennsylvania* (1787) is composed of letters, largely written by an Algerian official named Mehemet reporting back to Osman, Dey of Algiers, on conditions in postrevolutionary America. Disguised as a Frenchman, Mehemet has occasion to observe the high cost of intolerance while stopping in Gibraltar on his way to the United States. Casting out the Moors has, in his estimation, "weakened Spain at least as much as the banishment of the Protestants reduced the resources of France in the reign of Louis the XVIth" (14). Mehemet's next lesson in intolerance underscores the first in far more personal terms. On the basis of a rumor that he had converted to Christianity, Mehemet receives notice that "by order of the Dey, thy lands, house, furniture and slaves (two excepted) are confiscated to the state" (112). Should he hereafter enter "the territories of Algiers," cautions his correspondent, "thy life will be forfeit" (113). No more bound to respect his right to property than Spain was that of the Moors, Algerian nationalism expresses itself in religious intolerance.

Pennsylvania, on the other hand, offers both Mehemet and his estranged wife the land on which to set up households independent of each other. Pennsylvania, he writes, "has promised to succor and protect the unhappy, that fly to thee for refuge" (125). Mehemet considers American tolerance the reason why he thinks of himself as "formerly a Mahometan." He has renounced Islamic intolerance in order to enjoy, "in the evening of his days, the united blessings of FREEDOM and CHRISTIANITY" (125). If Christianity, more so than property, operates as a code word for tolerance, then how does it save Mehemet from the situation of the Moors in Spain or the Protestants in France? How, in other words, does it guarantee him the right of association? To conclude his story, Mehemet informs the reader that he and his wife have become Christians and acquired property. Lest we think that he has settled down, however, Mehemet makes a point of telling us that his marriage has dissolved and thus that they will circulate as members of one more disrupted household within a social network that will increase its heterogeneity as a result.

Samuel Lorenzo Knapp's *Extracts from the Journals of Marshal Soult* (1817) is narrated by a Frenchman who travels freely and finds much to admire in the United States. His journal entries break off abruptly as he is about to leave New England for the American South, which he expects to find even more congenial to his habits and sensibility. Before his protagonist could do so, Knapp decided against having a Frenchman narrate his novel and more or less rewrote the entire manuscript. Published a year later as *Extracts from a Journal of Travels in North America*, the second version of Knapp's fictional account of his travels in the United States surveys the nation from the perspective of an Algerian spy who is there to size up the possibilities for converting the American people to Islam. Given this sudden shift in the narrator's nationality and purpose in visiting the United States, we have to assume that Knapp was interested in raising the question of tolerance and testing the American capacity to practice it. It soon becomes clear that religious faith, as in Mehemet's account of his life in Pennsylvania, provides the test case: is it a nation's prerogative to make religious belief the condition for membership in the national community?

Ali Bey finds the sophisticated world of the Boston Brahmins unpropitious for conversion by virtue of their unanimity of taste and opinion. He assumes he will encounter an environment of dissent and division by visiting a political caucus. Again he "was surprised to find all the speakers coincide in their opinions" (41). In assessing the religious climate in America, Ali Bey finds that the American people are as contentious as they are otherwise tolerant, and he concludes that religious schisms "extend through the country. Scarcely a week passes but the belligerent parties assail each other from the press or pulpit. . . . The state of irritation produced by this warfare can be easily imagined. And a change that will restore harmony is doubtless considered a desideratum by all sober and reflecting spectators" (125). From the stranger's perspective, the various Christian sects that flourished in America would eliminate any possibility of national unity. But if he imagines that conversion to Islam will "restore [the] harmony" that "is doubtless considered a desideratum by all," the novel makes it clear that Ali Bey is mistaken. The American "press or pulpit" provided a framework for even the most divisive arguments. To disagree, those who took part in these debates had agreed to their opponents' right to use the "press or pulpit" and, in so doing, gave new meaning to Kant's concept of tolerance. This discovery on the narrator's part defines religious beliefs and practices as property in one's person to be protected by the state, not a condition for that protection. When foreign visitors come searching for the secret of American identity, they discover chiefly their inability to formulate a coherent character.

In 1797, Royall Tyler's *The Algerine Captive* offered an account of a young man who acquires training as a physician and attempts in vain to find a community where he can settle down, only to encounter various small communities through which he can, like Kant's stranger, pass safely but not settle down. In 1799, Brockden Brown similarly showed how property rights conflict with the right to association, as Arthur Mervyn breaks into one house after another during the yellow fever epidemic in Philadelphia. By 1836, Robert Montgomery Bird could turn the same form inside out and in *Sheppard Lee* perform similar dispersals within the phenomenological bubble of a pseudo-biographical experience. If Sheppard Lee encounters an insurmountable obstacle, it breaks him up, separating his memory from the body whose sensory experiences it recorded. In so dispersing the components of the protagonist, Byrd releases body and soul to live out a succession of separate futures. Sheppard Lee's body, which Locke considered a man's "first property," is thrust into the public domain and there for the taking. And so it remains—until Lee stumbles upon a lifeless body to house his subjectivity, restoring his mobility. But, like Mervyn, Lee soon feels captive and looks for a means of escape. The serial dispersal and recombination of this protagonist shifts the operative definition of property from property that constitutes one's identity to the possible identities that one could become in the future. The same process turns the novel into a string of short stories linked by the protagonist's death and rebirth as someone else.

The Later Life of Dispersal

Published in 1857, Herman Melville's *Confidence-Man: His Masquerade* continues to this day to challenge the category of the great American novel, to
which critics want it to aspire. The discrepancy between Melville's novel and
the literary concept of the novel has everything to do, we think, with Melville's reliance on the narrative trope of dispersal. By means of this trope, Melville deliberately calls into question any semblance of the continuous
developmental narrative of individual experience and, by proxy, that of a nation, which readers expect of a great novel. As we read it, this novel peels away
the irony from Ali Bey's portrait of the United States as a contradiction in
terms—an agreement to disagree—in order to demonstrate that conflicts do
in fact produce a community. We recognize of course that biographical criticism regards this novel as the bitter fruit of Melville's ignominious last years,
which offers either a cynical view of the nation or else a religious allegory.[9]
Such critical readings think of *The Confidence-Man* as a casualty of a century's
worth of critical commentary celebrating *Moby Dick* as the pinnacle of Melville's literary achievement. By contrast, we consider *The Confidence-Man* to
be a virtuoso performance of "dispersal" as the formal link between the novel
and the nation. What strikes most literary critics as Melville's cynicism makes
this novel the practice of cynicism in the classical sense, or what Foucault calls
"the courage to tell truth." Once divested of his personal and material property, man discovers the truth of human nature.

To make this point, we bring the concept of cynicism that Foucault developed in *The Courage of Truth* to bear on the scene of fierce religious debate
from which Ali Bey abstracted a common "desideratum for harmony." Foucault's account of the Cynic in his final series of lectures at the Collège de
France, from 1983 to 1984, argues that what makes religious belief necessarily
intolerant is the same principle at work in any radical belief system. That is to
say, tolerance is tantamount to accepting falsehood and thus a betrayal of
belief. Rather than elevate human existence above its material conditions, as
the religious zealot does, the true Cynic reduces that life to its ground zero
and lives as would a dog at the mercy of his fellow human beings and in full
public view.[10] To live this way is to reverse aggressively the logic of property
that compels us to remove our vital functions—especially defecation and
masturbation—from public view and so achieve false mastery over our most
basic needs and instincts. The Cynic puts his humanity at risk by exposing the

truth of its embodied life in this way, Foucault contends, and because it is predicated on such truth, the Cynic is an ethical man.

The Confidence-Man consists of a series of arguments among the odd assortment of characters traveling down the Mississippi on board a steamship provocatively named the *Fidèle*. These episodes take place in different parts of the steamship and bring together different levels of its social hierarchy in disputes that recall Knapp's description of religious factionalism in *Extracts from a Journal of Travels in North America*. At issue in the case of Melville's narrative is the question of belief. Rather than a question of how to define the will of God, however, the question of how to define human nature occasions the outbursts of intense hostility around which Melville organizes each chapter. There is no ship so big that it can contain all those who seem to debark and reappear at will, much less house the viewpoints that temporarily converge to erupt in conflict. The figure of the ship operates not as a container but as a point of conjunction and departure. The same holds true for the novel itself, whose characters and positions come from any number of sources and sometimes personify Melville's real-life fellow travelers: Emerson, Thoreau, and, most notably, those well-known confidence men, P. T. Barnum and Edgar Allan Poe.[11] What else but the question of human charity—and whether or not it, too, is a contradiction in terms—links the debates that momentarily crystallize a community out of otherwise dispersed characters?

That there are but two answers to a question so basic (i.e., either yes or no) perfectly suits Melville's purpose. If tolerance is an inappropriate response to this controversy, how does he avoid imposing a viewpoint that silences the opposition? Short of that, what does indeed organize the extraordinary mix of characters on board the *Fidèle*? No one has a stable identity or property in himself or herself. Within the sequence of performances that brings individuals into existence in relation to one another, no one is what he or she claims to be unless that individual's performance can convince the group. But whether or not their confidence means the performance in question—and they are always in question—is that of a confidence game or of the true individual is up for grabs. The unexplained appearance of a mute man in a cream color suit precedes a sequence of what can only be called performances designed to test belief. He holds up cards that, whether he intends to do so or not, announce the question informing his own performance as well as those to follow. This is a question of whether a man's performance exposes the truth of the person or whether his performance conceals that truth. Carrying this question over to the performance of the beggar that immediately follows, does the performance of neediness mean the performer is needy, thus deserving of charity, or does it brand him as a conman and thief? Depending on what epistemological assumptions we bring to his performance, the beggar will merit either compassion or violent expulsion from the community. In eliminating all middle ground, these options also eliminate any hope of tolerance. Melville's appeal to the nineteenth-century reader's fascination with hoaxes immediately casts a dubious light on the theater of religious debate—thus the performances of the public sphere that mystify Peter Markoe's Muslim narrator.

Attracted by a "grotesque negro cripple," dressed in cloth associated with plantation labor and walking on all fours, a number of passengers assemble and take to tossing coins into the cripple's mouth as if they were feeding an animal (17). Black Guinea swallows some when necessary, the narrator explains, "while still retaining each copper this side of the oesophagus. And nearly always he grinned, and only once or twice did he wince" (19). When at its height, the "game of charity" is interrupted by a "limping, gimlet-eyed, sour-faced" man, who begins "to croak out something about [the cripple's] deformity being a sham" (19). Operating on the principle that it takes one to know one, the crowd entertains the possibility that "the game of charity" is a hoax. But this distrust blossoms into debate only when "a Methodist" challenges the skeptical view of the man with the wooden leg and urges the crowd to "put as charitable a construction as one can upon the poor fellow" (23). But skepticism cannot be put to rest so easily, and the Methodist's intervention only escalates the conflict.

His turn of phrase generates much the same suspicion of human charity that Kant's notion of hospitality generated toward strangers: under what conditions can you consider a "stranger" a "guest" rather than an "enemy" intent on parting you from your property for his own surreptitious gain? Is Black Guinea the supplicant he appears to be, or is he performing that role to exploit the good nature of his fellow passengers? In urging the crowd to "put as charitable a construction as one can" on Black Guinea's performance, the Methodist is really telling them to consider any answer to this question a matter of interpretation. The skeptical man with the wooden leg refuses to tolerate the possibility that the cripple is merely performing neediness rather than in genuine need. Counter to the Methodist's call for a charitable reading, the skeptic insists, "Charity is one thing; truth is another" and, with only Black Guinea's act to go by, declares the man "a rascal" (22). In a situation where there is nothing to stop the relationship of con to gull from reversing the relationship of supplicant to donor, skepticism is the only safe bet. Better to remove oneself from the community than be reduced to such a position.

In a novel where characters exist only to the extent that their performances command a group's attention, however, playing it safe is not an adequate response to Black Guinea's performance.[12] The antidote to skepticism is not naiveté—whether willful, as in the case of the Methodist, or impulsive, as seems to be the case when a country merchant spontaneously takes on the role of donor. For lack of some basis on which to decide whether the cripple's performance of extreme neediness is true or false, the reader is thrown back on the performance itself. If it is that performance alone that merits confidence— as Black Guinea's dangerous performance of a dog catching coins in his mouth would seem to do—then performance is the truth of human nature. Viewing Melville's novel from this angle, we could in theory still agree with the tradition of reading that declares *The Confidence-Man* a cynical view of human nature—but that would be to miss the point entirely.

Foucault's reading of the classical figure of the Cynic helps to explain how the question of human charity forces us to think outside the logic of property that informs Kant's call for tolerance of cultural difference (*The Courage of Truth* 165–74, 191–211). It is indeed hard to ignore the uncanny similarity between Foucault's Cynic and the first avatar of Melville's confidence man: "Owing to something wrong about his legs," the narrator tells us, Black Guinea has been "cut down to the stature of a Newfoundland dog" and yet, the narrator continues, it was "curious to see him, out of his very deformity, indigence, and homelessness, so cheerily raising mirth in some of that crowd, whose own purses, hearths, hearts, all their possessions, sound limbs included, could not make gay" (17). Melville opened perhaps his most peculiar novel with a protagonist who lives, as Black Guinea himself puts it, as a "dog without a massa" (18). Melville's protagonist lives, as the Cynic does, namely, in a manner at once masterless and close to the bone, which corresponds to the cynical standard of a performance of human nature that exposes the truth.

Guinea seems to be enjoying the freedom of this role until his audience understands it as designed to exploit their charitable nature to deprive them of property for which they have no need, a possibility that Melville resolutely keeps alive by inserting "as if" to call attention to the performative dimension of Guinea's demeanor on being called a sham: "So far abased beneath its proper physical level, that Newfoundland-dog face turned in passively hopeless appeal, *as if* instinct told it that the right or the wrong might not have overmuch to do with whatever wayward mood superior intelligences might yield to" (19, our italics). Melville keeps in play the possibility that Guinea's act is indeed just an act by suggesting that what may appear to be the "waywardness" of the crowd's sudden change of mind is "not always waywardness, but improved judgement, which, as in . . . the present, operates with them" (20). In doing so, Melville holds open the possibility that what is left of human life once divested of its personal and material property is not what we call "bare life" but a performative capability quite different from constituted property.[13] Guinea's performance establishes social connections on a very difference basis. Lacking anything in the way of material property, he finds a home "all 'long the shore" (18). That his success in getting by on human charity might not depend on his lack of property in himself is no doubt what lays his performance open to suspicious reading. Like the con, Guinea possesses an innate ability to make use of the materials at hand to be whatever the situation requires. That every man embodies any number of possible or "constitutive" selves is the truth that he exposes and the basis for man's social being.

Grotesquely disfigured and dressed in "tow-cloth," he plays on a tambourine fashioned from an "old coal-sifter" and is, for all this, not "the least attractive object" in "the forward part of the boat" (17). When they grow tired of gawking, Guinea entices the otherwise dispersed group of passengers to treat him "like a dog" and toss him money as if it might actually nourish him. Here, the Cynic's aggressive performance of baseline humanity morphs into Malthus's human surplus as a hungry mouth. To see Guinea's humanity from a cynical perspective, we must abandon the notion that tolerance is all that stands between one man's appropriation of another's life without a law to stop him. To grasp the "truth" that Melville is exposing here, we must leave off defending the property of some against the needs of many. Like Foucault's Cynic, Melville seems to know that those who refuse to think of themselves in terms of material property risk everything but their potential property.

Kant had to acknowledge that their characteristic way of living off the land made Native Americans vulnerable to those who saw that land as theirs for the taking, because it had not been transformed into property. A similar danger casts its shadow over the scene where Guinea first appears in festive attire, only to be asked, "And who is your master, Guinea?" On hearing from the crippled negro that he is in fact "a free dog," the same "purple-faced drover" delivers this cautionary tale: "Well, on your account, I'm sorry for that, Guinea. Dogs without masters fare hard" (18). This is much the same as saying that the nation that establishes the man of property as its measure of a human being also made it virtually impossible to be human without it.

Melville designs Guinea's existence to challenge this equation. In the absence of human charity, Guinea emerges as a Shavian figure in his capacity to associate freely with anyone else, thereby providing one of the main threads connecting the semiautonomous chapters of Melville's novel. In doing so, Guinea also brings incompatible demographic groups out of self-contained worlds and into combustible proximity.

The fundamentally antisocial act of accruing property to oneself proves futile in novels that make the dispersal and circulation of such property a precondition for forming a network of social relationships. Writing around the same time as the novels that do just that, Kant and Malthus attribute the barbarity of slavery to abuses of property and, on this basis, side with abolitionism, Kant, on the basis of what he called "the science of right" and Malthus, because of his belief in the sanctity of marriage.[14] Of equal importance, both men thought the practice of slavery corrupted the character of their fellow Europeans in that it authorized them to tyrannize other human beings. Yet they saw the expansion of property rights as the only way to prevent people of property from extracting the labor of those who did not understand the use of land and labor in such terms. Although this proposition may seem hard to disagree with, we nevertheless feel obliged to ask how—given that they saw property as the rationale for Europe's violent appropriation of unprotected human resources—they nevertheless saw the principle of property as the only solution to the very problem it had caused.[15] The novels of the early republic disagree. By dispersing individuals, homes, and communities, these novels throw in their lot with the right of free association.

Dispossession

Abolitionist narratives characteristically expose the terrible effects of property on those whose very lives belong to others to buy and sell, but no novel does so perhaps more pointedly than William Wells Brown's *Clotel*. Nor could we think of a novel that better illustrates the shortcomings of property law as the means of establishing social relations between a class of owners and the people they formerly owned. In his opening salvo, Wells Brown quotes the law of slave states in terms that lay the blame for the dialectical positioning of master and slave squarely at the doorstep of property: "A slave is one who is in the power of a master *to whom he belongs*. The master may sell him, dispose of his person, his industry, and his labour. He can do nothing, possess nothing, nor acquire anything, but what must *belong to his master*" (59–60, our italics). Like Kant, Wells Brown insists that nothing short of a universal law ensuring property rights will put an end to the involuntary dispersal of people and the means of their livelihood. But because Wells Brown wrote a novel in order to make his point, he carries this logic further, showing how the periodic disruption and scattering of small communities intensifies a longing to reestablish those connections, which just may promote another way of maintaining them.

Wells Brown opens *Clotel* by posing the conflict between state laws of property as opposed to what he regards as a depraved twist on the marriage plot. Though addressing the reader from a perspective within a disenfranchised group, the narrator is not limited by that position. He simply knows more about the conditions of living under the laws of the United States from the position of someone subject to them: "Where the slave is placed by law entirely under the control of the man who claims him, body and soul, as property, what else could be expected than the most depraved social condition? The marriage relation, the oldest and most sacred institution given to man by his Creator, is unknown and unrecognized in the slave laws of the United States" (60). The slave's status as property severs the natural bond between man and woman as well as the ties to their offspring. Nor is there any question that a master could, like Thomas Jefferson, enter into unsanctioned sexual relations with women whom he owned and then feel little or no responsibility for the children of their union. *Clotel's* very existence testifies to the affective limitations of the founding father's definition of community. Upright slave owners were known, Brown claims, to become "uneasy in their minds about the rightfulness of permitting slaves to take to themselves husbands and wives, while they still had others living" (60). On applying to "their religious leaders for advice," however, these uneasy-minded slave owners were apparently told that "'in view of the circumstances in which servants in this country are placed . . . it is better to permit servants thus circumstanced to take another husband or wife'" (60). When they made property the basis for individual rights, the framers of the Constitution also legitimated the routine dispersal of those men and women who were denied the right to marry and raise their offspring.

Because she happens to be Thomas Jefferson's daughter conceived with one of his slaves, Clotel is destined, along with her mother and sister, to command a high price and be subjected to circulation as an object in the marketplace. The novel follows Clotel through methodical dispersals of her family as she struggles to establish bonds that can hold together the biological family. The first chapter of *Clotel* establishes the principle that will repeat itself throughout, as Horatio Green falls in love with Clotel and makes her his common-law wife, while Jefferson sells Currer and Althesa, Clotel's sister, in New Orleans to another owner. Later purchased by Henry Morton while passing as a white woman, Althesa marries him and has two daughters, only to have Morton die according to convention before manumitting them. The three are consequently sold and separated by the slave market, just as Clotel and her daughter are. Thus, it only makes sense that Wells Brown should present the marketing of Clotel's character, body, and soul in terms of dismemberment: "This was a Southern auction, at which the bones, muscle, sinews, blood, and nerves of a young lady of sixteen were sold for five hundred dollars; her moral character for two hundred; her improved intellect for one hundred; her Christianity for three hundred; and her chastity and virtue for four hundred dollars more" (67). This catalogue of her marketable features for the auction accompanies a similar reduction of her kin group and a dispersal of those parts to a succession of owners. It is therefore grotesquely appropriate that Wells Brown exploits the sentimental potential of suicide to rearticulate those body parts and grant the heroine command of them[16]: "On either hand, far down below, rolled the deep foamy waters of the Potomac, and before and behind the rapidly approaching step and noisy voices of pursuers, showing how vain would be any further effort for freedom. Her resolution was taken. She clasped her *hands* convulsively, and raised *them*, as she at the same time raised her *eyes* toward heaven . . . and then, with a single bound, she vaulted over the railings of the bridge, and sunk for ever beneath the waves of the river!" (219). Given the correspondence between disarticulation of Clotel's constitutive property and the dispersal of her kin group to successive owners, what does the coherence that she achieves in death say about relationships within that group?

When he set at least three plots in motion by selling Clotel as an object on the auction block, Wells Brown also set in motion a process that prevents her story from becoming a traditional captivity narrative. One such dispersal of the kin group begets another that produces a hybrid population connected by multiple lines of descent. Narrating this process grieves the author-narrator, who frequently intrudes to point out the pain and suffering generated when only some have an inalienable right to property and others can be owned and sold again and again. Observing the polemics of the novel, then, one must concede that happiness rests on self-ownership. As the source and product of unequally distributed property rights, the Jefferson household inaugurates a cascade of dispersals that produces what the novel's opening lines describe as "a fearful increase of half whites, most of whose fathers are slave owners and their mothers slaves" (59). This surplus population yields a body politic that arguably resembles Malthus's disfigured flower, a population so force-fed as to produce a "loose, deformed, and disjointed mass, without symmetry, or harmony of colouring."

But if, on the other hand, we focus on the social relationships that depend on the systematic dispersal of this subjugated population, we discover a social network remarkably similar to the one that forms in the other novels we have been discussing. Wells Brown indicates as much when, following her suicide, he continues Clotel's story from the icy waters of the Potomac through her offspring whose stories branch out like tributaries from her own. Running counter to the proverbial river that conventionally carries the slaves away from one another is the information that, when fueled by yearning for the vanished kin group, works its way indirectly through other contacts. Intensifying in proportion to the distance among its members, the affilation generated by these contacts not only eroded boundaries maintained by the Fugitive Slave Act but also transformed a dispersed and subordinated group into an independent social network.

Chapter 5

Population

The novels of the early republic so consistently refuse to formulate a protagonist who pretends to be a typical American or to represent some demographic group that we have no choice but to move the term "population" into the role of protagonist and do our best to explain how its performance differs as such from that of conventional protagonists. This will involve putting aside not only the monstrous figure that "population" usually assumed in the British literature and popular culture of the late eighteenth and early nineteenth centuries but also the statistically based maps, charts, and graphs by means of which early social scientists and city reformers sought to turn "population" into an object of knowledge. We focus instead on the aleatory narrative by means of which American novels of the same period animate a heterogeneous field of minor characters so as to displace a system of relationships based on property.[1]

The definitions of population that proliferated in Europe during the late eighteenth and early nineteenth centuries exploited either the early modern figure of the populace as a grotesque body or the use of body counts in times of epidemics to break up that body and subject it to control—whether by discipline or the security measures carried out by inoculation. We see both the grotesque and diseased versions of the popular body as the "other" side of managerial control and its enabling condition. Together, these obverse ways of looking at virtually the same object succeeded in suppressing the way that populations, like epidemics, organize themselves. Resembling the novels that uncovered that potential, the tropological behavior of population had to be coordinated in order to spread. Rather than the biographical form favored by the British novel, we argue, the novels of the early republic drew on a narrative tradition that saw population not as the very antithesis of a community made of individuals but as the basis for a community of a very different kind.

The Problem of Population

We have seen how Malthus portrayed population as a fundamentally ungovernable human mass bent on exponentially expanding the number of hungry mouths to feed. By contrast, philosopher Roberta L. Millstein, writing two centuries after Malthus, has little difficulty bringing population under conceptual control. Despite its variable and open-ended character, Millstein establishes basic biological criteria for a population that help us think our way back to the concept of population as the novelists of the early republic seem to have understood it. What determines the limits and internal organization of a population, according to Millstein, is "the causal interaction" among a number of biological groups over several generations: do they interbreed, do they compete, or do they support each other in the struggle for survival (269)? Individuals who interact causally in one or more of these ways constitute a population that can be regarded as a single biological body with its own lifetime, proclivities, and internal organization. The very capacity to think and act as one living being that inevitably made population assume such monstrous proportions in Malthus's imagination are exactly the propensities that allow Millstein to render it manageable in rational terms. With her remarkably simple definition of population in mind, this chapter turns to the novels of the early republic to see what social principles of organization they put in operation within the population of the United States during the early national period. In demonstrating how a heterogeneous population established relations among its various parts, we see these novels distinguishing an American concept of "population" from the scientific definitions that were emerging in Europe at that time.

Malthus reduced human life to a consistent proclivity for sexual reproduction and then compounded the results in order to define population as a fundamentally ungovernable human surplus that, even in times of peace and plenty, made it a phobic object. Although many of his contemporaries challenged this fatalistic view, Malthus nevertheless succeeded in producing an (in)human monster that seized the popular imagination, lending population a legibility that population science, even at its rhetorical best, would be hard-pressed to match throughout the century to come. Indeed, intellectuals and novelists so different as Mary Shelley, Thomas Mayhew, Friedrich Engels, Charles Dickens, and Bram Stoker reproduced the phobic figure of population as a clear and present danger to a modern person and his property.

Meanwhile, social scientists and city planners were busy turning population into a "set of elements that, on the one side, are immersed within the general regime of living beings and that, on the other side, offer a surface on which" government could intervene (Foucault, *Security* 74). As Robert Mitchell explains, the modern definition of population proposes that one can discern "in the *same* population constants and regularities that bear on many different qualities—responses to other diseases, suicide rates, height distributions, and so on—and each additional survey of the same population" therefore identifies "each individual as increasingly unique" ("Biopolitics" 374). Such scientific criteria turned Malthus's homogeneous mass into a dynamic field of individual variations whose relative numbers and characteristic behaviors could be retrospectively determined, the most advantageous points of government intervention identified, and the health and productivity of the entire field maximized. While they disagreed on the methods, the novels we examine in this chapter always considered it the raison d'être of government to promote the freedom to circulate and associate with others, so long as such freedom ensured the well-being of the entire body politic. These novels also departed from European notions of population on the issue of whether or not population can be seen strategically from outside and above—as an object of knowledge. Instead, the early American novel offered a fictional phenomenology that engaged readers in tactical experiences of government and, by this means, gave them access to rules of engagement both political and literary.

The social scientist and city planner survey the field of variations with an eye to maintaining an optimal state of equilibrium among various groups within a territorially bounded field of human actors. As Foucault's lectures published in *Security, Territory, Population* explain in fascinating detail, during the eighteenth century, European governments introduced an entire layer of bureaucracy to regulate the distribution of goods, people, and information so as to minimize the potential for famine and disease and to maximize the health and prosperity of the entire population. The optimal well-being of the population was not something to be achieved by passing laws or urging family discipline but required what Foucault calls "conduction": small but precise interventions in the habits of consumption, sanitation, the routes people took through the city, and even their forms of recreation. This way of regulating daily life could not be more different than the forms of discipline that not only shaped the novels of Richardson, Radcliffe, and Austen but also gave rise to an ethnos of "respectability" embraced by the modern middle classes.[2] Population does not aim to remove the individual from the welter of human bodies that live in common but rather encourages forms of conduct that maintain the circulation of goods and services on which the health and prosperity of a population depend.

In contrast to the top-down style of management that Foucault identifies with the European town, the early American novelists engaged population not as an object to be managed and labor power to be harnessed but as the heterogeneous field of those subject to material conditions they could not control. This composite subject was nonetheless the cause and agent of events, an organism shaped by the collective response to those events, the capacity to feel and respond to changes in the composition of the community as a whole, and the social network that became perceptible as a result. By contrast to objectifications of population that provide a strategic view—whether to incite fear or identify the advantageous points of intervention—the novels of the early republic see population as a leveling process that establishes horizontal rather than vertical relationships within a diverse and variable field of characters. These novels set narration to work negotiating such a field of variations, a field replenished by a succession of dispersals that create new opportunities for recombining social elements. Working within such a field, the question for the novelist was not how best to regulate the interaction of its elements but how to free those elements from the categories that contain and hierarchize an otherwise horizontally interactive field. It is population in this sense that serves as the protagonist of early American novels.

By characterizing such narration as tactical, we mean to challenge the assumption that strategy and tactics exist in the relation of top to bottom.[3] Where strategic thinking looks at its object from outside and above with a mind to subject population to laws that can conceptually manage it, the tactician does not depend on achieving a position of self-mastery where he or she oversees the whole. In contrast to the strategist, the tactician characteristically strolls through the city, taking things as they come, circumventing obstructions, moving this way and that with distractions, seizing opportunities as they present themselves, or simply changing as the wind blows. In a social field composed largely of immigrants—some fresh off the boat, others going several generations back, still others brought in chains—we can well imagine how easily such a protagonist might have run up against rules of conduct that developed strictly on the spot and in a makeshift fashion. Such rules would guarantee free circulation and designate alternate routes to follow, neighborhoods to avoid, and people with whom one should or should not associate.

Indeed, each new social element that entered such a field would put pressure on those rules of conduct that required some slight adjustment.

Conduction and Counterconduct

Foucault adds a further wrinkle to this transformation that bears directly on the conditions that gave rise to the novel in North America. In its attentiveness to "the conduct of all and each," he explains, government formed regulations in response to certain forms of "counter-conduct," which it considered abnormal and disorderly behavior. "There was," Foucault concludes, "an immediate and founding [and, we would add, ongoing] relationship between conduct and counter-conduct" (*Security* 196). This meant that specific struggles, say, for the rights of women, would neither remain separate from other struggles, like the abolition of slavery, nor lose their specificity. Under the right circumstances and working cooperatively, a number of such struggles could acquire the capacity to alter the general economy of social relations accordingly. The consistency with which novels of the new republic overturn the formal moves by which British novels produced a representative individual should tell us that in writing novels, Americans were practicing a form of counterconduct. To see how this tactical behavior converted a population of dispersed families into a community, let us begin where we left off in our discussion of "dispersal" in William Wells Brown's *Clotel*.

The figure of the dying slave is traditionally organized around a cruel contradiction. In British abolitionist poetics, the slave in question emerges as a fully human subject that can cross the color line and elicit sympathetic identification only when life as an individual is over. Saidiya Hartman has spelled out eloquently and at length what goes so wrong with the liberal politics of identification that informs this contradiction.[4] We like to think that Wells Brown decided to drain his heroine's suicide of the very sympathy readers would ordinarily feel for a mother who despairs of rescuing her child. That is to say, he rejected the sentimental way around the problem of slavery by using the heroine's suicide to imply that the problem was insoluble if one thinks in terms of saving one individual at a time. If our previous chapter argued that "dispersal" was necessarily antecedent to the novel's production of an acentric, nonhierarchical, and heterogeneous social body, then the purpose of this chapter is to consider how population displaces the heroine of sentimental

fiction as the protagonist of the American novel. Living in Boston but lectur-
ing in England when the Fugitive Slave Act was passed in 1850, Wells Brown
was hardly in a position to understand the positive implications of a fugitive
population.[5] An escaped slave himself, he was not about to become someone
else's property and stayed in England until his freedom could be purchased.
But, as we have claimed, the dispersal of Clotel's beloved family nevertheless
forces its members to start up new relationships in an attempt to maintain the
very ties that have been severed. As a result, the major characters reestablish
their relations through sequential mediations. Moreover, as information concerning Clotel's relations periodically travels back along the pathways of their
dispersal, that information links all those involved in transmitting it into one
and often several interlocking chains. By novel's end, these connections of mutual concern and cooperation have displaced the longing for a lost community
that had first motivated its members to reestablish those connections.

It is not simply as an alternative to the legally authorized family, however,
that the network of fugitive slaves becomes important to our argument. It is
also because the fugitive life becomes an alternative way of conducting daily
life that underscores the truth that there is never just one way of organizing a
population, no matter what most British novels of the period suggest. Subordinate to and yet independent of both family and state, the slave trade eluded
the apparatus of the well-intentioned household and the property laws designed to protect it. To read *Clotel* is to hold those very laws responsible, as
Wells Brown does, for creating a fugitive population. As the epitome of bad
government in both respects, the institution of slavery prohibited freedom of
movement and subjected its population to an intolerable form of captivity.
Under these conditions, as *Clotel* demonstrates, the slave trade itself gave rise
to a specific set of tactical maneuvers, or form of counterconduct, that transformed the population so defined into a community.

Thus, even as the Fugitive Slave Act of 1850 obstructs the heroine's attempts at removing herself and her children from circulation, it drives her to
seek alternative routes to freedom. Before Clotel resorts to suicide, she,
George, William, and Mary take advantage of their light skin and English
features to assume self-ownership and move freely on their own volition. In so
doing, they make it possible for us to see Clotel's suicide in an instructively
unsentimental light. In order to pass for white, one could say, these former
slaves relinquished their status as property of any kind—whether their own or
someone else's—and opportunistically performed identities that let them continue circulating unmolested. Insofar as their Anglo heritage masked their

identity as former slaves, who is to say that such performances falsified their identity?[6] Indeed, it would be more accurate to say that by passing back and forth between black and white, the members of Clotel's community were becoming no more than what they already were. Whether black passing for white, woman passing as man, or slave passing as free man, the act of passing from one side of such binaries to the other is neither authentic nor false but a realization of the actors' freedom from both. If passing erodes the sex, class, and racial differences legitimating Jefferson's family and personifies that erosion for the reader, then passing implies that any one person could become several others. In this respect, passing operates counter to the conduct of the slave trade as well as to the discipline that traditional households instilled in their women.

Equally important, in countering disciplinary practices, passing also works against the market forces of dispersal in producing a fugitive network that operates as a community. The distances that separate the members of Clotel's extended family, the secondary connections they make along the way, and the unrelenting threat of captivity all serve to intensify the fear of capture that pulses along plotlines that ultimately link each fugitive to every other. In providing a vanishing point for her role as the sentimental heroine, Clotel's leap into the Potomac thus provides the point of her emergence as the progenetrix of a community defined by its tactical evasion of the conduct that facilitated slavery. If characters seem flat and manipulated by the plot as a result, instead of rounded by self-conflict and capable of engineering their own stories, it is because their ability to master instincts and conduct themselves according to some norm is entirely beside the point. These characters operate as a community by virtue of their refusal to be turned into so many "bones," "muscles," "sinews," "blood," and "nerves" from which economic value can be extracted.[7] Passing provides at once a means of refusing such dehumanization and of repairing the emotional damage of repeated dispersals.

This is another way of saying that Wells Brown stresses not only the involuntary nature of the heroine's captivity but also the involuntary nature of her suicide, as the protagonist frantically looks for a way of eluding her captors. "God, in his Providence," the narrator avers, "had determined that an appalling tragedy should be enacted that night, within plain sight of the President's house and the Capital of the Union, which should be an evidence wherever it may be known, of the unconquerable love of liberty that the heart may inherit," in this case presumably from Jefferson himself (219). At the level of narrative, the unreflective character of her fatal act suggests that Clotel was

no more able to obey the rules of conduct for slaves and still remain the heroine than the African American child Topsy could obey her flinty New England mistress, Miss Ophelia, or the illegitimate Pearl could obey her mother
Hester Prynne and embody an alternative future for the nation. More clearly
than any other legal form of captivity, including even the dispossession of
Native Americans, the practice of slavery exposed the inadequacy of negative
rights to ensure freedom within the limits of property.

Slavery brings the operations of political exclusion to the fore. Occupying
the middle ground between the excessively large and abstract framework of
federal law, on the one hand, and a notion of family that was clearly too narrow, weak, and insolvent, on the other, the slave trade represents the very antithesis of the way of governing that American novelists considered necessary
to forming a national community. As in Wells Brown's *Clotel*, so in Harriett
Beecher Stowe's classic sentimental novel, *Uncle Tom's Cabin*, the slave trade
operated much as the yellow fever did in Charles Brockden Brown's *Arthur
Mervyn*—as a negative inversion of population management that realized its
own counterconduct as another form of community.

We want to linger over *Clotel* for another paragraph or two in order to see
exactly how the counterconduct generated by captivity produces a community. Thomas Jefferson's household demonstrates that being part of such a
household is ultimately a form of captivity for those to whom it denies the
ability to circulate of their own free will. Nor does the novel suggest that such
a household can be reconstituted by laboring bodies bought and sold by men
of property. Population resists the two-nations solution that Stowe proposes by
sending Topsy to Liberia once she arrives at a marriageable age. While both
authors show that the immunity property affords some people is lethal for
others, neither suggests another way to reassemble the scattered pieces of the
families rendered illegitimate by slavery. As it pulses backward along the forked
and looping pathways of the slave trade, however, the emotional residue of
broken families generates a new form of affiliation arguably common among
other groups within the new United States. The tactical moves by which *Clotel*
forms affiliations outside and independent of the household place it in a tradition of American fiction that extends back in time to the novels of the early
republic and, from there, as far back as colonial captivity narratives.

We have launched this discussion of "population" with a novel written
during the 1850s in order to focus on a narrative tradition that connects novels
considered works of "minority" literature directly to a body of fiction that itself tends to be marginalized by literary history and criticism. The dread that

gives rise to counterconduct in the face of the Fugitive Slave Act tells us that Wells Brown's novel was addressed not to slaves or even former slaves so much as to readers who never questioned their self-ownership. These same readers avidly consumed the captivity narratives permeated by a sense of impending violence strikingly similar to the vague sense of dread that suffuses novels by Brockden Brown, Bird's *Sheppard Lee*, and Melville's *The Confidence-Man*. A whole string of American novelists evidently sensed that only such a feeling could generate the counterconduct required to convert a population into a community hostile to the household celebrated as a model of discipline by their British counterparts.

Captive America

The later life of the American captivity narrative has persuaded us to dispense with the historical genealogy that locates the nation's genesis in the Puritan settlements of New England, as well as its eventual development into a secular culture of artisans, merchants, planters, indentured servants, and slaves along the Atlantic seaboard. As the story goes, the most enlightened among them coaxed the people of the United States out of theological absolutism and into a contractual government that promoted assimilation as the gateway to self-sovereignty. An enchanting tale it is that takes us from the ethnic purity of religious settlements to assimilation and a unified national culture—but it is not a story that publication statistics back up. It was, for example, only during the postrevolutionary period that Mary Rowlandson's narrative of captivity, first published in 1682, enjoyed peak popularity. This account of captivity and redemption in the seventeenth-century wilderness went through at least twelve reprintings in the last three decades of the eighteenth century. Of the 155 Indian captivity narratives published between 1682 and 1800, 115 appeared between 1780 and 1800, the same period when Mary Rowlandson's substantially earlier narrative was most frequently republished.[8] In other words, reprintings of the Puritan variety peaked exactly when the supposedly later—often semi-salacious—secular captivity narratives came into vogue.

To further complicate the picture, British North American readers for some time had been familiar with accounts of captivity at the hands of Barbary pirates. Yet it was only at the end of the eighteenth century, exactly when both variations of the Indian captivity narrative were enjoying their greatest popularity, that American readers developed an appetite for accounts of

Barbary captivity. Witness the fact that "between John Foss's 1798 narrative
and the numerous printings of James Riley's 1817 account . . . American publishers issued over a hundred American Barbary captivity editions" (Baepler
24). Riley's *Sufferings in Africa* (1817) went through no less than twenty printings. Before publication as a book, this story was well reported as a news
event, and afterward, the book was widely reviewed and anthologized. As a
result, hundreds of thousands of American readers became familiar with the
basics of the story.[9] Only modestly successful by comparison, Royall Tyler's
The Algerine Captive (1797) is one of the most explicit appropriations of a
Barbary tale by a novelist.

When we take into account the argument these variations of captivity
narrative were waging with one another, something very interesting happens
to the traditional opposition of Mary Rowlandson's concern for her Christian
purity and the native qualities that make it possible for Abraham Panther's
"Lady" to survive. Rather than displace the devout Mary Rowlandson with the
secular "Panther Lady," these American captivity narratives make better sense
if we think of them as mutually dependent arguments, the one encouraging
precisely the conduct on the heroine's part that the other variation condemns.
Both use privation, or what Malthus named scarcity, to define inversely the
form of government that would eliminate it. Mary Rowlandson's account as-
serts the absolute difference between the Native American and Christian forms
of government, the one completely lacking what the other guarantees. To ward
off any hint that her survival under that regime might have entailed some
compromise of her purity, Mary Rowlandson's narrative takes every opportunity to turn physical privation into proof of her refusal to assimilate. Thus, she
claims never to have lost her disgust for the unclean food she ate in captivity
while near starvation. As for the integrity of her womanhood, alone in the
company of Indians and other captives, "sleeping all sorts together," she insists,
"not one of them offered the least abuse of unchastity to me in word or action"
(Rowlandson 171–72). To the degree that her virtue remains intact through
enormous hardships, Rowlandson's privation testifies, as in the title to the first
American edition, to "The Sovereignty and Goodness of God."

Attributed to the pseudonym Abraham Panther, "A Surprising Account
of the Discovery of a Lady Who Was Taken by the Indians" (1787) shows how
a secular or assimilationist narrative seemed to argue against God's sovereignty
by transferring that authority to the individual subject. Published more than
twenty times, Panther's narrative features a heroine who disobeys her father
and elopes with a lover. Panther compromises his heroine's sexual purity in

order for his Lady to reclaim it by slaying a giant who has murdered her lover and then threatened to force himself upon her. By means of the ritual decapitation and burial of her captor, Panther's Lady deftly appropriates the father's prerogative in defense of her own chastity. The slaying of the giant is consequently less important for the physical violence it seems to share with Indian practices than as the means of distributing sovereignty—vis-à-vis the monopoly on violence—from God, father, or husband back to the individual subject. In contrast with the colonial captivity narratives, Panther's account pays less attention to what the Lady refuses to do than to the measures she takes to maintain mobility. Thus, it should come as no surprise to see the heroine's improvisational talent run roughshod over the prohibitions observed by her Puritan counterpart.

The Lady's brutal murder of her would-be rapist amounts not only to the theft of the Native American's indigenous qualities but also to the usurpation of male authority that should place her at the opposite pole from Mary Rowlandson. The point here is evidently not to exonerate a woman who adapts to Indian ways and usurps masculine prerogatives but to transform her into a heroine as she assumes self-mastery. Why else have her perform an arduous cultural script prescribing the procedures for slaying the villain and burying his dismembered remains? That the publication of narratives that endorse racial and sexual passing coincided with the many reprintings of Mary Rowlandson's narrative in the 1780s and 1790s is provocatively suggestive. These narratives may seem dead set against each other now, but during the late eighteenth century, they nevertheless appealed to the same readership. This implies that while the two forms of captivity narrative disagree about the sort of heroine who should provide the center of the household, they do so in order to insist on the household as the model of government. Put another way, one can say that the colonial captivity narrative and the later secular variation of that narrative can disagree about what guarantees an individual's freedom but still agree on the more fundamental issue of property. Both narratives therefore ask the reader to see the protection of property in oneself, whether sacred or secular, as the whole point of government.

Enter the Barbary captivity narrative, which imagines government on an entirely different basis. Accounts of captivity in the hands of Barbary pirates appropriate the same argument Kant mounted on behalf of the universal right to property but then use it to insist that good government should have nothing to do with property. Against the background of a decade-long debate on the immigration question, the popularity of novels that questioned the limits of the nation's hospitality—who was a fellow countryman, who a guest, and who an enemy?—should not surprise us.[10] But what does deserve attention is how these narratives question the limits placed on citizenship. In choosing *The Algerine Captive* as the title for his novel, Royall Tyler provided readers with a reason to read through the first volume that, as we suggested in Chapter 3, offers a dim view of fellow feeling in the new United States, counting on readers to keep reading in anticipation of the more exotic fare promised by the title. Tyler's protagonist, Updike Underhill, spends the first volume sifting through the differences he encounters along the eastern seaboard of the United States. As a New Englander, this protagonist is consistently met with mere hospitality as he traverses a patchwork of independent communities that are in no respect united, save in their refusal to accept him as a member of the community. Broke and unable to find a satisfactory place to settle down, he signs on board the good ship *Sympathy* as a surgeon and is soon captured and enslaved. What had presented itself as a quasi-autobiographical record of regional conflict, boundary violations, and failed social relationships breaks off as the narrator begins his story anew—in the double role of protagonist and narrator of a Barbary captivity narrative. In keeping with this tradition, he finds himself thrown into the company of "a Negro slave, five Portuguese, two Spanish sailors, an Italian fiddler, a Dutchman . . . and his Hottentot servant" (114). This assortment of individuals appears to be as diverse and unstructured as the American communities he visited were unified and rule bound.

The wonder of it is that, having been routinely excluded from communities within the United States, Underhill considers himself American once captured, taken to North Africa, and enslaved. Having no value in himself, he acquires value in the eyes of his captors as an object of exchange in the international economy of the North Atlantic. He also acquires value in the eyes of his fellow captives for the literacy that allows him to speak as someone involuntarily subjected to those in a position of authority. In literary terms, moreover, Underhill finds himself in the advantageous position to author a detailed, firsthand ethnographic description of the northern coast of Africa, considered one of the more interesting corners of the triangulated Atlantic world. So situated, he is no longer just anyone writing to anyone. If the slave's narrative sees the United States from the abject position of those subject to the market in laboring bodies, then the Barbary narrative reverses the power differential and offers the reader a view of the barbaric practices of North African pirates from the perspective of an American citizen taken captive. His ability to record his experience in writing distinguishes his voice not only from the reader's but from that of his fellow captives as well.

In Volume I of *The Algerine Captive*, we can say that the narrator speaks as anyone to virtually anyone else who shares his literacy, but in Volume II, he breaks completely with the biographical form and performs as the spokesman for an American perspective in the Atlantic world. As a Barbary captive, Underhill doesn't need to argue in the abstract for tolerating a range of ethnic differences. Though a professional man with considerable knowledge of the world, his captors have deprived him of the privileges that come with property and rendered him an object among other objects. But when reduced in their eyes to human cargo that might demand a good amount of ransom money, Underhill finds that his literacy and medical skill can improve the condition of this micro-community provided he apply them tactically as the occasion presents itself. In contrast to any top-down measure for protecting nations from the free circulation of strangers throughout the Atlantic world, the Barbary captivity narrative clearly promotes forms of counterconduct that maintain free circulation.

Two roughly contemporary strains of cosmopolitanism—Kant's principle of universal hospitality and the Barbary captivity narrative—gesture toward each other across an ontological gulf that separates the concept of the man of property from that of a human population.[11] Kant felt that "the inhospitableness that coastal dwellers (e.g., on the Barbary Coast) show by robbing ships in neighboring seas and by making slaves of stranded seafarers, [was] contrary to natural right" ("Perpetual Peace" 118). But because it "extends . . . the privilege of aliens to enter, only so far as [it] makes attempts at commerce with native inhabitants possible," his principle of hospitality maintains those rights (118). As if to expose the antisocial side of hospitality, Tyler sets the first volume of *The Algerine Captive* in postrevolutionary America and dwells on the minor differences that divide one region from another—to the extent, as Tyler's protagonist complains, that his "every attempt at familiarity, in a young stranger, habituated to the social, but respectful intercourse, customary in the northern states, excited alarm" (82–83). Here Underhill is received, however hospitably, as a foreigner who, like Kant's stranger, can pass through but not belong. But once on the high seas, he is outside of the world of protected property and understands himself as part of a population. As such, he hopes "that the miseries, the insults, and cruel woundings, I afterwards received, when a slave myself, may expiate for the inhumanity, I was necessitated to exercise, towards these MY BRETHREN OF THE HUMAN RACE" (96). The novel itself breaks out of its biographical form as Underhill proclaims his allegiance to the principle of population.

Narrating Population

The American appetite for Barbary captivity narratives coincided with the appearance of novels that similarly entangled Americans in and distinguished them from a large cast of international characters. Leonora Sansay's *Secret History* (1808) takes its reader through circuits of exchange between Philadelphia and Haiti, Haiti and France, back to Philadelphia, then to Jamaica, and on to Cuba, as a pair of sisters try to evade capture by the tyrannical plantation owner married to one of them. The narrator of *Arthur Mervyn* (1799) reports by novel's end that Arthur and his wife will soon "Hie to Europe." At the conclusion to *Wieland* (1798), Clara writes that she is living with her uncle in Montpellier, and *Ormond* (1799) ends as Constantia Dudley arrives in England. It is significant that the single most popular gothic novel in nineteenth-century America, Isaac Mitchell's *The Asylum; or, Alonzo and Melissa* (1811), tells a story of lovers who cannot marry because the Revolutionary War created a disparity in their respective family fortunes. The very novels that seem most bent on fulfilling the traditional desire for the security of home—for instance, Susanna Rowson's *Charlotte Temple* (1791) and William Hill Brown's *The Power of Sympathy* (1789)—in fact block and divert the marriage plot with a consistency that defines household and nation as obstacles to overcome. Observing the tropes of the Barbary captivity narrative, these novels hijack the need to make a home for oneself apart from the population and replace it with a contrary urge for a mobility that links the dispersed elements of a population as a common body.

The difference between Books I and II of *The Algerine Captive* demonstrates, and does so in bold type, that while the protagonist cannot speak for others as their representative, his peculiar form of literacy allows him to speak from within the population and for everyone. In taking this decidedly tactical turn against the strategic perspective of European novels, however, the population novel does not hand over its authority to democratic writing. To show exactly how a style of narration exploits this double move, let us turn to a narrator who refuses to do so in an effort to maintain a biographical perspective on experience. Originally published in 1782, J. Hector St. John de

Crèvecœur's *Letters from an American Farmer* is somewhat off the beaten path for a study that focuses on the early American novel. Published a year later, again in English and with minor corrections, the 1783 edition has been read so widely, demonstrates the impossibility of individualizing experience so well, and uses the trauma of the American Revolution so directly that it is relatively easy to see how this fictional collection of letters from an American farmer to a British correspondent adapts the captivity narrative to describe the condition of the Loyalist during a year of revolution.[12]

As he recounts how his father worked American soil into a farm, which "in return . . . has established all our rights; on it is founded our rank, our freedom, our power as citizens, our importance as inhabitants of such a district," Farmer James rolls out his Lockean credentials, and his letters build on that base to measure his own success (54). Between his second to last letter and the last, however, something stops in its tracks what tries to be a pseudo-biographical account of a representative individual. After a failed attempt in 1779 to escape the turbulence of revolution, an attempt that landed him in prison, Crèvecoeur arrived in England at some point in the early 1780s and published his *Letters from an American Farmer* from that relatively secure position. But he does not see fit to grant his surrogate and narrator the same opportunity. In his final letter to an English gentleman, Farmer James describes himself as part of a "convulsed and half dissolved" society that recalls both Hobbes's headless multitude and the disfigured population of Milton's Hell. Overcome by the same frenzy that dissolves the property beneath his feet, he describes himself as "seized with a fever of the mind" and "transported beyond the degree of calmness which is necessary to delineate our thoughts" (201). Desperate to remove himself from a population moved to violence, he decides to relocate his family "from the accursed neighbourhood of Europeans" to the western frontier, where they can live in a manner "sufficiently complete to answer all the primary wants of man and to constitute him a social being such as he ought to be in the great forest of Nature" (211). In doing so, this protagonist reproduces the fantasy that once brought his father to the American wasteland, the British fantasy of transforming America into a world of property.

If we now fast forward from the aftermath of the War of Independence to the decade leading up to the Civil War, we see Harriet Beecher Stowe taking up this "broken" form as a form of openly sentimental misconduct. *Uncle Tom's Cabin* lays the foundation for this tactical move as it attempts to resolve two narrative traditions that struggle for the upper hand in determining the outcome of her novel. These are the same traditions that compete for control of Crèvecœur's *Letters*, Tyler's *Algerine Captive*, and, indeed, virtually all the novels of the early national period under consideration here: one narrative devoted to the disruptions produced by the international circulation of goods and people and another dedicated to consolidating a household around the man of property. Chattel slavery would appear to doom from the outset attempts to reconcile these two traditions. Whether or not the novel ultimately comes down on the side of Crèvecœur, as opposed to that of Tyler, the process yields a broken form. What does Stowe accomplish by producing such a break in her narration?

It seems somehow predictable that she should use a domestic novel to think about the consequences of a nation divided over the issue of slavery. In *Uncle Tom's Cabin*, as in *Clotel*, a house divided raises the possibility that such a division could be reconciled within the household. Even though domestic fiction is conceptually bound to property, Stowe uses the site of the sentimental family to expose that way of imagining community as egregiously inadequate to the task of dealing with the problem of population. Like Wells Brown, she locates the source of the problem in a household that lacks the legal obligation and economic will to protect its members from the transatlantic trade in human beings. The novel's title refers to the humble abode of stereotypically happy slaves over which Uncle Tom presides as their mock patriarch. By situating this home within the Shelby property and that property within the American South, Stowe contains the problem of slavery within the territory of the nation. So situated, it demonstrates what happens to the nation when Tom's sentimental value as a member of the family comes into conflict with his economic value as a member of an enslaved population. As it breaks Tom apart, his double status exposes the failure of men of property both to remove the household from the international slave trade and to sustain that household without slave labor. Tom's symbolic journey down the Mississippi consequently sets off a cascade of dispersals in which household after household collapses as he is sold and bought down the river. This tells the reader that a slave narrative based on accounts of Barbary captivity has taken over a novel and eliminated all possibility of a domestic resolution.

To bring this narrative form to bear on conditions in the United States during the years preceding the Civil War, Stowe simply reversed the roles of the American captive and his North African captors. Where captivity achieved its effect in *The Algerine Captive* by demoting Underhill to the social nonbeing of a slave, *Uncle Tom's Cabin* elevates Tom to a sentimental emblem of the sacrificial victim. Tom's apotheosis begins as he rescues Eva St. Clare from the river and is rescued in turn by her father to provide her with a playmate. But Stowe takes the process up several notches in recounting Tom's death scene, as his spirit departs from the body purchased and destroyed by Simon Legree. His former owner, the well-meaning George Shelby, arrives as Tom departs the mortal world to utter sentimental platitudes. Tom's response renders George "awestruck at the force, the vehemence, the power with which these broken sentences were uttered": "'Don't call me poor fellow,' said Tom solemnly, 'I *have* been a poor fellow, but that's all past and gone, now. I'm right in the door, going into glory! O, Mas'r George! *Heaven has come!* I've got the victory!—the Lord Jesus has given it to me! Glory be his name!'" (421). Tom's journey into the gothic heart of the system managed by satanic slave master Simon Legree generates the same dread that accompanies Poe's narrator across the tarn into the ill-fated House of Usher. Like those captives who land in the dungeons of Algiers and, later, Tripoli, human beings who end up under Legree's government are subject to the same barbaric treatment that exposes the failure of government to protect its citizens when they venture beyond national boundaries. By staging that failure within the borders of the United States, Stowe indicts the U.S. government for licensing this barbarism.

Yes, this novel engages in the same antislavery discourse that William Wells Brown's novel does. Rather than read the horrific descriptions of physical abuse in *Uncle Tom's Cabin* with the slave narrative in mind, however, we want to suggest how, in different ways, both Stowe and Wells Brown drew upon the tactics of the Barbary captivity narrative. Like Wells Brown, Stowe stops short of plucking her protagonist from the population whose fate he shares. In contrast to Wells Brown, she stops short of endowing Tom with anything like a human life to give away and pursues an alternative strategy: a sentimental rendering of the captive that aims to persuade her readers that enslaving a population is a barbaric practice and should be abolished. The ritual manumission of the remaining slaves—who stay there voluntarily after Mr. Shelby sets them free—does nothing to repair the tear in the household caused by his loss, and Tom consequently continues to serve as the absent center—the ghost of the sacrificial slave—around which a sentimental household struggles and fails to reconstitute itself (615–17). The novel thus limps to the resolution that Ann Douglas famously condemns for compromising the rigor of the Puritan tradition. Though convinced that Stowe deliberately broke with both the spirit and letter of religious rhetoric, we also find ourselves completely at odds with those who want to see the novel's call for a change of heart with a surge of democratic sentiment. Thus, while Stowe went one better than William Wells Brown in winning over potential abolitionists, she nevertheless grants the point that freeing a slave one household at a time would never solve the problem created when rights were linked to property.

All things considered, then, one can well understand why Stowe decided to append a forthrightly polemical ending to her novel. In her "Concluding Remarks," she detached the author's voice from that of the sentimental narrator of *Uncle Tom's Cabin* and addressed her readers as an educated and distressed member of a nation on the brink of war. In other words, she performed the same counterconduct—or breakdown, if you will—that Crèvecoeur did. If the War of Independence nullified the future of the colony of Pennsylvania for the Loyalist and man of property, then the Fugitive Slave Act would have cast the future equally in doubt for an abolitionist writing during the decade leading up to the Civil War. Stowe breaks into the narration in order to declare the problem one that could never be resolved within the limits of the very form in which she chose to write. If the routes of the slave trade organized the entire Atlantic world, then any solution would of necessity be systemwide. It is from the position of an American within the international trade in human beings that Stowe retooled her sentimental narration to call into being an international crisis: "A mighty influence is abroad, surging and heaving the world, as with an earthquake. And is America safe?" No, is her answer. In terms that echo Crèvecoeur's, she writes, "Every nation that carries in its bosom great and unredressed injustice has in itself the element of this last convulsion" (619). We want to insist, though, that Stowe's second ending is still a sentimental one in that it figures the captive population strategically as an abused and unwholesome body that recalls Malthus's phobic figure of a mass that threatens to burst its container. To be sure, while Stowe sees the population as an object to be cared for, she also sees it as one to be managed—not one that can manage itself. In materializing the enslaved population as a single body and cause of increasing dread, however, Stowe recants the sentimental apotheosis of Uncle Tom, which forces us to consider what brings an established author to the tipping point where she abandons the strategic position of a major novelist and speaks from within a population.

Chapter 6

Conversion

By the late 1780s, the European model of society had come to stand, in the eyes of many, for the tyranny of a landed elite.[1] While this put the American novelist in the position of imagining a society for which the footprint did not yet exist, the negative criteria—or social rules he or she sought to counter—were only too clear. Just as unchecked power on the part of any one branch of government would be considered dangerous to the authority of the other branches, so the formation of a federal government would compromise the sovereignty of states, and so the laws of each state would impinge on the autonomy of local communities. Any novelist who wanted to imagine the United States as a single body politic had to negotiate these conflicts, and as we have argued, many of them indeed developed ingenious forms of counterconduct. But to imagine how any set of individual tactical moves could mobilize a community capable of enduring over time, the first American novelists had to perform the move we call "conversion." They had to stage an event, often a chain of events at the level of plot, that (1) disabled the exchanges that bound individuals to their property and through that property to one another in hospitable relations and that (2) generated an excess of emotional energy sufficient to link the scattered elements of population in a continuous social network. By means of such an event, the randomly linked if not disconnected field of characters suddenly became perceptible as a community. Appearing to come from nowhere and having no particular objective, this transformation defied explanation in terms of past experience or a once possible future. Such an event is, as Alain Badiou suggests, an impossible occurrence until the moment when it changes the rules determining what can henceforth be considered real.[2] With the help of this concept, let us consider how the novels of the early republic reversed themselves and, in doing so, revised the conditions for imagining a sustainable system of social relationships. To perform this move, novelists obviously had to do more than tinker with the models available; they had to reimagine the very foundation on which a society could be built. To ensure that readers would understand what they were doing, as we have argued, a considerable number of these novelists encouraged their readers to imagine property as a form of captivity.

In this respect, the first novelists who wrote as and for Americans were dealing with much the same dilemma that Duncan J. Watts and Steven H. Strogatz formulated in their mathematical modeling of "small worlds" (see Buchanan 48–60). In the most general terms, small worlds are social systems whose members can get from any one point to any other by traveling the relatively short distance between familiar contact points. Small worlds come in a number of varieties, have strong centers, and tend to disintegrate when that center is damaged. Their formal similarity in all these respects to what, for lack of a better term, we have characterized as a traditional household offers us a way of addressing a set of questions as to how property operates in novels of the early republic. These questions are precisely the ones that readers don't ask of novels that use the family to naturalize a household: How is such a closed community organized? How does it maintain that organization? Under what circumstances can it expand and diversify? Under what circumstances does it fall apart? Are there one or several forms of household, and how do they differ? We raise these questions in order to suggest that these were the very questions that novelists addressed in order to develop the tactical maneuvers that gave the novels of the early national period their distinctive form.

To explain "conversion," then, we have to identify the formal mechanism that transforms the negative procedures of counterconduct into procedures that kick-start the circulation on which the vitality of the entire field of characters depends. Before it can provide social connections that can expand and diversify along with the nation itself, these novels must expose some affirmative potential in destroying traditional social categories and leveling the hierarchies they support. They must, in other words, hand over control of writing to a principle that is not so much against property as for something else. To understand the formal operations of "conversion" in this sense, we need to rephrase our question as Watts and Strogatz would: how do you turn a small world inside out and so make it part of a larger system of social connections? This, as we have suggested, requires any number of small, independently motivated ideas, desires, and behaviors not only to spread but also to coalesce in opposition to an established pattern of social behavior. But then, under what circumstances do these tactical maneuvers suddenly change gears and provide the means of managing the popular energy they have put in motion?

In *Clotel* and *Uncle Tom's Cabin*, as we have noted, a pervasive sense of dread accompanies the metastasis of oppositional practices. What Brian Massumi calls "the affective event" begins in much the same way, with the generalized fear that something terrible is about to disrupt irreversibly the habitual practices of daily life. Fear that the worst will happen intensifies until it triggers the counterconduct that actually disrupts those practices. The anticipation of the actual event (e.g., the deaths of those denied legal ownership of their bodies) becomes an event in its own right for the reader. Both novels bring us to the tipping point where fear is so infused with outrage that it overwhelms the premise that property must be defended. But although both novels call for "conversion" in the form of thoroughgoing reorganization of the body politic, neither one can acknowledge the form that body would take. In *Clotel* and *Uncle Tom's Cabin*, the trope of conversion consequently operates as an affective event or revolution of the heart. To move beyond oppositional resistance, beyond even the fantasy of universal rights to property in one's own person, novelists had to imagine the possibility of a limitless network of horizontal affiliations from a perspective within a diseased and tumultuous mass body. Simply put, it took nothing short of an impossible event for novelists writing during the early national period to rethink the basis of realism.

On this point, Nancy Ruttenburg makes a strong case for understanding the evangelical movements of eighteenth-century America as perhaps the first formulation of revolutionary ideology.[3] To make this argument, she reads the conversion ritual practiced by the evangelist George Whitefield as the genesis of what she calls a "democratic personality." Motivated by a critical attitude toward the established clergy, as Ruttenburg explains it, Whitefield's performance simultaneously humbled the convert and exalted that person to membership in a spiritual community.[4] Whitefield's autobiographical account and the widespread influence of his movement make it clear that conversion, as he conceived it, empowered virtually anyone moved to speak in a divinely authorized voice to virtually anyone else. Still more to the point was the expansion of Whitefield's ministry into an international network. "Endlessly circulating throughout the United Kingdom and the British-American colonies," Ruttenburg explains, Whitefield

> exulted in the opposition he so assiduously courted, claiming it as a sign of his professional efficacy that mandated in turn his

transgressing the boundaries of established parishes and co-opting
the prerogatives of settled pastors in order to gather a congregation
of the newly regenerate that neither church wall nor parish line
could contain. He augmented his far-reaching influence . . . by traveling with an entourage of devotees who functioned as a press corps,
advertising his itinerary and the remarkable success of his field sermons in local newspapers, and disseminating his journals and sermons in local publishing networks. (84)[5]

Transpiring beyond the jurisdiction of any government, the conversion ritual
placed those converted outside their social positions as well. This may sound a
lot like Rancière's description of democratic writing, a style that earlier American novels adjusted to address their respective local readerships, but Whitefield's enthusiastic performance of conversion is historically a world away
from the event these novels at once described and performed.

From Population to Security

John Marrant's well-known "Narrative" (1785) of his religious conversion
takes its reader through the transition from the one concept of conversion to
the other, a transition in which demands that expressed themselves in insur-
gent forms of popular democracy eclipsed the focus of the religious movements. One might be tempted to claim there is no better testimony to the
transformative power of Whitefield's sermons than Marrant's account of how
the evangelist converted him to Methodism. His conversion began, as he recalls the experience, with "many lights" and a crowd flowing into a meeting-
house, where Marrant had planned to blow on his French horn and disrupt
the service.[6] But as he pushed his way through the crowd with this mischief in
mind, the voice of George Whitefield "struck [him] to the ground," where he
"lay both speechless and senseless near half an hour" (206–7). Marrant blamed
his loss of self-possession on an internal battle with Whitefield's voice for possession of his soul. As he recalls, "Every word I heard from the minister was
like a parcel of swords thrust into me, and what added to my distress, I
thought I saw the devil on every side of me" (207). No less than three doctors
predicted Marrant's death from the ordeal, and the feckless musician did indeed pass away in preparation for his rebirth as one of Whitefield's followers
and fellow evangelists, an event that he describes as a release from captivity:

"[N]ear the close of [Whitefield's] prayer, the Lord was pleased to set my soul at perfect liberty, and being filled with joy I began to praise the Lord" (207–8). This borrowed voice takes over his story and transforms the very substance of his character. But as Marrant goes on to recount his postconversion life, paradoxically, the narrative does not turn out to be a version of a pilgrim's progress. To the contrary, Marrant's narration performs the very moves that anticipate the distinctive style of the first American novelists.

Renouncing his family, Marrant handed over his life to Jesus and wandered in the wilderness, living on grass and water until taken captive by Native Americans and condemned to death. With a Bible in his hand and a mind to acquire language, Marrant's voice freed him to pass "among [Native American tribes] without danger, being recommended from one to the other" (215). Quite as interesting as this conduct, which runs counter to Puritan captivity narratives, is Marrant's sudden decision that, having become a stranger to the white community, he could rejoin them: "My dress was purely in the Indian stile; the skins of wild beasts composed my garments; my head was set out in the savage manner, with a long pendant down my back, a sash around my middle without breeches, and a tomahawk by my side" (216).

It is a curious thing that his savage appearance in combination with his spiritual conversion prevented Marrant's assimilation no matter where he went. Arriving at the home he had left in order to become a musician, Marrant performs an elaborate resurrection of his old identity from the death to which his family had consigned him. With "the commencement of the American troubles," if not before, Marrant makes it clear that he had no intention of writing a narrative conducting the reader from this world to another (218). Neither destination—the religious conversion that set him to wandering nor the spiritual community into which it promised to admit him after death—determined the story of his travels among the Indians and between them and the British settlements. Rather than return to the fold of the family, Marrant is "pressed upon the Scorpion sloop of war, as their musician" (221). Wounded in "the engagement with the Dutch off the Dogger Bank" (227), Marrant ends up in a hospital in the West Indies and transported from there to London, where he was ordained to preach and encouraged to write an account of his transformation from an aimless boy into a man of the world. Where Marrant's voice had sought to place him among Whitefield's future community of saints, his story branches out into an expansive network that moves easily across demographic divisions. As it does so, his "Narrative" records a decisively secular drift in the concept of conversion itself. In that the impossible event of his transformation from a local troublemaker to a preacher of international renown retains some of the magic of religious conversion, John Marrant's story nevertheless provides a parable of what happened to the figure of "conversion" in the decades that followed.

The century preceding the expansion of the evangelical community in North America saw passage of a law that anticipated this transformation in legal terms. The law that forbad "troving" covered only those alterations of someone else's property caused by accident and injury, not criminal intent. The offense occurred when someone happened upon someone else's property and so changed its substance that the owner could not reclaim the object he had lost. If, for example, one found a goose and made a meal of it, that person could be found guilty of troving.[7] Whether or not the alleged trover intended to alter the property—whether, say, he confused the found goose with one of his own and ate it—is beside the point; all that matters is whether or not its substance changed while in the finder's possession. The contrast between the "conversion" (in the language of the law) of property from one substance to another and the conversion of matter into spirit reveals what is at stake in the one as opposed to the other. The spiritual rebirth of the secular man, as recorded in the "Narrative" of John Marrant, performs a categorical violation that went a long way toward destabilizing institutionalized religion. No less qualified a political thinker than Alexis de Tocqueville saw popular democracy as working in the opposite direction from religious conversion as it converted individual citizens into an irrational mass with a propensity to trample individual rights. By making it a crime to alter the very substance of property, the legal prohibition of "troving" sought to establish an absolute difference between a resource that anyone could appropriate and a resource whose owner is entitled to use it as he will, thus a difference between common resources and property.

The Power of Weak Ties

It was with considerable uneasiness that we turned to a well-popularized concept from network theory to consider not only how but also to what purpose a substantial group of novels challenge the efficacy of property as a basis for community. There was nevertheless something about the idea of a network composed of "small worlds," as Mark Buchanan explains it, that we found too helpful to resist.[8] In the most general terms, small worlds are social groups held together by strong triangulated or quadrangulated ties that bind each party to every other. Let us suppose, as in the early American novel, that these small worlds are households in which everyone is related to everyone else. Let us say, further, that ties nearly as strong connect those households to one or two others, so that to know someone in a neighboring household is to know nearly everyone that person knows and vice versa. This is the small world of Jane Austen's *Emma* as well as the Southern town in which Royall Tyler's Updike Underhill hoped to settle down as a physician. In both instances, the novels must establish weak links between small worlds in order to create a workable model of community. Where the small world of Austen's Highbury takes care to rule out Mr. Elton and Frank Churchill as unfit to enjoy intimate relations with its heroine, each eventually marries someone in that otherwise shrinking community. If after a flirtation with the world at large, Austen's small worlds close back in on themselves, their strong ties replenished, then Royal Tyler fashions a protagonist who embodies what Buchanan defines as a weak link and, in this capacity, serves as surrogate for the novelist himself. When allowed to do their work, Buchanan explains, "Even a tiny fraction of weak links—long-distance bridges within the social world—has an immense influence on the number of degrees of [social] separation" (55). The threat that such links invariably pose to small worlds accounts for many if not all of the formal resemblances among early American novels. While the content it described might link a novel directly to a particular readership, the narrative aspects we are here identifying would nevertheless provide a weak link to American novels that addressed other local readerships.

When the ties that hold a small world together include a random element, one or more of its members are bound to know someone that other members don't. In thus compromising the organization of a small world, as Buchanan points out, one weak link or more actually gives it the flexibility that a small world requires to survive in the long run. To maintain connections through attacks and dispersals, it must have bridges that provide one or preferably several routes between itself and other small worlds. The individual whose social existence depends on the strong ties of intimacy will be likely to imagine his or her community as one in which everyone knows everyone else. Thus, where Volume I of Tyler's *The Algerine Captive* demonstrates the impossibility of establishing weak ties among such communities, Volume II shows that weak ties enable more contacts that in turn ensure the survival of a small group better than strong ties can. Indeed, to demonstrate the spectacularly destructive behavior of strong ties seems to be the point of *Wieland*, Brockden Brown's first published novel.

The novelist designed a patriarchal household of German immigrants as so inappropriate a way of forming social relationships in the United States that he devoted a novel to destroying it. Wieland the elder immigrated to the United States in hopes of spreading his idiosyncratic interpretation of the Bible in the manner that Whitefield had. Convinced that he had failed to carry out this mission, Wieland spent his later years brooding in his own pavilion, a fitting place of worship for a religion of one, where he apparently underwent spontaneous combustion and died. "Such was the end of my father," Clara, the narrator, recounts: "None surely was ever more mysterious. . . . The prelusive gleam, the blow upon his arm, the fatal spark, the explosion heard so far, the fiery cloud that environed him, without detriment to the structure, though composed of combustible materials, the sudden vanishing of this cloud at my uncle's approach—what is the inference to be drawn from these facts? Their truth cannot be doubted" (18). Not a good beginning for a novel, one might think, unless we assume that the absence of any psychological explanation for a self that could so disfigure itself would appeal to readers who relished an account of an impossible transmogrification of the human body that they were asked to accept as true.

There is a long tradition of case histories featuring impossible events that include Daniel Defoe's "A True Relation of the Apparition of Mrs. Veal" and the medical account of Mary Toft giving birth to rabbit parts, Washington Irving's "Rip Van Winkle," Robert Lewis Stevenson's *Strange Case of Dr Jekyll and Mr Hyde*, and Sigmund Freud's *History of an Infantile Neurosis*, better known as the case history of "the Wolf Man." All report an event that could not possibly have happened but, for one reason or another, could not be disproved. In thus changing the rules governing what is possible, these accounts necessarily call into question such basic categories as the difference between a living body and a dead one, between a human baby and animal parts, between the British king and the first president of the United States, and so on. True to this tradition, Brockden Brown's account of Wieland's death invites us to consider what categorical violation the novel stages by subjecting the title character to spontaneous combustion. One doesn't have to read very far to know that by demonstrating the powerlessness of the Wieland family in the face of the random links forged by Carwin, a ventriloquist, Brocken Brown meant to argue against the principle of strong ties. We take it that was his way of rejecting the household as the foundation of and footprint for community in the United States.

Having rid itself of the founding patriarch, the Wieland family reproduces itself in the next generation. Wieland's son, Wieland, and daughter Clara in turn fall for a pair of siblings who are in fact their only friends. Having completed their education by a maiden aunt who also serves as their sole parental surrogate, brother and sister divide their father's property and live within a stone's throw of one another, so that they can meet frequently and keep each other company. More's the pity, for into this harmonious picture enters a disruptive voice, which, as we learn only many chapters later, is sometimes but not always or necessarily the voice of Carwin, a stranger of vaguely elite origins who appears in rustic dress at Mettingen, the Wieland family estate in Pennsylvania. In person, Carwin's speech is so grammatically correct and lucid, so void of personal markers, that it offers no clue as to who he actually is. If Carwin's voice could be anyone's, then anyone's can in turn be his. With this as his distinguishing feature, Carwin personifies the dangers of democratic writing. His appearance on the scene injects what must have been a familiar sense of dread into the novel and allows it to acquire paranoid dimensions in anticipation of the actual disintegration of the Wieland family. The affective event is the means by which weak ties overpower strong ones.

As a person of property who crossed paths with Henry Pleyel in Spain before renewing their acquaintance in Pennsylvania, Carwin also reveals the limitations of the weak tie. As if to punish the Wieland family for neglecting to forge relationships to those outside the family, Brocken Brown summons a character capable of appropriating strong ties and converting them into weak ones. Though a stranger, he alone can speak with the voice of an intimate family member without becoming one, and he consequently knows everything that they know without their knowing what he knows in return. His voice consequently destroys the sense of trust that comes with knowing both each member of the community and everyone they know. In contrast to the voice that Whitefield performed and passed along to others, Carwin's disembodied voices, as Ruttenburg summarizes their impact, "promote the conversion of spatial into personalized claustrophobia, a progressive isolation and entrapment of the individual that constitutes the novel's plot" (211). We can indeed read Carwin, as she does, as the means of critiquing the egotism that turns strong ties into a form of captivity.

In reading the novel as what amounts to a critique of a disembodied voice on the order of Whitefield's, we can also regard Carwin's intervention as the means by which Clara's narration of that experience converts her personal letters into the voice of a distinctively American novel. Caught in a violent near-death hallucination engineered by Carwin, Clara engages in a struggle that reverses the outcome of the process that converts John Marrant from a horn player into a man who can speak with God's authority. Clara struggles against the very possibility that a disembodied voice could persuade her to turn her life over to a dream that shows her dying at her brother's hand. Rather than ponder the psychological motive or rational cause behind the script of what she is convinced is an impossible event, Clara sets about to de-mystify it. Her relentless interrogation of the ventriloquist renders her family's inexplicable destruction into an explanatory narrative that anyone can read and understand. We might see Brocken Brown's second novel doing better than his first one in staging an impossible event. If the point is to expose the weakness of the strong ties organizing the European family, then making Ar-thur Mervyn the agent of rumor does a better job than Carwin's pointless ex-ploitation of ventriloquism at converting small worlds into a potentially limitless and yet lasting social network.

To read *Arthur Mervyn* as the sequel to *Wieland* makes it a good deal eas-ier to spot indications that such a network is emerging from the destruction that Carwin engineered. We can infer, for example, that if a small world is linked to several others, and provided no one member of the network is con-nected to everyone, that network will have several centers, none of which can dominate the others. *Wieland* indicates that it takes such a polycentric system of social relations to weather migration, upward and downward mobility, and even mass extinction. Should a number of connections be knocked out—as happens in Philadelphia during the yellow fever epidemic—relationships can start up from any point and make the connections needed to bring the city back to life. In making this happen, Mervyn's semiotic behavior can be com-pared to Lev Vygotsky's "chain complex," a principle implicitly hostile to strong ties and friendly to network formation. According to this principle, as Rodney Needham summarizes it, "the definitive attribute keeps changing from one link to the next; there is no consistency in the type of bonds, and the variable meaning is carried over from one item in a class to the next with 'no central significance,' no 'nucleus'" (350).

Needham associates Vygotsky's principle of linguistic behavior with Lud-wig Wittgenstein's figure of the rope used by the British Navy to illustrate his concept of "family resemblances": "the rope consists of fibres, but it does not get its strength from any fibre that runs through it from one end to another, but from the fact that there is a vast number of fibres overlapping" (*Blue and Brown Book* 87). In communities where the repetition of any one feature is sporadic, there is no reason, according to both models, why someone known by one member should be known by any other, so long as each knows at least one other person. The community, like Vygotsky's linguistic chain and Wittgenstein's rope, will indeed be the stronger for it. It may seem likely that one would encounter nothing but strangers in such a community, until we sort out the intermediate connections that carry over some feature from one person to any other and from that person to yet another. Such a community understandably gives rise to suspicion, even paranoia, until the actual sequence of connections is exposed. That is the price of tolerating the random connections enabling the free circulation and expansiveness of social contacts that characterize Brockden Brown's style.

Once we compare *Wieland* with *Arthur Mervyn*, it becomes apparent that the skeptical and probing voice that informs Clara's letters opens her small world to and places it within a more comprehensive network based on family resemblances. This pairing reveals in turn that Brockden Brown exploited this opening in *Arthur Mervyn* in order to produce a network of almost exclusively weak ties. But it remains for us now to explain the event that makes a latent and largely unacknowledged system of social connections suddenly assume control of *Wieland* and bring order to the field of characters that Carwin has dispersed and scattered. How does the system of contact within the novel reach beyond the limits of the printed text, linking one of Brockden Brown's novels to those written for other readerships within the United States? How do ideas, rumors, desires, and fears detach themselves from human agents and move infectiously from one person to the next, lending visibility to the circuits that they trace?

Like Clara's narration, this form of intelligence develops from firsthand experience of the connections among very different sectors of a population and yields an explanation of how the entire system works. In such moments as the one where Brockden Brown co-opts Clara's interrogative voice to reflect on his own narrative machinery, his *Wieland* betrays the fact that characters were never independent or free to determine their stories. Where a more traditional narrator would induce us to read characters as if they were indeed individuals capable, like readers themselves, of minimally independent decision making and limited power to act, the early American narrator demonstrates that characters exist only insofar and in the manner that they take part in a social network and subject themselves to its protocols. It is by means of this event that Brockden Brown's novels achieved the power to link any number of local communities as a single readership.

The Event of Democracy

It may seem odd to choose a short story for purposes of showing how novels mobilized this event, but such is indeed our claim. We consider this particular story an unusually concise descriptive theory of exactly how an account of "an impossible event" could convert the story of individual development into the footprint for the unique polity that Tocqueville titled "democracy in America."[9] Because the point of Nathaniel Hawthorne's "My Kinsman, Major Molineux" is nothing other than to show how this conversion might work in practice, we shall read it as a "how-to" book of sorts for revising the world made of property as an alternative to European liberalism. Hawthorne's story allows democracy to unleash the popular energy that liberal government is designed to harness for productive ends. The story then proposes a way of managing this excess that would make the world of property more inclusive and, at the same time, leave its economic inequities pretty much intact. Although popular democracy is not made to last in this story, the possibility is definitely there.

Assessing the state of American democracy during the early 1830s, Tocqueville was obviously fascinated with the possibility that the end of monarchy had given rise not to the liberal individualism of Europe he seemed to admire but rather to an alternative form of self-government capable of nullifying the principle of individual rights. As he explained, "It may almost be said that the people [of America] are self-governing in so far as the share left to the administrators is so weak and so restricted and the latter feel such close ties with their popular origin and the power from which it emanates" (70–71).[10] His familiarity with early nineteenth-century America convinced him that by freeing men to think for themselves, the British had created a power vacuum that could be filled by a dangerous form of popular democracy. Finding in America few of the traditions and institutions responsible for an expanding citizenry in England and France, Tocqueville fastened on the abstract concept of "the people" as the force that had so far managed to hold all those different attitudes, interests, and practices together as the United States. As he famously put it, "The people reign in the American political world like God over the universe. It is the cause and aim of all things, everything comes from them and everything is absorbed in them" (71). Without central institutions to maintain and expand access to all of "the people," Tocqueville foresaw the new democratic ideal foundering on the shoals of its own universalism.[11] The second volume of his *Democracy in America* begins on a note of concern about the dangers posed by this new form of sovereignty—dangers that owe "their birth to factors alien to, or even opposed to, equality" (489). In order for men to coexist and prosper, Tocqueville reasoned, "all the citizens' minds must be united and held together by a few principal ideas" (499).

How does the unification of disparate local beliefs and practices come to pass? In democratic societies, he observed, "the general public . . . does not impose its beliefs by persuasion but inserts them in men's souls by the immense pressure of corporate thinking upon the intelligence of each single man" (501). From this it followed that, for lack of enduring traditions, "beliefs" will arise in America and acquire a "dogmatic character" (498). Recast as a "general public" coerced into a highly volatile unity under the pressure of popular belief, Tocqueville's figure of popular sovereignty displays an ominous new face—no longer that of a unified ideal but the tyrannical potential of embodied factions that Rousseau had foreseen. Men, Tocqueville wrote, "normally . . . seek the source of truth in themselves or their fellow men" (500), but "as citizens become more equal and similar . . . the predisposition to believe in mass opinion increases and becomes progressively the opinion which commands the world" (501). In order to protect their personal liberty, paradoxically, individuals will gradually cede it to the group until some group belief has emptied men of their independent thought and usurped the place of a public sphere where varying opinions could be openly debated. Tocqueville pursued this argument to the inevitable conclusion that democracy was in danger of destroying the founding principle of individual freedom when men pursued their freedom unchecked by custom and institutional constraints. By forming a democracy, he cautioned, "men will not have achieved the means of living independently; they would simply have lighted upon . . . a new face of enslavement" (502).

Michel Foucault's *Discipline and Punish* takes issue with the idea of liberalism as a form of government that empowers individuals to govern themselves. To mount this argument, he appropriates Jeremy Bentham's architectural design for a new kind of penal institution as the prototype for all modern social institutions and, as such, a paradigm of liberal government. He credits the scenario that unfolds within this institution for producing individuals who feel their behavior could at any moment be exposed to public view and so behave accordingly. In contrast to an "ascending individuality" that depends on a name, position, and property within the patriarchal family, Foucault characterizes the form of individualism that developed under liberalism as "descending" (193). Thus, in contrast with the man of property, the new liberal individual does not acquire political power over others as he or she achieves self-government but finds instead that he or she has become increasingly subject to abstract norms of reason, morality, and work-time discipline. Especially in England and France, the impersonal forces of law, medicine, and education conspired with the very institutions that Tocqueville found noticeably missing from American culture to make each individual ever wary lest his or her appetites and urges elude self-control. When it turned over command of their bodies to those who felt their identity would be endangered by any failure to regulate that body and its impulses, Foucault laments, liberal society saw to it that "the adventure of our childhood no longer finds expression in '*le bon petit Henri*,' but in the misfortunes of 'little Hans' " (*Discipline* 193–94).

On this note, his historical account of liberal individualism threatens to converge in a complementary relationship with the very political theories he intends to dispute, namely, those that consider individualism the only means of liberating individuals from the category into which they were born and predestined to fill. Indeed, whenever Foucault embarks on a critique of liberalism's theme of individual development, his argument seems to stall out and begins to oscillate between the figure of an ungovernable populace and that of the individual imprisoned in an identity that he or she achieves at the cost of spontaneous forms of self-expression. But where Foucault uses the baleful figure of the prisoner to characterize his disciplined individual, Tocqueville invoked the antithetical figure of the agitated mob to characterize what he saw as the alternative to self-discipline. Tocqueville found Americans only too eager to "escape the spirit of systems, the yoke of habit, the precepts of family, the opinions of class, and, to a certain extent, the prejudices of nation" (493). Thus, while Foucault understood these alternatives as two ways of looking at a single political formation, he rarely afforded a glimpse of the implied dialectical third term. As a result, the stakes of his work on liberalism sometimes appear to be much the same as Tocqueville's—that is, to identify the line separating liberal individuals from those nonindividuals who pose a threat to person and property. The relative porosity of that line in Foucault's account promotes the fear that one could grow careless and slide over to the other side, while the apparent impermeability of the barrier separating the immigrant from the propertied classes in Tocqueville's America infuses his descriptions of popular power with the combined fear and elation that accompanies the fantasy of bursting out of the category to which any number of people obviously felt captive. Hawthorne's fiction explores the social possibilities that open up at the convergence of the narratives forming these opposing fantasies, as a sudden consolidation of counterconduct gestures toward another way of organizing a population.

"My Kinsman, Major Molineux" opens conventionally enough by inviting its reader to regard a fictional event that took place "not far from a hundred years ago" (3). Hawthorne lets us assume that this event will show that the colonial governors appointed by the kings of Great Britain "seldom met with the ready and general approbation which had been paid to . . . their predecessors" (3). Then he endows "the people" with a capacity to look "with most jealous scrutiny to the exercise of power, which did not emanate from themselves" (3). In this statement, the people appear in the plural form, "themselves," as the source of a negative reaction to the exercise of power on the part of colonial government. By the end of the first paragraph, however, the narrator has revoked the suggestion that we read this account of events in a New England town as an allegory that explains the cause of the War of Independence. Instead, he cuts that bait and asks us to see the "temporary inflammation of the popular mind" as an affective event rather than the harbinger of political crisis it initially promised to become (3).

The story begins as Robin, a young country boy, crosses a body of water by ferry and enters "the little metropolis of a New England colony" with "as eager an eye, as if he were entering London city" (4). In seeking out his kinsman, Major Molineux, Robin sets off a conflict between two systems of affiliation, one designated by the term "kinsman" and another by the term "multitude," both of which recur throughout Hawthorne's story. According to the one system of affiliation, the meaning of the name "Molineux" cancels out the meaning that the same name acquires in the other system, so that by invoking that name, Robin identifies himself as a stranger precisely where he expects to be recognized and rewarded—as might his English counterpart—for having a distinguished relative. The question of under what conditions a stranger can be welcomed into a community rather than kept out is a definitively nineteenth-century question and one this story aims to answer.

Another Story

Stopping to inquire after his notable relative at an inn that the narrator describes as "a Turkish Caravanasary," Robin enters what seems like a haven of
cosmopolitan tolerance (6). The inn is run by a Frenchman and harbors a
cross section of the community, including a few "strangers" from the country
with whom Robin initially "felt a sort of brotherhood" (6). But the minute he
inquires after his relative, the demand triggers "a sudden and general movement in the room," and when Robin resists the innkeeper's suggestion that he
should move on, that same "general movement" manifests a "strange hostility
in every countenance" (7). Should he persist in demanding that the townsfolk
receive him in a manner befitting Molineux's kinsman, he is warned, Robin
will be put in the stocks. Is this a demonstration of intolerance that violates
the principle of hospitality—or has Robin done something to warrant being
treated as a criminal? It would not seem so from the perspective of someone
who obviously sees himself as the protagonist of a family romance. To become
the protagonist of Hawthorne's story, however, Robin will have to abandon
that fantasy and perform as part of a population.

Hawthorne provides little more than a snapshot of what the spectacle of
charivari has done to Molineux, but it is more than enough to show Robin
that the ritual has transformed his kinsman from a man "of large and majestic
person" to a mass of agitated flesh (16). Despite his "civil and military rank,"
Molineux's body is no longer his to command (13) and now belongs to the
same category as the "wild figures in the Indian dress" that ceremonially escort
him from town (15). These savage figures provide Hawthorne with a way of
addressing the question a townsman puts to Robin: " 'May not one man have
several voices, Robin, as well as two complexions?' " (14). Here, race ceases to
establish the external limits of community and instead marks the line within
that community between the majority who express its will and those who are
subject to it. As Hawthorne's narrator declares in the story's opening paragraph, however, the event of Molineux's humiliation is not the event with
which the story is primarily concerned. The spectacle of charivari triggers "a
temporary inflammation of the popular mind" that alters the conditions of
possibility for Robin's conversion.

As the second son of "a clergyman, settled on a small salary, at a long
distance back in the country," Robin will make a living, he hopes, with some
help in the way of patronage from his kinsman (13). But once subjected to the

deracinating force Tocqueville regarded as "the tyranny of the majority," Robin hops storylines and becomes an entirely new character. The surplus of popular feeling that expresses itself in the ritual humiliation of his kinsman produces a phenomenological break in Robin's narrative. As it spreads infectiously from person to person, this feeling acquires the power to suspend the rules of conventional realism and release self-expression from confinement to property-based positions within the town. Lacking anything in the way of property, Robin has no protection from this force: "The contagion was spreading among the multitude, when, all at once, it seized upon Robin, and he sent forth a shout of laughter that echoed through the street, every man shook his sides, every man emptied his lungs, but Robin's shout was the loudest there" (17). We might be tempted to gloss his "shout of laughter" as an expression of the elation that accompanies Robin's sudden release from the isolation of a protagonist confined to a family romance. But the literary texture of Hawthorne's story urges us not to draw this conclusion. Elation soon passes. Having severed the bonds of family, he has become an exile in a world of exiles. His involuntary connection to the community will allow him to circulate and associate with others with a freedom that he previously lacked. In creating this possibility, however, what seem like purely contingent ties have disenchanted the world of property in opposition to which this possibility has materialized. Without any connection to Molineux, indeed without strong ties of any kind, Robin's future depends not only on his capacity to act but also on the expansion of his social connections and whether they, too, will grow and prosper (12). How does the ritual inversion of the socioeconomic order of the town hierarchy convert that system of strong ties into a more democratic system of relationships?

To address this question, we need to shift attention from that spectacle to "the shout of laughter" that "echo[es] through the streets" of the town. This is a community in which Robin can now claim membership. His performance of that borrowed laughter has converted him from someone who depends on his wealthy kinsman to a member of the very population that has expelled that kinsman from their midst. In giving voice to "the loudest" shout of laughter of all, Robin has been infected with what Hawthorne calls "the inflammation of the popular mind" and then distinguishes himself by the gusto with which he performs (17). His conversion has reversed the direction of Molineux's. To the Major's "strong square features, betokening a steady soul," the narrator attaches a string of details—the "red and wild" eyes and "foam [that] hung white upon his quivering lip"—that temporarily collapsed the social ladder Robin had hoped to climb on entering the town (16). But even so radical a change in social position is a matter of surface rather than of substance in Molineux's case, for the inner man still supports the abject body and expresses itself through that body even in losing control of it. By contrast, the alteration of Robin's position in relation to the town alters the inner man. The event that severs the ties of kinship making Robin a Molineux involuntarily incorporates him in the population of the town where he is an altogether different individual, if we can say he is an individual at all.

Despite the festive spirit and trappings of carnival, the ritual of charivari depends on a horizontal system of relationships already at work in the town.[12] Upon his first demand for the hospitality due a Molineux to the confrontation of his kinsman covered in tar and feathers, Robin grows increasingly suspicious that a conspiracy is afoot in the town that aims at humiliating and then excluding him: "no sooner was he beyond the door, than he heard a general laugh, in which the innkeeper's voice might be distinguished, like the dropping of small stones into a kettle" (7). Robin's paranoia is further substantiated, as what was initially "a murmur" grows into "a noise of shouting" amplified by "frequent bursts from many instruments of discord" and punctuated with "wild and confused laughter" (11, 16). The sleeping town comes to life in a manner that defies explanation: "windows flew open on all sides, and many heads, in the attire of the pillow, and confused by sleep suddenly broken, were protruded to the gaze of whoever had leisure to observe them" (15). This many-headed creature breaches the walls dividing the household from the street at the very moment when "[a] mighty stream of people now emptied into the street, and came rolling slowly towards the church" (15). The sense of still unnamed dread increases as "many [more] heads" burst from households and merge with the "mighty stream of people" (15). By including among "the mass of people, inactive, except as applauding spectators" a number of women who "ran along the sidewalks, piercing the confusion of heavier sounds, with their shrill voices of mirth or terror" (15), Hawthorne points out that those normally excluded from the life of the town have turned its house-lined streets into a space for exercising popular power.

Looking at the situation in America through the lens of European liberalism, Tocqueville saw a nation torn between two competing concepts of individualism. According to one, only the individual could govern his thoughts, feelings, and behaviors and not encroach on the self-sovereignty of other citizens, but according to the other concept of individualism, anyone achieved individuality along with visibility only as he or she spoke with the voice of his

group. In *Democratic Personality*, Ruttenburg makes a valiant attempt to show
how these different concepts of individualism, though ideologically hostile,
managed to avoid stepping on each other's political toes. She reminds us that
forms of popular sovereignty had indeed been around since early colonial
times and continued to influence literature throughout the nineteenth century, well after liberal concepts and practices were incorporated at the national
and state levels of government. In theory, these concepts of individualism
could pose a direct contradiction and in practice go their separate ways. The
fact that they belonged to the domains of jurisprudence and religious belief,
respectively, mitigated the conflict between the right to accumulate property
and the right to move and associate freely. Thus, where Tocqueville saw these
antagonistic concepts of rights poised to cancel each other out, Ruttenburg
shows how the one form of individualism haunts the other as a spectral excess
throughout nineteenth-century literature, with no one concept proving capable of incorporating or suppressing the other. As Robin and his kinsman meet
and then part, however, "My Kinsman, Major Molineux" suggests that these
two notions of individualism did not go their separate ways. Quite the contrary, charivari converts what had been a mutually exclusive relationship between two concepts of individualism into two sides of the argument defining
the problematic of liberalism itself and thus a mutually defining relationship.

  As in a number of early American novels, so in Hawthorne's story the
agent of conversion takes the form of a peculiar affect that spreads like a disease: "The contagion was spreading among the multitude, when, all at once, it
seized upon Robin, and he sent forth a shout of laughter" (17). Though no
different in quality from anyone else's in affect, Robin's laugh was "the loudest
there" (17). Here, "the inflammation of the popular mind" promised in the
opening of the story makes mockery of self-control, as Hawthorne updates an
earlier notion of "contagion" to characterize popular democracy: "every man
shook his sides, every man emptied his lungs" (17).[13] And much like an epidemic, Hawthorne's multitude passes on, leaving Robin drained of his former
vitality, his cheek "somewhat pale, and his eye not quite so lively as in the
earlier part of the evening" (17). In that it empowers the townsfolk to act as a
group, paradoxically, the individual's performance of democratic personality
as well as the joy that accompanies it comes at the cost of any distinction he or
she might otherwise claim, whether from the prestige of lineage or the enthusiasm of his or her performance. Thus, when asked by a "gentleman" spectator
if the encounter with Molineux has altered his ambitions, Robin replies
"rather dryly. 'Thanks to you, and to my other friends, I have at last met my

kinsman, and he will scarce desire to see my face again. I begin to grow weary of a town life, Sir. Will you show me the way to the Ferry?'" (17).

On the other hand, in so depriving Robin of the wish that his family tie to Molineux would provide a ticket to success, the conversion experience also constitutes a brand-new beginning for this protagonist: "'If you continue to wish it,' the gentleman replies, 'I will speed you on your journey. Or if you prefer to remain with us, perhaps, as you are a shrewd youth, you may rise in the world, without the help of your kinsman, Major Molineux'" (17). Though personally exhausted by his performance of mass affect, the joylessness that settles over his story comes from an entirely different source. To offer possibilities for becoming someone to anyone at all, Hawthorne momentarily levels the playing field where there are neither representative nor exceptional individuals, and Robin will begin again as a man of interests.

Does the story's arrival at this stalemate make it more democratic than the family romance that it displaces? Hawthorne knew full well that popular energy—once historically detached from its evangelical roots—would acquire an entirely different character. He clearly thought it lost its utopian potential, which was inevitably recaptured, if not by the economic logic of rational choice, then by some realization of the incipient totalitarianism Tocqueville saw in popular opinion. To consider whether or not the novel *could* become democratic, however, is a different question: could there be a future, where democracy, like conversion itself, no longer operated as a transitional state between systems of social organization but replaced property as the basis of community itself? As we will suggest, the novels of the early republic use the trope of "conversion" to ask this question.

Chapter 7

Hubs

Is there a future in which popular democracy would no longer be a dangerously messy transitional state between two forms of government but become
a form of government in its own right?[1] Having called property into question
as the foundation at once of self and of society, were the novels of the new
republic content simply to test the possibility of another basis for community?
Or did they offer a system of social relationships that later novelists and literary critics would mistake for a transition between forms of community, thus a
community in a state of crisis? Our reading of the short story, "My Kinsman,
Major Molineux," follows an ominously unclassifiable affect as it spreads and
intensifies, quickly leveling the social field of Hawthorne's characters to reveal
a horizontal system of social affiliations. We also saw how those affiliations
dissipated soon enough, as the townspeople returned if not to homes, then to
the inn or public house that geographically reinscribed them on the basis of
property. To form a durable system of relationships, this story suggests, it is
not enough to turn the prevailing social hierarchy on its head. A work of fiction must also put into play alternative social rules that had not been imagin-
able until that moment. Hawthorne's story stops short of fulfilling this
promise.

It is only within the framework of the world of property that the release
of popular energy will have lasting consequences in that story. The ritual humiliation of his kinsman may have altered the conditions for Robin to move
up the social ladder, but his involuntary participation in that ritual does nothing to undermine the presumption that there is a higher position to which
one can aspire. As the well-meaning gentleman puts it, " 'If you prefer to remain with us, perhaps, as you are a shrewd youth, you may rise in the world,
without the help of your kinsman, Major Molineux' " (17). Though Robin no

longer considers access to his kinsman's wealth and influence a means of rising, property is nevertheless the basis of his interest in doing so—what he hoped thereby to gain, as well as the sign of his having achieved a higher place in the world of property.[2] There is no comparable drive in this story—no other lasting affiliation among the townsfolk—to counteract this desire to acquire property. What Tocqueville viewed through admiring but apprehensive European eyes as a precarious form of liberalism, Hawthorne saw as a social order that was only the stronger for its ability to accommodate moments of radical democracy within an institutional framework.

By contrast, the novels of the early republic rejected both the ethnos of the propertied classes *and* the competitive ethos that, as Hawthorne's gentleman predicts, is bound to displace the traditional hierarchy of New England towns a generation hence. To do so, these novels set "dispersal," "population," and "conversion" to the task of putting people, goods, and information into circulation. The formation of "hubs" within the resulting field of characters is, we argue, what promises to control the links that form among those characters as well as the expansion of their connections into new territory.[3] The concept of "self-organization" associated with modern chaos theory and cybernetics goes back as far as Aristotle and arguably developed a subversive edge during the late eighteenth century, which might explain why it seems remarkably compatible with the descriptive theory we have been drawing from early American fiction. The collapse of the traditional household in Brockden Brown's *Wieland* spells out in detail why a small world where any one member knows pretty much what every other member knows cannot last in a world of strangers, a problem that certainly would not have been lost on Brockden Brown's readers. Carwin, a ventriloquist, finds it relatively easy to substitute his voice and the misinformation it conveys for the bonds of intimacy that form the Wieland family. It takes only this one deceptive link, when strategically activated and deployed, to displace the trust that accompanies direct contact among members of a small world.[4] Family ties become instantly uncanny relationships that reduce a system of ties connecting each to every other member of the group to two tenuous connections: Clara's compromised relationship with her former suitor, Henry Pleyel, and her vexed relationship with the man who persuaded Henry to distrust her.

Her job as heroine is to assemble a community that does not duplicate the small world of her origins. While this more or less rules out a village where each knows the other's every move, her principle of open communication remains key to controlling deceptive links. In renewing old social contacts,

Clara also turns writing into the means of managing the information she circulates about what would otherwise seem the impossible events at Mettingen. The final chapter of *Wieland* consists of a letter that corrects the misinformation that Carwin introduced into her family over a period of two generations to knock out the household and prevent it from reforming itself anew. This letter transforms a deceptive link into reliable information but roots out the seeds of mistrust that Carwin had planted. In that it establishes that words don't necessarily mean what they say, this information paradoxically reestablishes trust between Clara and Henry Pleyel. Where the letters that precede it in the novel offer what must strike the reasonable person as a chain of impossible events in the Wieland household, her final writing converts her personal account into a public record that anyone can read and consider possible. Emerging from within the same network it describes, the very form of the novel, it suggests, assembles a community of those who read it, each knowing what the other knows. As to why one would want to do so, *Wieland* offers only the negative incentive of protection for one's property (see Esposito).

Of all the novels that one might compare with such a pervasively defensive novel, Leonore Sansay's *Secret History* is perhaps the last that comes to mind. *Secret History's* narrator goes to as much trouble to seek out strangers as the narrator of *Wieland* does in trying to avoid them. The difference between the two is the difference between the security that property provides and the pleasure of social circulation. When read through the moral lens of novels organized around a marriage plot, Sansay's account of two American-born sisters who find themselves in Saint Domingue during the Haitian revolution initially makes the sisters seem weak. Insofar as they cannot separate themselves from political turmoil but frequent parlors and ballrooms that encourage promiscuity, they also strike us as corrupt. Elizabeth Maddock Dillon considers *Secret History* more important for offering an American perspective on the Haitian revolution in particular and the instability of Caribbean social institutions in general than for condemning creole behavior on moral grounds. As they oscillate between scenes of heightened sensual pleasure and the senseless carnage of colonial warfare, Dillon observes, Sansay's pair of heroines operate as a sort of tag team that produces the account of their Caribbean exile. The sensual pleasure that Clara enjoys in parlors and bedrooms across the region provides her somber sister with a sequence of vantage points to reflect on the horrors that the pair has just avoided. The thoughtless escapades of her pleasure-seeking sister entice the reader to persist through numerous brushes with violence, confident that moments of sensual indulgence are soon to follow. In the process, the censorious sister, Mary, learns to appreciate the virtues of creole women and to see herself, a white woman from the United States, as a member of a creole nation. By actually experiencing what it feels like to belong to a tyrannical French plantation owner husband, Mary comes to understand and ultimately approve of her sister's need for constant movement and amusement.

From the novelist's perspective, this is only to the good. Without Clara, the narrator's account of her Caribbean travels would barely rise above the level of a salacious version of Mary Rowlandson's Puritan account of her Indian captivity. Of the creole women whom she initially condemned, Mary observes, they never complain, "nor vaunt their industry, nor think it surprising that they should possess it" (119). She comes to the conclusion that the same social behavior that consigned a woman to social perdition in more traditional novels "may be a resource [under conditions of] a reverse of fortune" (119). Under conditions of hardship, the creoles' unfailing generosity of spirit "excite[s]" the narrator's "warmest admiration" for these women (119). This shift in the tenor of its narration from the puritanical dread of a woman in fear of losing her virtue to the warm anticipation of sensual pleasure allows Sansay to invert the codes of good conduct. Where *Wieland* provided a clear example of what form of social relations would produce a viable community, Sansay's attempt at a positive model will depend on her narrator's ability to translate sexual conduct in the French and Spanish Caribbean into a style of social relationships, or counterconduct, that can be tolerated in the United States.

Fleeing from place to place to avoid Clara's husband, the sisters are invariably offered hospitality for the pleasure of her company. This happens because, as Mary puts it, "Clara's fate is to inspire great passions. Nobody loves her moderately. As soon as she is known she seizes on the soul, and centres every desire in that of pleasing her" (109). The intensity of those connections rests on a power of attraction that in turn renders Clara "insensible to all around her" (109). Let a strong tie begin to form, and she will flee it as surely as she flees her husband. Clara's role in the sisters' narrative is virtually indistinguishable from the power of attraction that motivates the narrative itself. All by itself, however, the pleasure principle is never enough to form a lasting social network. Casting its shadow over Sansay's protracted inquiry into the possibility of forming one is the question of the difference between the conduct of social life in various regions of the Caribbean and the standard maintained in Philadelphia, where Mary would like to settle and travel in the same

circles as her correspondent, Aaron Burr. Unless the censorious Mary can re-
value his sister's amatory adventures, Clara's power of attraction is bound to
strike Americans as a sign of moral corruption.

Mary understands that her job as letter writer is to redeem the pleasure
principle as the condition for returning with her sister to the United States. In
this capacity, Mary is, as she explains in her final letter to Aaron Burr, "more
than ever necessary to my sister." She credits Clara in turn for "many of the
sentiments expressed in this letter" (154), a statement that comes close to declaring Mary's attachment to the prominent American politician who was
known to say, "The rule of my life is to make business a pleasure, and pleasure
my business." It made sense, then, for Sansay's narrator and surrogate to con-
fess her intention to "infuse in [this man's] bosom those sentiments for my
sister that glow so warmly in my own" (154). So interchangeable are their
pronouns at this point in her final letter that if Clara finds in Aaron Burr "a
friend and protector," then Mary will as well. At some point midsentence,
writing catches up with Clara's radiant charm and converts the eroticism of
escape into a power of attraction that sustains social relations. The novel's
conversion of the energy of political revolution into a power of attraction capable of extending Philadelphia society to the pair of sisters depends as much
on Mary's suspicious sensibility. Her initial reluctance to relax moral protocols
in the pursuit of pleasure provides a basis for trusting the attachments she
prefers. However we imagine Burr responding to Mary's unorthodox proposal, we will have granted Sansay's point. We will have granted her the power
to open up the household to preferential attachments.[5]

How to Manage the Risk of Circulating Freely

No one variation of the novel shows how the disintegration of family ties
strengthens a social network with more clarity than the American seduction
novel. If one adds the sheer number of seduction stories appearing in maga-
zines to the frequency with which seduction plots appear in the sentimental
fiction of the period and that sum in turn to the seduction novels that cannot
be classified in any other way, the result would show the seduction novel to be
the most popular variation of the American novel published during the early
republic.[6] Key to the success of seduction narratives throughout the antebellum period was their reduction of the heroine to an unanchored and perme-
able body no longer eligible for the role of wife. So disqualified as the means

of legitimate biological and social reproduction, what the British would consider a morally compromised heroine served early American novelists as the means of regulating a very different form of social network. How can removing an otherwise quite eligible woman from the marriage market possibly bring strength and elasticity to her community? If *Wieland* proved that the household composed of intimate ties could not last more than a generation in early America, then *Secret History* exposes the risk of a social network that lacks any intrinsic means of control. Both Clara and Mary write in a style that manages the risk of circulating freely.

Social networks with strong hubs connecting smaller hubs can automatically reroute people, goods, and information even when several small hubs within the social network disappear.[7] The practical advantage of thus providing alternative routes between social contacts soon becomes apparent in households that can facilitate relationships between characters that would otherwise be strangers. Such a household would defeat its purpose and disappear were it to prevent strangers from passing through on their way to other locations within the same field of characters. On the other hand, the indiscriminate mingling that tends to occur on the frontiers of a social network prevents a household—and by implication a novel—from coalescing as a sustainable set of social connections. Cast in these terms, the problem becomes one of how to regulate weak ties—relationships with strangers—so as to extend and diversify the household without endangering its future. Even in the best eighteenth-century British circles, courtship procedures apparently required a number of near misses before a woman identified the man who best assured her future within a respectable household.[8] Should she err in the direction of promiscuity, a woman would be out of circulation, which in the world of the novel means nothing short of social death. But let her err in the direction of purity, and the woman all but vanishes from a network capable of connecting anyone to anyone.

Enter the American seduction novel. By using the heroine's reproductive role to take her out of circulation, this variation of the novel positions her to serve in two capacities at once—not only as the means of promoting social circulation but also as the means of regulating sexual reproduction. The seduction narrative negotiates this apparent paradox by opening up the possibility of indiscriminate connections in order to expose the risk of doing so. But such didacticism alone would not, in our view, explain why Hannah Webster Foster's *The Coquette* enjoyed "rapid sales" when it was first published and went on to be reprinted at least ten times over the course of the nineteenth century.[9] It is also necessary to factor in the familiarity, on the part of Foster's readers, with the novels of Samuel Richardson—not only the full-blown epistolary versions of *Pamela* and *Clarissa* but also the redactions that pared down the original to a seduction plot whereby the libertine takes the heroine captive, forcing her to resort to letter writing.[10] Thus, in the redacted version, how the heroine carries on her social life despite the libertine's success does not matter nearly so much as the impact of her letters on the readers among whom they circulate: can those letters repair the social network in the heroine's absence and diminish the risk of open social circulation?

Foster based *The Coquette* on the highly publicized "Elizabeth Whitman mystery," a newspaper account of an unmarried woman writer of wit and breeding who died alone, after giving birth to a child, at the Bell Tavern in Danvers, Massachusetts. While we certainly agree with critical opinion that Foster's novel capitalized on this scandal, we are primarily concerned with how Foster remodeled Richardson's disrupted household rather than with the feminist position that she assumed in doing so. The medium, we argue, is in this instance indeed the message. The story of Elizabeth Whitman spread like wildfire through New England newspapers. Foster then transformed it into an epistolary novel that presumed to give readers a sense of the personal decisions on the part of its fictional heroine, Eliza Wharton, that might have led to the newspaper accounts of Elizabeth Whitman's death.[11] Foster folds one such factual account into the novel, as the heroine's closest correspondent, Julia Granby, describes the lifeless body of Eliza echoing the newspaper reports of the discovery of Whitman's lifeless body: "We had no doubt of Eliza's being described, as a stranger, who died at Danvers, last July. Her delivery of a child; her dejected state of mind; the marks upon her linen; indeed, every circumstance in the advertisement convinced us beyond dispute that it could be no other" (170). In writing *The Coquette*, Foster not only transformed this anomalous event into one that could happen to any woman who was adept at attracting men but also situated the woman who got herself in trouble doing so at the center of a social network created by that style of writing.

As the newspaper accounts of Elizabeth Whitman's demise revise Richardson's sentimental classic, *Clarissa*, Foster arguably accomplished both objectives. Early in *The Coquette*, before the heroine becomes hopelessly ensnarled in the deceptions of Peter Sanford's seduction plot, we learn the basis on which Foster plans to revise Richardson's narrative procedures. When the coquette's hostess of the moment, Mrs. Richman, disapproves of "the sacrifice of time, which you have made to the amusement of a seducer," Eliza responds, "I hope, madam, you do not think me the object of seduction!" To which Mrs. Richman answers, "I do not think you seducible; nor was Richardson's Clarissa, til she made herself the victim, by her own indiscretion" (65). Foster's revision of "Richardson's Clarissa" turns on "indiscretion," which clearly means leaving oneself open to deceptive social connections that can remove her from circulation. Richardson's heroine is all response and reaction. Her power of attraction rests largely on Clarissa's stubborn refusal to say yes save in the one fatal instance, when she required Lovelace's assistance in order to say no to a forced marriage. By openly and directly pursuing the pleasures of sociability, Eliza is by contrast reluctant to say no and endeavors to prolong the courtship period during which women of the respectable classes were relatively free to circulate and make new associations. What makes Eliza the protagonist of Foster's novel is her power to make what we mean by "preferential attachments."

That she refuses a man whom she admires and later claims to love on the grounds that he would limit her ability to make new attachments concerns Mrs. Richman. "Pardon me, Eliza," she states the case: "this [Peter Sanford] is a second Lovelace. I am alarmed by his artful intrusions" (65). Mrs. Richman's suspicion is completely justified, for in Foster's novel, as in Richardson's, the libertine operates as a deceptive link to turn the coquette's power of preferential attachment against her own interests. In manipulating her social inclinations, the libertine puts an end to the heroine's ability to make new attachments and consequently forces her to exercise that power exclusively in and through writing. Once removed from direct participation in the social network, the written account of her misadventures follows the pathways of the seduction plot, exposing the deception that captured and destroyed Eliza's social agency. As it casts suspicion on the machinations that aim at immobilizing her, the novel restores her agency as a form of risk management and repairs the rupture created by her involuntary removal from the social network. Eliza's performance as an epistolary heroine converts the newspaper accounts of Elizabeth Whitman's death into a novel that counters Richardson's and corrects what Foster obviously considered bad information.

We must quickly add that *The Coquette* never holds Sanford's deception responsible for Eliza's downfall but suggests that the heroine has only herself to blame for failing to suspect the motive behind his flattery. Eliza also regrets that in pursuing the pleasures of circulating freely, she caused another suitor embarrassment and pain. That twinge of regret notwithstanding, she refuses to blame herself for adhering to the pleasure principle that her former suitor, like Sanford, would have monopolized. She regrets only that she allowed Sanford to steal her power to make attachments and hoard it for himself. In identifying this as the lesson that Eliza learns too late, the novel rejects conventional morality that tries to limit all preferential attachments to a concept of love that condemns sexual pleasure to the silence of married life. As her closest friends marry and move away, Eliza maintains each relationship, and they in turn maintain one another's.[12] The heroine therefore fulfills her purpose as a coquette as she moves from one social circle to another between Boston and New Haven, settling nowhere, attracting new admirers at each minor hub, and so maintaining the network that expands as she circulates within it. Like seduction, marriage would not contradict this principle unless it were to circumscribe her social agency.

On learning that Sanford has stolen time alone with Eliza, Mrs. Richman (herself married) never condemns Eliza for extending him hospitality but simply advises Eliza to be more suspicious of his "insinuations." Nor is her hostess concerned with Eliza's lack of moral discipline but simply that the coquette's "heart is too sincere *to suspect* treachery and dissimulation in another" (65, our italics). If happiness depends on the freedom to travel from place to place in New England and connect with virtually anyone, then any disruption of Eliza's mobility will diminish the pleasure of the entire community unless that disruption provides a means of correcting the problem. Foster's coquette thus counters Clarissa's punctilious morality with a pragmatic ethic aimed at minimizing the risk of circulating and associating freely. Had she approached strangers with appropriate suspicion, the pleasure of making new associations would have increased her social value without decreasing her moral value and allowed her to marry well. Recast as Foster's Eliza Wharton, Elizabeth Whitman acquires a life in letter writing that operates in some respects like Friedrich Kittler's account of the discourse of 1800 (27–69). The vernacular print medium spread, according to Kittler's model, as readers began to hear a particular voice—a woman's voice at first—while reading, and they sought to reproduce that voice in writing. By opening the interactions that form Eliza's network to public scrutiny, the novel circulates an account of her misadventures that aimed to make other women cautious in circulating too freely. It is in thus rendering herself ineligible for marriage that Eliza provides a hub, a way of managing the risk of encountering strangers, a formal means of regulating social contact no less essential to the network envisioned by early American novels than the traditional household was to the fantasy of the world as property to which those novelists strenuously objected.

Sinners in the Hand of an Angry Man

To see *Hobomok* (1824) as the legacy of the early American seduction novel, we must first consider how Lydia Maria Child revised the form of historical romance for which Sir Walter Scott and James Fenimore Cooper were widely celebrated. She did so abruptly and in such a conspicuous manner, moreover, that we must assume she knew exactly what she was doing when the Puritan heroine—the perfect means of establishing a British household in colonial New England—elopes with a Native American. Where Foster had Eliza "fall" precipitously on the scale of moral value that qualifies her to travel in respectable social circles, Child has Mary Conant violate the principles of the Puritan colony that her father established in British North America. By "going native" in the New England of Mary Rowlandson, then, a woman forfeited her claim to Christian virtue along with her British identity.[13] On this basis, we can say that by eloping with a Native American more than a century later, Child's sentimental heroine abandoned the celebrated position of Mary Rowlandson in order to survive the harsh conditions of Indian captivity.[14]

Like one such survivor, Mary Jemison, whose account of Indian captivity was transcribed and published in 1824, the same year that *Hobomok* appeared in print, Child's heroine displaces the Puritan heroine with a household that, by contrast to that in *Wieland,* accommodates a more diversified and open society.[15] *Hobomok* leaves little doubt that it takes magic to transform a Puritan heroine into one suited to the American novel, as Child uses a seduction narrative to revise a story of Indian captivity and maintain the heroine's fitness for that role. As in *The Coquette,* so in *Hobomok,* when the sentimental woman "falls," she takes the pleasure principle with her, detaching it from a concept of love that ensures the reproduction of the same strong ties that would limit community to members of the family. This allows Child to relocate pleasure in the heroine's ability to attract and be attracted by strangers who increase the scope and diversity of a household perishing for lack of new blood. She does so by remodeling a household that insists on strong ties so that it can tolerate weak links that expand and diversify the Puritan community and so qualify as the means of imagining a future national community. We offer this account of how *Hobomok* converts one household into another in order to suggest that tolerance for strangers remains the key issue on which the two concepts of the household that were in play in the American novel inevitably converged and then parted ways.

Even if we think that the world could be made entirely of property, as Kant imagined, we would have to allow strangers to pass through it, as he also acknowledged, in order for that world to benefit from international commerce. It would take nothing less than a universal liberalism to ensure that neither host nor guest do violence to, much less alter, the other's property. Accordingly, the concept of tolerance underwriting Kant's "law of hospitality" implicitly distinguishes strong from weak, contingent, or random ties and trusts to intimacy as the means of sustaining the ethnos of the community that he imagines. By contrast, the early American novel posits a soft opposition between trust and suspicion, whereby even a charlatan like Wellbeck in *Arthur Mervyn* becomes trustworthy once one understands that whatever performance he may be putting on is bound to be deceptive. Here, we have quite a different concept of tolerance than the one that Kant proposed in the interest of securing property. To make this point, *Hobomok* exposes the inadequacy of tolerance in a social environment populated by strangers eager to steal one's daughter and undermine the religious faith of the community, which determines the identity and maintains the limits of an immigrant community.

The novel situates a sentimental British heroine in the setting fit for a Mary Rowlandson. Transported to America, Mary Conant finds herself in an isolated Puritan community with strong but unreciprocated ties to the beloved English grandfather and the Episcopalian suitor from whom she was "removed" by her father's quest for religious freedom in the colonies. In England, as Child's narrator tells the story, Mary appeared to thrive: "her eye sparkled as brightly, and the rich tones of her voice were as merry, as they could have been when her little aerial foot danced along the marble saloon of her [English] grandfather" (9). But in America, she is confined to an unbearably contentious household that tolerates no more than splitting hairs within the framework of Puritan orthodoxy. Consequently finding "the moral as well as the natural atmosphere [in Massachusetts], was chill and heavy," Mary "grew more and more weary of the loneliness of unreciprocated intellect" (91). This is a novel in which sentimental women die for lack of the pleasures of social life, and Mary has not developed immunity to this sentimental affliction as her companion, Sally Oldfield, clearly has.

Sally has the power to enjoy being alive, young, and attractive to others even in the dour company and dreary climate of Puritan New England. Never mind that she lacks the class markers that Child describes as the "latent treasures of mind" or "rich sympathies of taste," qualities that waste away in her more refined companion. By means of this buoyantly ordinary girl, Child temporarily revives the drooping heroine and reveals what she and thus the community must have if they are going to last: "the heart must have sympathy; and amid the depression of spirits, naturally induced by the declining health of her mother, and the disheartening influence of the stern, dark circle in which she moved," Mary found "welcome relief" in her "untutored friend" Sally (36). Having made this point, the novel finds a husband for Sally, whisks her off to Plymouth (where she is positioned to extend the social network), speeds up the decline of Mary's mother, and sinks her suitor's ship off the coast of Africa. "What more had life to offer?" the narrator asks. "If [Mary] went to England, those for whom she most wished to return, were dead. If she remained in America, what communion could she have with those around her?" (121). The novel condemns a system of morality that overvalues the needs of the human soul over the common pleasures of social life and God's company over a community of friends and neighbors. But this attack on Puritan morality does not address the question that Child poses by means of her novel's title and its heroine's fall: why have Mary elope with Hobomok and bear him a child?

By what stretch of imagination could that doubly scandalous liaison provide the basis for a system of social relations that would auger well for the future United States? We chalk up this turn of events to a novelist pulling out the stops in rewriting a seduction novel as high romance. This liaison not only hastens Hobomok's disappearance but also indigenizes the heroine. Not so obvious is why Child mitigates the act of going native by recasting the Native American as the lovesick swain who waits on the sidelines until the heroine needs to be rescued and then sanctifies their marriage in a Native American ceremony, much less why Hobomok disappears at his own volition when it turns out that Charles Brown was not lost at sea off the coast of Africa after all. Having engineered their marriage, Child takes equal care in engineering Mary and Hobomok's divorce, as if to suggest that the fallen woman is not fallen after all. If she were in fact the heroine of a romance, Mary Conant would have to remain true to the Mary Rowlandson prototype and follow her mother to the grave. By going native, Mary Conant consequently becomes the protagonist of a very different story.

If there is danger in an open household through which strangers are free to pass, then there is a compensatory danger, as we have seen, in the closed community of exclusively strong ties. Being nomadic, the indigenous community is constituted of weak ties that, though elastic and portable, are not made to endure in this novel. Until he establishes a household with Mary,

Hobomok fades in and out of visibility, showing up when and where social connections are necessary to overcome the exclusionary principles of the household. Early on in the novel, he mediates between the Puritans and a hostile tribe in the region, but it is a folk ritual that lays bare the role that Hobomok plays in the heroine's rebirth. This romance in the forest begins with her preparation of a magic circle in hopes of conjuring the figure of Charles Brown, her British lover:

> She rose with a face pale as marble, and looking around timidly, she muttered a few words too low to meet my ear; then taking a stick and marking out a large circle on the margin of the stream, she stept into the magic ring. . . . The following were the only words I could hear,

> Whosoever's to claim a husband's power,
> Come to me in this moonlight hour. (13)

But as "she looked anxiously around," the narrator continues, "I almost echoed her involuntary shriek of terror, when I saw a young Indian spring into the centre" (13). Hobomok's leap from the seclusion of the trees where he was observing the ceremony into the very center of the national imaginary looks ahead not only to their marriage but also to the impossibility of reconciling the two different concepts of community at play in this scene, one sprung from American soil that overvalues the body as the source of life and another passed down through the father whose overvaluation of the life of the spirit would destroy the body.

On these grounds alone, the organization of the Conant household is wrong—so wrong that an indigenous society appears to offer the heroine freedom and a reason for restarting a community in North America. When her mother dies and her beloved is shipwrecked, Hobomok reappears before a heroine whose "faculties" are "partially deranged by grief" and pulls her back from the grave. In her condition "even Hobomok, whose language was brief, figurative, and poetic, and whose nature was unwarped by the artifices of civilized life, was far preferable to [the members of the Puritan community]" (121). In making her marriage vow, she acknowledges only that Hobomok is at that point her sole connection to life: "I love him better than any body living" (125). There is no one else. Within two years, however, Mary has replaced her tie to Hobomok with a preferential attachment in which there is no tinge of irony. Indeed, borrowing Adam's words upon first setting eyes on Eve, Child's narrator tells us, "Mary looked on the little being, which was 'bone of her bone, and flesh of her flesh'" and, in doing so, "felt more love for the innocent object, than she thought she should ever again experience" (136). Her strong tie to baby Hobomok prepares the way for Hobomok himself to disappear and be replaced by what we must regard as a proper head of household; within just a page or two, "Charles Brown stood by [Hobomok's] side" (138).

Mary Conant assembles the basis for a future Anglo-American community not by reproducing an English household on American soil but by allowing men to pass through, depart, and return. Once she went into the forest with Hobomok, Mary found herself suddenly accessible not only to Sally and her young daughter who enjoys the company of little Hobomok but also to her former lover whose religion can now be tolerated. The entire community has indeed loosened its boundaries, shifted its center sideways, and reorganized itself by accommodating weak ties that defy kinship, embrace hybridity, and refresh themselves with each departure and return. Child locates the household so assembled "near Mr. Conant's," who becomes particularly attached to little Hobomok and designates half the legacy of Mary's British family for her son's education: "[Hobomok] was afterwards a distinguished graduate at Cambridge; and when he left that infant university, he departed to finish his studies in England" (150). Key to the elasticity of the reformed community is the capacity to maintain connections when it members are spatially dispersed.

Into the Forest

When Mary goes into the forest, the Puritan household declines into obsolescence, leaving only the deposed sovereign to debate theology with his one remaining interlocutor, as Hobomok the elder pulls together what theology has put asunder and scattered across time and space. Hobomok the younger expands those connections by traveling back along his mother's immigration route, and by means of a secular education, he integrates the conflicting perspectives of his multicultural heritage as that heritage vanishes along with the Native American. Like Mary Conant's father and his one remaining interlocutor, the Puritan community in Nathaniel Hawthorne's *The Scarlet Letter* attributes authority to a higher power. In both cases, the heroine's sojourn in the forest secularizes political theology.[16] Thus, like *Hobomok, The Scarlet Letter* uses the pleasure principle to convert the difference between good and evil into the relative difference between friend and enemy, a difference that allows their respective communities to expand and diversify.

Despite his disdain for what he regarded as the scribbling of sentimental women writers, with Hester Prynne, Hawthorne does something remarkably similar to Child's Mary Conant. Indeed, we might say that he goes one better than Child by having the heroine of *The Scarlet Letter* "go native" with a Puritan minister. Where Mary Conant eloped with a Native American as a sort of holding pattern until she could unite in a traditional romantic relationship with Charles Brown, Hester Prynne consummates a romantic relationship with the Reverend Dimmesdale at the cost of permanent alienation from her legal husband and the entire Puritan community. This move transforms her irreversibly from a heroine in the tradition of Mary Rowlandson into the fallen woman who operates as the exclusive inclusion of the Puritan colony; as the town beadle puts it, her emergence from the prison where Hester has been condemned for adultery is actually a "blessing on the righteous Colony of the Massachusetts, where iniquity is dragged out into the sunshine" (41). Hawthorne makes it clear that she is so positioned by the Puritan community because she embodies a future, along with the beauty, vitality, freedom, and sensuality of the American wilderness, that displaces theirs. It was "as if a new birth, with stronger assimilations than the first, had converted the forest land, still so uncongenial to every other pilgrim and wanderer, into Hester Prynne's wild and dreary, but life-long home" (56). Hawthorne reveals the implications of this claim in a spectacular production of the impossible event—the redemption of the fallen woman and her bastard offspring.

If Chapter II offers an account of the religious ban placed on Hester for adultery, Chapter XII repeats the scene on the scaffold in order to convert the ritual of exclusion into an affirmative basis for horizontal affiliations. In this second scene, Hester again ascends the scaffold, "holding little Pearl by the hand." Only now Dimmesdale acknowledges his paternal relationship to Pearl: "The minister felt for the child's other hand, and took it. The moment he did so, there came what seemed a tumultuous rush of new life, other life than his own, pouring like a torrent into his heart, and hurrying through all his veins, as if the mother and child were communicating their vital warmth to his half-torpid system. The three formed an electric chain" (101). To mark this event as equivalent though inversely related to divine revelation, Hawthorne illuminates it with a meteor "in a strange and solemn splendor, as if it were the light to reveal all secrets, and the daybreak that shall unite all who

belong to one another" (101–2). He points out that what triggers the "tumultuous rush of new life" is none other than Hester herself, who consequently
emerges from this second scene a secular saint "quick to acknowledge her sisterhood with the race of man . . . Hester's nature showed itself warm and rich;
a well-spring of human tenderness, unfailing to every real demand, and inex-
haustible by the largest" (105).

As the novel proceeds to reembroider her "token of sin" with the mythol-
ogy of the Magna Mater, it also transforms Dimmesdale in language that suggests that he has been born again. Meeting her once more in the woods where
Pearl was conceived, "his inner man gave him other evidences of a revolution
in the sphere of thought and feeling. In truth, nothing short of a total change
of dynasty and moral code, in that interior kingdom, was adequate to account
for the impulses now communicated to the unfortunate and startled minister"
(138). This curious conversion experience sets him both free in body from the
constraints of his overburdened conscience and free in spirit from the constraints of his debilitated body. The strength of the impulse that derives from
his connection to Hester would seem to be just what Dimmesdale needs to
acknowledge publicly about his relationship to Hester and Pearl. This repetition of the scene on the scaffold reverses Hester's humiliation and threatens to
undo its conversion of beauty and pleasure into sin and degradation. As it
negates the negative, this repetition of the public ritual in the forest reveals the
basis for conduct fueled by but counter to the impulses that Puritanism
sought to locate in strong women, who could then be stigmatized. While the
counterconduct imagined in this scene cannot reverse Hester's abjection,
Dimmesdale's guilt, or Chillingworth's vengeance, it does augur an alternative
to a community organized by the opposition between good and evil in the
secular opposition between friend and enemy. Hawthorne allows us to glimpse
this possibility in the symbolic rehabilitation of Hester's scarlet letter and her
daughter Pearl.

To appreciate what the second public reenactment of the scene on the
scaffold accomplishes by reversing the positions of the men and the women
performers, we must first consider how this third and final performance on
the scaffold undoes the sentimental resolution that Child negotiates at the
end of *Hobomok*. Mary Conant's sojourn in the forest decentered and opened
the patriarchal household by making a number of weak ties where there had
been either strong ties or none at all. The two households are ultimately compatible, as Charles Brown steps in for Hobomok and little Hobomok both
loses his Indian name and acquires a British education; the Conant family

genealogy biologically incorporates the Native American so that he can be excluded as a demographic fact. What might easily have been considered little more than "bare life" in the figure of his son acquires rights to government protection, as this process endows that life with key markers of individuated personhood. For Hawthorne, there can be no such return to his or her community of origin for the individual who has ventured "into the forest." Hawthorne has seen to it that Hester's subjection to the ban acclimates her to being "outside" political theology, where she has indeed created a community by making "friends," as the term is used in all the novels we consider in this chapter.

Like Charles Brown, Roger Chillingworth was captured at sea, eliminating all possibility that Hester's marriage could fulfill the legal requirements of the community and still satisfy the human need for sexual love and human companionship. Like Mary Conant, Hester Prynne is drawn into the forest by a pleasure principle on the verge of perishing in the name of purity and an afterlife in heaven. Once they have violated the standard set by the heroines of Indian captivity narratives, however, the parallel between Child's and Hawthorne's novels ends. In contrast to the noble savage, the man to whom Hester gives herself (thereby usurping the father's prerogative) is a Puritan minister whose mission is to warn his flock away from exactly the pursuit of pleasure that leads to carnal sin. Hester's lawful husband, the unfortunate castaway whose disappearance occasioned the sojourn in the forest and procreative act, does not become the true companion of Hester's soul. Chillingworth plays the vengeful serpent in the garden who severs the bond that nature had conjoined as one. Even that is not bad enough to make Hawthorne's point: the malicious trickster takes Hester's place as Dimmesdale's roommate in hopes of becoming the secret sharer of the convulsions of his soul. Hawthorne turns Hester's legal husband into so craven a fiend as to justify figuring forth the natural family in redemptive splendor by restaging the scene on the scaffold in the forest that once made them fall from public grace. But as readers already would have known from the occasion for the tale, he invoked this resolution in order to revoke it in an equally sensational manner when he staged the final scene on the scaffold to expose the romance in the forest and its consequences to public scrutiny.

Hawthorne is no more willing to allow this romance of the forest to materialize than to grant Hester Prynne to return to life in her natal England. The transformation wrought by no less than three repetitions of the scene on the scaffold has rendered her a different form of social being historically as well as geographically beyond the Puritan community. This and not romance is what turns the ritual on the scaffold against itself, so that social purification becomes a form of inoculation and exclusion provides the basis for mutual aid. Hawthorne not only rejects the sentimental resolution he uses to entice the reader to wander with Hester into the forest of his imagination but also rejects the possibility that a religious community could be capable of redeeming Hester and legitimating Pearl. Where Child uses Hobomok as a placeholder to sustain the heroine until a liberal version of her father comes along and marries her, Hawthorne will brook no such compromise formation. Rather than replace a restrictive version of the family with one that tolerates preferential attachments, Hawthorne sees married love as a form of subjection that reduces women to property of one kind or another.[17]

With Dimmesdale's death and Pearl's departure, the magic of romance vanishes from Hawthorne's nature, its ghost lingering in Dimmesdale's disconsolate hope of their reunion in the unforgiving afterlife imagined by the Puritans. Killing off both men to whom Hester is attached makes it possible, at the same time, for Hawthorne to pick up and run with a common thread that connects his novel to *Hobomok* as the means of organizing social life outside and in a supplementary relation to the restricted and restrictive community of citizens. Hester's cottage, as opposed to the household she might have formed with Chillingworth, connects a portion of the wilderness both to the Puritan settlement and to England. An abandoned peasant cottage, it is in no way hers save when she is using it, and it offers her no legal rights or protections. Thus positioned, she marks both the outer limits of the town, or what that community must exclude in order to retain its moral authority over others, and its inner limits, the debased foundation of that moral hierarchy.

To read the novel as the legacy of earlier American fiction, not only Childs's *Hobomok* but Brockden Brown's *Wieland*, Foster's *The Coquette*, and Sansay's *Secret History* as well, we need to call attention to what happens to the abject woman as she carries the symbolic weight of the scarlet letter through three performances of the ritual shaming that completely redefines her. The process begins soon after Hester has taken up residence in the abandoned cottage outside of town and, as the narrator explains, "came to have a part to perform in the world," sewing beautiful garments for the people of the town, including the regalia for the religious administrators. "With her native energy of character, and rare capacity, [that world] could not entirely cast her off, although it had set a mark upon her, more intolerable to a woman's heart than that which branded the brow of Cain" (58). Once banished from social intercourse with "the little world to which she was outwardly connected," she began to feel "that the scarlet letter endowed her with a new sense . . . that it gave her a sympathetic knowledge of the hidden sin in other hearts" (60). The sense that her fallen condition is a universal one makes Hester "quick to acknowledge her sisterhood in the race of man" and to put that awareness to work by offering help in "all seasons of calamity." Hester came, the narrator tells us, "not as a guest, but as a rightful inmate, into the household that was darkened by trouble" (105). It is not only her compassion for others, then, but also the fact that she does not "have" a household—or even a daughter—of her own that entitles Hester to come in friendship and pass freely through any household in a time of need. These two characteristics—the consequences of her social ostracism—empower Hester to rewrite her own character.

In the register of "population," her story reembroiders the scarlet letter that classifies hers as the body of a fallen woman. Her fidelity to the vital impulse on whose denial the community is based gradually rehabilitates that impulse in Hester's practice of mutual aid. In thus translating the biblical meaning of the mark of Cain into a notably clumsy pun that secularizes Abel, Hester joins the tradition of women writing with the power of the outsider: "The letter was the symbol of her calling. Such helpfulness was found in her,—so much power to do, and power to sympathize,—that many people refused to interpret the scarlet A by its original signification. They said that it meant Able, so strong was Hester Prynne, with a woman's strength" (106). In so rewriting the American heroine, Hawthorne dispels any lingering similarity between *The Scarlet Letter* and *Hobomok*, bringing his dispute with sentimentalism into bas-relief. So inimical, in Hawthorne's view, is the Puritan model of community to social life in North America that his heroine cannot assimilate. Once Hester had ventured into the forest with Dimmesdale, she not only left the Puritan community but also became the founder of another.

In time, even the members of that community read the letter that once stigmatized Hester in positive terms. Dimmesdale returns to the Puritan community to seek Christian redemption by etching a scarlet letter in the skin that would otherwise conceal his heart. Where the final revelation of his liaison with Hester breaks the curse and offers him possible redemption in another world, Hester remains true to her role as the stigmatized woman and founds a community that contrasts starkly with the family envisioned in her second sojourn in the forest. Having deposited her daughter in "that unknown region [presumably in England] where Pearl had found a home," Hester returns to the site of her banishment and picks up where she left off:

"people brought all their sorrows and perplexities, and besought her counsel, as one who had herself gone through a mighty trouble. Women, more especially—in the continually recurring trials of wounded, wasted, wronged, misplaced, or erring and sinful passion,—or with the dreary burden of a heart unyielded, because unvalued and unsought,—came to Hester's cottage, demanding why they were so wretched, and what the remedy! Hester comforted and counselled them, as best she might" (165–66). Adjacent to the Puritan town, Hester's cottage is open to those who "[demand] why they were so wretched and what the remedy" (165). Promising future dissidence along with mutual aid, she has authored a network that both exposes the limits of the traditional household and imagines the possibility of a system of social relations both indigenous to North America and embedded in the literary past.

Chapter 8

_____

Anamorphosis

In what would become James Fenimore Cooper's signature move, the last sentence of *Hobomok* simultaneously incorporates the Native American within the romance resolution and excludes him from the future nation: "the devoted, romantic love of Hobomok was never forgotten by its object; and his faithful services to the 'Yengees' are still remembered with gratitude" (150). The process that immortalizes Hobomok also turns him from a metonymic link between the settlers and the larger American population into a conventional metaphor for genealogy itself: "the tender slip which he protected, has since become a mighty tree, and the nations of the earth seek refuge beneath its branches" (150). Using disenchantment as the antidote for sentimentalism, Hawthorne crafted Pearl in stark opposition to the hybrid offspring of Child's romance in the forest. To signal that he planned this demystification from the start, Hawthorne arranges a second visit to the forest so that Hester can retrace the steps that led to the encounter with Dimmesdale and the subsequent birth of Pearl, and this time she is accompanied by her daughter. Pearl is perfectly in her element in the forest. As she catches a beam of sunshine that casts Hester in relative shade, Pearl stands "laughing in the midst of it, all brightened by its splendor, and scintillating with the vivacity excited by rapid motion" (119). A living pun on the term "natural child," this daughter of the American wilderness is, as Harriett Beecher Stowe might have said of Topsy, just too full of wild energy to be captured by any social denomination. "She wanted," the narrator cautions, "what some people want throughout life—a grief that should deeply touch her, and thus humanize and make her capable of sympathy" (119). Overturning the aesthetic principle that reduced her joyless mother to an emblem of the fallen woman, Pearl's status as a sprite of nature empowers her to speak an Adamic language that Hawthorne here and elsewhere links to witchcraft.

But only when Dimmesdale acknowledges his paternity in the final scene on the scaffold is that "spell . . . broken," and we discover, counter to all preceding evidence, that "the great scene of grief in which the wild infant bore a part, had developed all her sympathies; and as her tears fell upon her father's cheek, they were the pledge that [Pearl] would grow up amid human joy and sorrow" (162). This puts an end to the use of nature as the stage for a struggle between good and evil. Things and people cease to vibrate with symbolic life and take up positions within a differential system of signs that organizes an altogether different culture: "None knew—nor ever learned with the fulness of perfect certainty—whether the elf-child had gone thus untimely to a maiden grave; or whether her wild, rich nature had been softened and subdued, and made capable of a woman's gentle happiness. But, through the remainder of Hester's life, there were indications that the recluse of the scarlet letter was the object of love and interest with some inhabitant of another land. Letters came, with armorial seals upon them, though of bearings unknown to English heraldry" (165). There you have it—all there is to know. Thanks to a dowry from her mother's late husband and the sudden transformation of her womanhood from creole unruliness to the polite demeanor of the English ruling class, Pearl becomes an entirely different being. She has undergone nothing short of a change in literary lineage in order to become the heroine of a sentimental marriage plot. What emerges from the figure of this American girl is an English woman so altered in form and behavior that the armorial seal on the letters Hester received provide the only proof that the radiant imp of the forest has indeed become the heroine of a sentimental novel.

In forging this connection, these signs of her miraculous cultural rebirth also assure us that Pearl no longer belongs in an American novel any more than Mary Conant's mother did. Fading at the outset, the conventional English woman expired halfway through Child's novel, abandoning her daughter to the eager arms of Hobomok. While playing by the same rules as Child, however, Hawthorne uses Hester's sojourn in the forest to sever the very genealogy that Child had established by linking a hybrid colonial male to his English heritage. Hester provides an alternative existence in North America for those who, for whatever reason, could not find a home within a traditional household. This community neither reproduces itself nor promises a more inclusive family. Indeed, once Pearl was rewritten as a marriageable woman, she no longer belonged in the same world as Hester, and Hawthorne packed her off to Europe, never to return. Even the "articles of comfort and luxury" that Pearl sent back to her mother are out of place in a New England home for, we are told, Hester "never cared to use" them (165). Rather than maintain the continuity of British culture as it moves westward across the Atlantic, then, Pearl's sudden and decisive change of character exposes the irreparable rupture that Child took such trouble to conceal.[1]

The fact that young Hobomok and Pearl are born in North America means that their respective stories project antithetical futures for the same national community. Where young Hobomok's generic Englishness allows him to circulate seamlessly from Plymouth to Cambridge and on to England, Pearl's radical transformation during the final scene on the scaffold ends the illegitimate status that had justified her exclusion from respectable society; only then could she reclaim British lineage. Her transformation splits senti-mental womanhood off from the natural vitality that Hawthorne embodies in this heroine, so that America's future rests on the mother who went native. Whereas Mary Conant's marriage to Charles Brown resolves symbolically what the wilderness had put asunder, Hester's story transforms that impulse into a way of life resistant to any concept of marriage. Where Child's novel encourages us to imagine the nation as a polycentric community of structur-ally equivalent households, Hawthorne's novel thinks in terms of a loosely interwoven system of weak ties that allows each group to maintain the prac-tices that render it incompatible with others. In order to diverge on this point, however, Child and Hawthorne engaged an argument that would ultimately validate both alternatives. The next and final chapter of this book will show how James Fenimore Cooper circumvented the impossible marriage of an in-digenous culture with a xenophobic community by means of an openly het-erogeneous social network that earned him the status of an American Sir Walter Scott.

How Incompatible Parts Form a Whole

As art history would tell the story, "anamorphosis" was rediscovered during the seventeenth century in a number of experiments spurred on by the inven-tion of linear perspective.[2] To establish the authoritative sightline from which an object should be viewed, European painters and cartographers developed perspectival conventions that distorted the object so that it would position the viewer accordingly. As artists and artisans proceeded to do so in various ways, the burst of images that ensued gradually undermined the Cartesian method of localizing points in space according to their relative distances from intersecting perpendicular lines. It became apparent that no such two-dimensional method could account for a field of social information where multiple, often mutually hostile cultural perspectives simultaneously converged in forming a single object. Artists made use of anamorphosis to challenge the concept of an authoritative center. Hans Holbein's painting *The Ambassadors* is only one example of a work of art that renders an object unintelligible to a spectator accustomed to seeing things and people in relation to a dominant perspective. While the disorienting effect of the blot in the foreground of that painting resists intelligibility to such a spectator, Holbein made it obtrusively apparent that his view did not cover everything within the framework of the painting. Anamorphosis achieves its disorienting effect by positioning viewers between two incompatible perspectives, where they must shift positions in order to grasp the entire field of sensory information. The art of anamorphosis therefore resides not in the skill or originality with which the author or artist depicts the object in question but in the ingenuity with which he or she conjoins incompatible perspectives.

As Holbein's painting famously demonstrates, the perceptual doubling that constitutes an anamorphic object breaks up the viewer's gaze.[3] In moving to the left, the gaze confronts a skull that appears on the rug squarely in front of the major characters oblivious to its presence within the framework they presume to dominate. While the subjects of the painting, namely, the ambassadors, continue to look straight ahead, the skull turns and looks back along the line of the oblique perspective that it objectifies. Consequently unmoored from a position fixed by the gaze of the figures in the painting, Holbein's spectator has to move back and forth between centered and eccentric positions to see what is marked as unintelligible from any one perspective. Given that neither perspective can incorporate or completely occlude the other, what we get is a composite image. Stephen Greenblatt describes a painting that demands such movement as implicitly undermining "the very concept of locatable reality upon which we conventionally rely in our mappings of the world" and so "subordinates the sign systems we so confidently use to a larger doubt."[4] Cast in this light, anamorphosis would never free the observer to view the object from his or her own perspective but would rather set the object free to demand how it should be seen, even at the risk of becoming unintelligible. The American novel takes this same risk in order to challenge the concept of perspective very much like the one that E. M. Forster drew from the major works of British fiction.

From their first appearance, the novels of the early republic relied on the principle of anamorphosis to eliminate the possibility of any one view dominating the rest. One does not read a novel so organized for the pleasure that accompanies achieving a position of strategic control over and above a field of characters but rather to enjoy the tactical dexterity it takes to negotiate a field of information that would seem absolutely incoherent from a strategic point of view. In this respect, we can regard Hawthorne's Pearl as an anamorphic object and say that Child's baby Hobomok is not. The fiction that concerns us in this chapter exploits the oscillation between dominant and peripheral perspectives in order to prevent any one view from incorporating the others. This situated early American readers in a polycentric world, where they could shift from one cultural perspective to another without relinquishing their own. But neither, on the other hand, could they assume that each individual brought his or her own distinctive view to the act of reading. Eluding the classic alternatives of the one as opposed to the many, the early American novel produced a world by means of apparently random encounters between disparate people and things who present themselves to each other however they will and establish relationships designed to fall apart almost as soon as they are made. As antagonistic to the very idea of "form" as such a narrative process may seem, the metonymic method in this fecklessness resulted in a form of novel distinctive to the new United States. Rather than expand the small worlds of various regions to make an inclusive whole, this form invariably conjoined incompatible perspectives of the same event to make a composite reality. On this basis, it is fair to say that the novels of the early republic were anamorphic objects in their own right.

Looking at the landscape of South Carolina with the botanical investment of an English naturalist, Crèveceour's Farmer James recalls that he wandered off the beaten path in search of a spot where he could examine the "unfamiliar plants" he had just collected. There, he heard a sound that told him that he was not alone but which failed to indicate what or who had intruded on his solitude. Looking up from his specimens, he saw at "about six rods distance something resembling a cage, suspended to the limbs of a tree, all the branches of which appeared covered with large birds of prey" (*Letters* 178). Having disrupted the traveler's self-composure, this curious object prompted him by "an involuntary motion of my hands" to fire at the thing he

could not identify. With the birds gone, Farmer James could see what someone more familiar with the brutality of slavery would have understood at a
glance: "a Negro, suspended in the cage and left there to expire," his eyes already plucked from their sockets by the birds (*Letters* 178). Farmer James's first
impulse was to put the slave out of his misery, but having no ball for his gun,
he handed the dying man a glass of water instead. Here, then, Crevècoeur has
inserted, within a field of vision he attributes to the Pennsylvanian farmer, a
human figure distorted beyond recognition as such to someone unfamiliar
with the local practices of a slave state. As it revealed the human body disfigured by slavery, however, the anamorphic object also exposed the limits of the
Loyalist's repertoire of responses. Such a narrative presents knowledge of the
whole system of relations from a local perspective within that system that
provides those who share that position with self-knowledge. The differences
between such a perspective and another is not, under these conditions, a difference in scale of micro to macro or periphery to core; they are different ways
of organizing information within a single system so as to understand what
that social system really is. Given that each such perspective considers itself
more accurate or realistic than the others, no one perspective is qualified to
synthesize, much less to dominate the rest.

To understand anamorphosis as the means of meeting the challenge of
cultural incompatibility that allows such atrocities to happen also casts new
light on the American predilection for gothic fiction. A brief look at Washington Irving's well-known story, "The Legend of Sleepy Hollow," offers a clear
example of how the dead comes to life and pokes a hole in the economic fab-
ric of an itinerant schoolteacher's misbegotten sense of superiority. While the
spectacle of resurrection can certainly be read as a momentary triumph of folk
practice over book learning, the joke played by a local suitor on the itinerate
schoolmaster serves an alternative purpose as well. In that the joke exploits
local knowledge to counter the deracinating effects of Anglo-American culture, it keeps the courtship practices of the Anglo-Dutch community intact.
Reading this way, one is bound to think of the local and the national as the
same community on different spatial scales in which the smaller and more
particular defines itself in terms of its resistance to the larger culture of which
it is but a part.

But suppose we were to read the spectacle of the headless horseman according to the formal trope of anamorphosis. In that case, we would no longer think of its appearance as the means by which the story stages a conflict
between local and national communities but rather as the link that makes two

distinct local communities meaningful in relation to each other on the basis of their respective ways of organizing the same social information. Thus, if in the first instance we take Irving's story to be an account of how the ethnic community (or part) resists the nationalizing force of New England culture (or whole), then the second way of reading would situate us at the conjunction of two incompatible ways of understanding the appearance of the headless horseman. According to the first—and more traditional—reading of the story, Ichabod's fateful encounter with the headless horseman accomplishes much the same thing as Lydia Maria Child's version of the marriage plot. The presumptuous schoolmaster plays the stranger who threatens to disrupt marriage practices that maintain the boundaries and secure the future of a relatively closed community. The sudden appearance of the headless horseman would, from this perspective, operate like the reappearance of the shipwrecked Charles Brown to provide the means of neutralizing the threat of disruption. While it accomplishes its immediate objective of humiliating the dominant culture, the momentary realization of superstition nevertheless yields to common sense, leaving what will become the prevailing rules of realism virtually unchanged. The affective event of the spectacle will not stop the inevitable dissolution of local kinship practices. As to what future might arise from the sort of weak tie that Ichabod Crane failed to make, we turn to the most popular gothic novel of the early national period.

American Gothic

We are so familiar with the way of reading the American novel that Leslie Fiedler proposed, back in the 1950s, that many of us adopt his method without feeling obliged to acknowledge the source, much less question what it takes for granted with respect to the novel form. So many critical readers have indeed accepted whole cloth certain assumptions from Fiedler that we felt it was necessary to revise them. Here is the kernel of his argument: "it is the gothic form that has been most fruitful in the hands of our best [American] writers: the gothic *symbolically* understood, its machinery and décor translated into metaphors for a terror psychological, social, and metaphorical. . . . Such a mode can, of course, not be subsumed among those called 'realism.' Our fiction is essentially and at its best nonrealistic, even anti-realistic" (28). Fiedler goes on to proclaim that the American novel never aspired to realism but is written in a "symbolic" style that harkened back to the culture of colonial

North America. This tradition "was born of the profound contradictions of our national life and sustained by the inheritance from Puritanism . . . of a typical way of regarding the sensible world—not as an ultimate reality but as a system of signs to be deciphered" (29). This evocation of nature as Adamic language is really all the ground he requires for reading the figural operations of the gothic text as symptomatic of the unacknowledged collective guilt of founding a nation on the violent appropriation of land and labor from those who used to own them. Yet, in order to celebrate what he saw as the symbolic expression of this guilt in the American novels that warrant critical attention, Fiedler found it necessary to dismiss one of the earliest attempts by an American author to write a "serious" gothic novel. We find his reasoning curious.

Between June 4 and October 30, 1804, Isaac Mitchell published his serial novel titled *Alonzo and Melissa. An American Tale Founded in Fact* in *The Political Barometer*, a weekly newspaper that he owned and edited with Jesse Buel. Enlarged and published in two volumes in 1811, *The Asylum; or, Alonzo and Melissa* was then pirated and republished in various versions over the next four decades. All told, Mitchell's novel went through twenty-five editions to become one of the most popular novels of its time. Yet despite its evidently wide and enthusiastic reception, Fiedler disparages Mitchell's attempt to imagine a gothic country house on Long Island, "as not merely unconvincing but meaningless" (144). In addressing the reader of British novels, he contends, "the haunted castle of the European gothic lost all point" when it appeared "fifty miles from New York City" (144–45). A critic of unerring taste, Fiedler may not be wrong in declaring Mitchell's contemporary, Brockden Brown, the novelist who adapted the gothic novel for American readers and so bequeathed that form to the geniuses of Edgar Allan Poe and Nathaniel Hawthorne. But Brockden Brown did not, as Fiedler implies, perform this transformation alone, as a serious look at Mitchell's deterritorialized castle should indicate.

Both volumes of *The Asylum* feature captive women as the subject around which to unfold a novel of sensibility like those of Samuel Richardson or Ann Radcliffe. But where Mitchell's Selina flees before her father can force her into a loveless marriage in Volume I, in Volume II, Melissa's father fails to keep his daughter stashed away in the very "castle-like" mansion on Long Island Sound that Fiedler singled out as the object of scorn. Yet, in our view, the volume that Fiedler finds unworthy of critical consideration (we suspect for its lack of psychoanalytic resonance) is nevertheless the far more interesting of the two. Partly in ruins, this edifice "of real Gothic architecture" is surrounded by a moat and entered by way of a drawbridge (154). In such a country house, as we have argued elsewhere, the same purgatorial isolation that tested a Mary Rowlandson's virtue also provided Richardson and Radcliffe with the captivity narrative they used to string together a sequence of heightened emotional displays that expose the heroine's inner life.[5] To challenge Fiedler's claim that we should view *The Asylum* with contempt, we have to challenge his literary genealogy. If such novels as *Clarissa*, *The Mysteries of Udolpho*, and *Mansfield Park* can be read as descendants of the American captivity narrative, then wouldn't turnabout be fair play? Rather than think of *The Asylum* as a bungled attempt at transplanting an English form to an American setting, it seems easily as reasonable to see the gothic features of *The Asylum* as Mitchell's way of bringing the captivity narrative back to its native soil. The novel's obvious popularity with an American readership indeed suggests that he succeeded in doing just that. Contrary to Fiedler's characterization of *The Asylum* as completely useless to later novelists, then, we want to show how Mitchell's novel updated the gothic so that Hawthorne (in "Rappacini's Daughter") and Poe (in "The Fall of the House of Usher") could rewrite that form in a full-blown literary style.

Consider the "castle-like" mansion that suddenly appears on the shores of Long Island Sound, where Melissa's father stashed his only daughter early on in Volume II of *The Asylum* to keep her from running off with Alonzo. Here, Melissa has a dream of a blood-spattered, knife-wielding intruder accompanied by a chorus warning her to flee for her life. She does so at once and without a second thought. This supernatural visitation is, like Irving's, a performance designed to expose the machinery of economic conflict among groups within the Atlantic world, a conflict that can be and is resolved as the novel forms a reparative circuit of information. In order for it to do so, however, Mitchell had to change his protagonist's plans to marry his beloved. Thus, just as Alonzo arrives at the castle gate to rescue her, the novelist whisks Melissa off to another location before sidelining her for the duration of the novel. Taken in by a kindly uncle who had recently lost a daughter also named Melissa, she is as good as dead, freeing Alonzo to pursue a narrative course resembling that of Arthur Mervyn.

The novel calls upon one gothic intrusion to deprive Alonzo of his love object and then calls upon another to transform him from a desolate hero of romance into the agent of an information network. Well before he happens upon her cousin's obituary and mistakes it for that of his beloved, Alonzo confronts Melissa's corpse in a dream, which is immediately followed by another dream in which she appears full of life, suggesting that, though dead, Melissa may also be alive. To further confuse the matter, this sequence repeats itself with the appearance in a window of a shadowy figure having "very much the appearance of Melissa." Within a few hours, however, Alonzo discovers that "the lineaments of her countenance, when viewed by the light of day, were widely dissimilar" (180). Appearing first as one person and a mere copy, the figure of "the veiled woman" exposes the gap between his wish for the dead woman to be alive and the fact that, once dead, she cannot return.[6] This is the novel's way of establishing that no one else possesses exactly Melissa's "delicate features, pale and dejected as when he last saw her, her brown hair, falling in artless circles around her neck, her arched eyebrows and pensive aspect" (179). The appearance of the veiled woman eliminates the possibility of a future substitute.

Nor can Alonzo recover the family estate whose loss initially cost him the blessing of Melissa's father; creditors have seized the old man's "lands, tenements, and furniture, [and plan to sell that property] at public auction for less than half its own value" (136). "With your acquirements," his father tells Alonzo, "you may make your way in life. I shall have no property to give you" (136). Stripped of both a past and an anticipated future as a man of property, Alonzo is, like the man of interests, capable of becoming any number of different men as the opportunity arises. To signal this shift in role, he joins a convoy that "was at that time preparing from parts of the United States for the protection of our European trade" (186). It is entirely fair to see Mitchell's use of gothic machinery as aggressively hijacking Melissa's story, a romance fashioned on the Mary Rowlandson story, and then engineering another popular narrative tradition that delivers Alonzo to a London prison.

Mitchell's readers would certainly have appreciated the ease in which the characteristic devices of the Barbary captivity narrative transformed what had been an aimless display of gothic tricks into a transatlantic network. With his love object removed, the protagonist is reborn. Tearing his clothes into strips from which to fashion a rope, Alonzo descends from prison into the London streets "literally stark naked" (194). There, a British sailor encounters him, provides Alonzo with a "decent suit of clothes," and hides him until he can make arrangements to smuggle him into France. "'Say nothing,' says the generous tar," when Alonzo attempts to thank him: "'We were born to help each other when in distress'" (197). If his nakedness allows him to bridge the gulf between men of warring nationalities, then Alonzo's new clothing "refits" him for a cosmopolitan life in Europe where he crosses paths with Benjamin

Franklin. To this point, very much the same lawless economy that motivated Kant's proposal for an international "law of hospitality" has determined the course of Alonzo's life. But Mitchell had a very different notion than Kant as to how to bring that lawlessness under control.

As Alonzo's exchange with Franklin in Paris establishes the means of connecting information from two sides of the Atlantic, it also creates a virtual link between Europe and key individuals in the new United States that will eventually complete a circuit of information. Their exchange consequently allows information concerning the movement of people and goods to catch up with the actual movement of people and goods to expose the infrastructural ruptures that destroy people's reputations and scatter their property. By filling in the gaps and holes in Alonzo's story, Franklin simultaneously repairs the damage done to Alonzo's family and provides the hub of an information network that exposes the swindlers and pirates who operate behind a cloak of secrecy. With legibility comes legitimacy.

This network begins to form the instant Franklin asks Alonzo "to recite his history." On learning the "particular circumstances of his father's misfortune," Franklin writes a letter, which in turn secures employment for Alonzo with a British bookseller in Paris (198). From this point on, as information travels from one location to the next, the novel observes the principles of a distributed network and establishes multiple connections among members of a community dispersed by an unregulated system of international trade and speculation.[7] Outside a bookseller's establishment, Alonzo finds a miniature portrait of Melissa "after she had been sometime dead," which gives him cause to wonder, "by what providential miracle am I possessed of the likeness?" (199). A published description of the lost portrait locates the owner, none other than Melissa's brother, who confirms her death. The ensuing friendship indirectly reestablishes contact with Melissa's family where her death had severed it. But by the time Alonzo calls upon Franklin a second time, the cascade of dispersals set off by the loss of his father's investments has already ground to a halt and begun to reverse itself. The freshly desolate Alonzo returns to Franklin only to learn that now that he has no use for it, his father's fortune has been recovered. Having no reason to return to America until Franklin delivers this information, Alonzo returns simply to convey the good economic news. Once his protagonist has fulfilled his mission as the agent of information and brought a sense of order to an otherwise unintelligible commercial economy, Mitchell trots out the figure of the veiled woman and undoes the doubling that made Melissa vanish.

To set the stage for her unveiling, the novelist himself assumes the role of narrator in order to debunk Alonso's claim that it would require a miracle to bring Melissa back from the dead. It is especially important, Mitchell reminds the reader, for the author of an impossible event to remember that "he is no magician. Or, if he is, he cannot raise the dead. Melissa has long since mouldered into dust, and he has conjured up some *female* Martin Guerre or Thomas Hoag—some person from whose near resemblance to the deceased he thinks to impose upon us and upon [Alonzo] also, for Melissa" (218). Deception is no better than magic, in the author's view, because it substitutes, as in the cases of Martin Guerre and Thomas Hoag, individuals who "in countenance, stature, voice, and manners so nearly resembled other persons that their own wives could not discriminate between them" (218). In that similitude introduces a deceptive link into the social network, the woman behind the veil "must be the identical Melissa herself, or it might as well be her likeness in a marble statue." Once a novelist actually kills off his heroine, on the other hand, "it is totally beyond his power to bring her back to life—and so, his history [will be] intrinsically *good for nothing*" if he does so (227). *The Asylum* must, like the British gothic, strip the event of the dead come back to life of all supernaturalism, but it must do so in such a way as to counter the British gothic. The American novelist refuses to do so in the name of common sense. Just as the figure once allowed the genuine Melissa to disappear into her semblance in the light of day, so the second appearance of the veiled woman now allows the original to return to Alonzo alive and well. It is by thus conjoining the original to its semblance and then reversing that sequence that the novel pulls off the impossible event of the dead come back to life.

We might assume that the last way a novel, much less a gothic novel, would think of resolving a problem posed by a supernatural disruption of domestic order would be to bring intelligibility to the international economic infrastructure. But this is how *The Asylum* proposes to demystify and bring conceptual control to the irrational forces of dispersal that disrupt the social field. Never a conventional man of property, Alonzo's father always depended on the free circulation of trade to increase his fortune, which opened him to risk and ultimately cost him his home and respectability. With his investments restored, he has no incentive "to enter into mercantile business, but placing his money in safe hands, lived retired in the country" (232). Nor does his retirement mean his removal from the world of trade and speculation in the manner of an Enlightenment gentleman but rather that he can count on a steady and sufficient income from investments. Self-regulation can only go so far, however. To make the point that control is not control unless it is system-wide, Mitchell connects Melissa's story to Alonzo's. Rather than fall into each other's arms and form a household, the pair goes right to work exposing deceptive links in each of their stories, a task that obviously requires any number of different perspectives.

The time has clearly come to explain the blood-spattered specter that sent Melissa fleeing from the castle-like country house as a Loyalist deception. The dream was all a ruse to distract her from the distribution of illegal arms and counterfeit money that was as much a part of the lawless economy as swindlers and pirates. This disruption of cooperative relations, rather than the machinations of a disinherited relative, was behind the gothic spectacle that drove Melissa into hiding. As the pair retells their respective stories, the novel turns bad circulation against itself by means of corrective information. The discovery of one deception leads to another. Thus, in cleaning out the nest of Loyalists, Alonzo meets up again with none other than "the affectionate tar" who rescued him in London, now captured by American forces and left to languish in prison. Although the "tar" in question had been operating as an enemy, just as Alonzo had been when he was seized by the British navy, Alonzo secures his friend's release and provides him safe passage back to England with the capital to buy a tavern he will call "The Grateful American." As it ties up this loose narrative thread, we see the novel converting national rivalry into international reciprocity.

By calling his novel *The Asylum*, Mitchell simultaneously invokes the country manor house and transforms its closed community into a social network that, in key respects, looks ahead to the waystation provided by Hester Prynne. In addition to a social nexus for friends, family, and former acquaintances, the house provides asylum for dispersed, lost, and otherwise homeless people, as well as the point from which Alonzo will venture forth in the defense of his country, a conflict in which "he took a very conspicuous part" (242). This reparative network emerges from a sequence of tactical maneuvers that depend on local knowledge to keep the circulation of goods, people, and information moving. By definition, such a narrative cannot articulate a single strategic view if it acquires force and functionality by accumulating information from various tactical vantage points whether directly or through others. As in the Holbein painting of *The Ambassadors*, so in American gothic, only knowledge on the spot from the spot can make that spot intelligible. Operating on this principle, Mitchell uses the tropes of a gothic romance set during the period of the War of Independence, much as Charles Brockden Brown

uses Philadelphia during the time of yellow fever, to produce a communication network that diminishes the risk of social circulation. Mitchell bombards
his protagonist with dreams, spectacles, obituaries, advertisements, a miniature painting, and any number of personal accounts that, once combined, will
protect that community from unregulated trade and circulation. The story-
telling procedures that combine these disparate viewpoints so as to expose the
source of their inconsistencies are arguably what Poe and Hawthorne inherited not only from Charles Brockden Brown but from Isaac Mitchell as well.

Unspeakable Life

Were it to yield no new insight into the classics of American fiction, even the
cleverest reading of Mitchell's *The Asylum* could not earn that novel a reprieve
from Fiedler's curt dismissal. To meet this challenge, we look first at Edgar
Allan Poe's "The Fall of the House of Usher" and reconsider what critics tend
to see as a clash between common sense and abnormal hypersensitivity as a
gothic account of the dissolution of the man of property. Under what conditions, this story seems to ask, does common sense itself cross over the line that
evaluates all difference on a scale of normalcy and become, according to those
same criteria, a symptom of mental dysfunction? Once classified as normal, in
Foucault's account, a person is not entitled so much as subjected to the protections of his person. The more inappropriate his response to material phenomena, paradoxically, the more unlikely that individual will be held
accountable for inappropriate, even criminal behavior.[8] To go thus off the
scales is to lose the property in himself that is subject to such judgment. Poe
captured the simultaneous collapse of such property in the person and its
manifestation in material property in the double meaning of his title "The Fall
of the House of Usher."

    With this in mind, we second Siân Silyn Roberts's proposal that Poe's
fiction as a whole challenged the opposition between reason (in the person of
the hyperrational detective Dupin) and the irrational forms of cognition on
display in Poe's horror stories but most memorably personified by the narrator
of "The Fall of the House of Usher." Where the protagonist's madness serves
"as a placeholder for categorical dysfunction that preserves the everyday order
of things and behavior," according to Silyn Roberts, what the narrator regards
as his host's abnormal state of mind is actually his struggle to come to terms
with the reality that he has buried his catatonic sister alive (99). Intent on

exposing the limitations of common sense in this respect, Roberts shows how American literature rethinks Lockean epistemology and so modifies the individual that acquires mastery over the world by enlarging common sense to deal with "unexpected forms of experience" (100). Such an adaptation is necessary, she concludes, if one is to "feel at home in a nation of many different local or regional cultures" (102). We want to pursue this observation in another direction.

We agree that common sense is no longer common sense once Poe sets it in motion geographically. When deterritorialized, common sense becomes one of so many local views that for the most part coexist without calling one another into question. They might have indeed continued to coexist without perplexing one another, in this case, had Poe not so positioned both common sense and an alternative perspective as to bear witness to the same impossible event—none other than the return of a woman from the dead. Under the regime of common sense, death is irreversible. It is up to Poe, as it was to Isaac Mitchell, to pull off the impossible event so that it both observes this immutable law of living matter and changes the limits of what can henceforth be considered fact. From a local perspective—familiar with the architecture of the Usher house and the locations of its creaks and groans, as well as with the symptoms of the family malady—this event, though too awful to acknowledge, is perfectly intelligible. In this respect, the figure of Madeleine Usher's reanimated body has something in common with the veiled woman in *The Asylum*, as it does the figure of the skull that emerges in the foreground of the Holbein painting when each is viewed from an oblique perspective.

In these cases, fear has nothing to do either with things that go bump in the night as it does in a Radcliffe novel or with "the uncanny." Where the lack of intelligibility in the one instance results from a well-engineered deception, the lack of legibility in the second instance arises from unnamable feelings of apprehension that distort some otherwise familiar object beyond all recognition. In both instances, fear suspends the usual patterns of life and diverts the narration of experience into an interpolated tale of the dead come back to life. Whether it actually stages this violation of the everyday in the protagonist's bedroom or presents it as a dream or hallucination, the Radcliffe novel will ultimately yield to a rational explanation that expels the distortions wrought by fear and restore the normative perspective with an expanded and more sophisticated grasp of things.[9] Not so with the American gothic. Rather than provide an occasion for expanding and updating the explanatory power of any one perspective, Poe uses the interpolated tale to conjoin viewpoints, each of which makes a seemingly impossible event legible in its own way but neither one of which makes much if any sense to the other. Here again, the dead woman's return to life creates a blot of illegibility within the framework of common sense that exposes the limits of what otherwise might become the dominant perspective.

Mitchell's shift of focus to the mysterious operations of an international economy widens the blot of unintelligibility within the field of characters that Alonzo traverses and transforms his movements into a sequence of connections that introduces a new means of control. Reversing Mitchell's priority on the international economy over domestic life, Poe shows that as goes the woman, so goes the family's fortune. A mystery when still alive, once entombed, Madeline's presence generates dread until it consumes the entire household. Refusing to add up in terms of common sense, the details of her death and burial accumulate until gothic description completely derails what presents itself as factual narration. This process is hardly a subtle one. After lingering to describe the rotting vegetation that surrounds the crumbling mansion, the narrator takes us "over a short causeway" and through "the Gothic archway of the hall" (233). By so identifying the descriptive mode in which the narrator records his immersion in this alternate reality, Poe prepares us to read it as both a tale of terror and as an elaborate joke at the expense of the kind of fiction to which common sense resorts when facts exceed the scope and flexibility required to read them. Resembling the spectacle that so terrified Ichabod Crane, this joke is designed to expose a reading of the world that presupposes an absolute distinction between fact and fiction.

Betting his reason on this distinction, Poe's narrator writes off Roderick Usher's mounting apprehension as a figment of an imagination that has lost its foundation in the world of fact. From the first paragraph of his account, this narrator classifies as abnormal whatever eludes his notion of common sense, and he mobilizes a gothic style to do so. The house he is about to enter is "melancholy" and conducive to "an utter depression of the soul," "a sickening of the heart," and "an unredeemed dreariness of thought" (233). The narrator clings to this habit of thought even as the "shadowy fancies that crowd upon [him]" defy his conviction that these gloomy premonitions are "beyond doubt" products "of combinations of very simple natural objects that have the power of thus affecting [him]" (233). As Roderick realizes that his sister revived to find herself entombed and has begun to claw her way out, biological fact and gothic convention converge in a figure that is at once one man's truth and another's fiction. In that anamorphosis inserts some part or detail in a familiar object or scene that simply doesn't belong there, it will necessarily take on the flavor of a joke, which requires the viewer to rethink the classification system to which the object ordinarily belongs. In thus calling into question the difference between life and death, Poe's story forces the narrator to question the difference between the world of fact and that of fiction.

Convinced that he is the one with feet firmly planted on the ground, this narrator blames the fact that he and his former schoolmate have come to see the world through different eyes. Suspicious of what he regards as Usher's abnormal responses to his environment, the narrator looks to his friend's preferences in art and music to learn how Usher's imagination has distorted what is actually out there. As the narrator explains, these preferences "admitted me more unreservedly into the recesses of his spirit" than anything Usher could say outright (236). This claim takes us to the crux of anamorphosis, an art object in which two perspectives meet and call each other into question. Puzzled as to why his friend is so fascinated with a painting "of an immensely long and rectangular vault or tunnel with low walls, smooth, white, and without interruption or device," the narrator fails to recognize the features of the very crypt where he assisted Roderick in burying Madeline (237). Where Roderick sees the empty crypt, the narrator sees only a painting. That Roderick finds all music unbearable save that which observed "the narrow limits to which he thus confined himself upon the guitar" provides the narrator with evidence that his friend is abnormally sensitive to sound (237). For further confirmation that the source of Usher's intensifying anxiety is indeed located in his mind, the narrator seizes one of his lyrical improvisations as testimony to "full consciousness on the part of Usher of the tottering of his lofty reason upon her throne" (237). Inserted verbatim in his narrative, the narrator reads the "The Haunted Palace" as a metaphor for mayhem of its owner's inner life.

The poem might indeed yield to such an allegorical reading had Poe not also loaded his prose with evidence to the contrary. The narrator chooses this moment in his account not only to recall Madeline's burial in terms that echo his earlier description of the empty vault in Roderick's painting but also to acknowledge that he, too, hears "certain low and indefinite sounds which came, through the pauses of the storm, at long intervals," the very sounds that bedevil Roderick (241). Never mind that the details of Madeline's burial chamber match those in Roderick's painting. Never mind that her body when laid to rest displayed, as he put it, "the mockery of a faint blush upon the bosom and the face, and that suspiciously lingering smile upon the lips which is so terrible in death" (241). To hang onto common sense in the face of so much evidence is to hang onto a fiction, allowing the blot of illegibility to spread until it commands the entire framework of Poe's story.

In a last-ditch effort to distract himself from the now obvious sounds of Madeline's approach, the narrator decides to read aloud from the "Mad Trist," an ancient tale by Sir Launcelot Canning. The narrator attempts to escape into fiction only to find it coming true. As Sir Ethelred uses a mace to force his way through a door to a hermit's shed, according to the story, "'he so cracked, and ripped, and tore all asunder, that the noise of the dry and hollow-sounding wood alarmed and reverberated throughout the forest'" (243). As he reads this sentence, fact begins to converge with fiction: "it appeared to me," the narrator acknowledges, "that from some very remote portion of the mansion, there came, indistinctly to my ears, what might have been, in the exact similarity of character, the echo . . . of the very cracking and ripping sound which Sir Launcelot had so particularly described" (243). To stay within the protective bubble of fiction, he disavows the evidence once again: "It was . . . the coincidence alone [of literary description and sensory phenomena] which had arrested my attention . . . the sound, in itself, had nothing, surely, which should have disturbed me" (243). With Roderick's anguished cry, "*We have put her living in the tomb!*" the impossible event emerges from fiction and displaces the regime of common sense.

The Anamorphic Subject

To conclude this study of anamorphosis, we want to consider the vaunted ambiguity of Henry James's fiction as his way of calling into question the possibility of drawing a clear and discernible difference between the subject's private experience and his or her social milieu. On this possibility hinges the reader's ability to distinguish the affective event of the story from one that changes what can henceforth be considered possible, thus the difference between reading *The Turn of the Screw* as a gothic story and as a novella that expands the purview of realism. To regard James's "ghost story" as a narrative that depends, for the affect it generates, as much on anamorphosis as the narratives by Mitchell and Poe requires us to counter the critical tendency to see *The Turn of the Screw* as the record of a delusional narrator. We assume instead that James wanted to understand what would happen if he took this particular narrator, a governess, out of one locale and put her in another. How would someone in her position—as were many young women of modest education and little exposure to the world—experience the sudden shift in position from relative obscurity to authority over an understaffed British country estate home to two parentless children of the upper class? How would her radical dislocation not only expose the limits of the interpretive equipment she brought with her from one closed environment to another but also intensify her desire to grasp the situation? The gap between her means and the drive to succeed in her supervisory role produced the gap that the gentleman who reads the governess's account of her experience aloud characterizes as "another turn of the screw," or how the story accommodates two diametrically opposed views of her role in what is an unquestionably horrific event.

The Turn of the Screw keeps both views in play: either the ghosts of former caretakers are, as she says, influencing the children, or the evil spirits she alone can see are products of her own lack of worldly experience and the gothic novels she has obviously consumed. If one considers the ghosts of Bly's former caretakers a fact to reckon with, as the governess does, then she has saved the children from certain damnation, but if, on the other hand, we consider the ghosts a product of a libido aggravated by the loneliness of her situation and perhaps too much novel reading, then we are likely to assume that an overactive fantasy life prompted her to frighten to death the boy whom, for lack of parents, she was in charge of rearing. All there is in the way of evidence that the dead actually came back to life is a manuscript written by the governess well after the event. Given that she describes events on the basis of her recollection and includes no counterevidence, what has persuaded so many of James's readers that the account records the governess's descent into paranoid delusion?

Obviously unfamiliar with a polite discourse that resorts to ellipses rather than name an offense that couldn't be challenged if it did, the governess is quick to fill in those gaps with language that would make sense of the child's offense for a person of her class position and religious background. When the housekeeper inquires as to why the boarding school "declines" to take young Miles back after the holidays, the governess informs her that the school administrators "'go into no particulars. They simply express their regret that it should be impossible to keep him. They can have but one meaning'" (128–29). In the absence of any "particulars," the governess supplies the only reason she would consider worthy of expulsion: "'That he's an injury to others'" (129). Familiar with the boy himself, Mrs. Grose is reluctant to agree and does so in a way that throws the governess's suspicion of the school administrators back onto the governess. "'It's too dreadful,'" responds the loyal housekeeper, "'to say such cruel things'" (129). The struggle between their different ways of making sense of the same event sets the stage for James to challenge the British gothic much as Poe did in "The Fall of the House of Usher." This bit of dialogue ups the ante from "no particulars" to "cruel things."To counter the impression that the hypersensitive responses of the governess will overwhelm the common sense of Mrs. Grose or that common sense will fail to grasp the situation, James brings the reader into the community that hears the governess's manuscript read aloud, a group of urban elites gathered around a hearth at Christmas—so very English.

Having agreed to exchange stories that were "gruesome, as on Christmas Eve in an old house a strange tale should essentially be" (115), one of the company, when prodded, explains the kind of ghost story he is of a mind to tell the group. He does so in the same cryptic style as the governess's manuscript. "'It's beyond everything. Nothing at all that I know touches it,'" the narrator claims, in terms evacuated of content (116). This account provides nary an inkling as to why the governess who confronted what he describes only as "dreadful—dreadfulness" wrote an account of that experience—or why she entrusted it to the safekeeping of a gentleman named Douglas, much less why the narrator, after forty years of silence, has decided to read it at this particular social gathering. We are told only that before his death—"when it was then in sight"—Douglas committed to his care the very "manuscript that . . . with immense effect, [the narrator] began to read to our hushed little circle" (119). Like the governess and then Douglas, this narrator leaves it to readers to connect the dots.

Before the manuscript can arrive at the house where the group had assembled, the women grow impatient with the narrator's coyness about the story's source and genre. They jump to the conclusion that "love" is what links the governess to her gentleman employer in Harley Street; brings about the failure of her predecessor, Miss Jessel; ties the governess to her charges; and binds Douglas to her and the narrator of the frame tale, in turn, to Douglas. By filling in the blanks with this all-purpose emotional glue, the women in the group not only rule out the possibility that Douglas's story is a love story gone wrong but also make the mystery of what happened all the more intriguing. Recognizing that the generic expectations they bring to a conventional story will not make sense of this one, the women drift away; a select group of men remains. Like the skull in Holbein's painting, the object of horror in James's story becomes perceptible only when viewed from an oblique perspective. Such a story speaks chiefly to those curious about how life within a manor house appears from the perspective of a stranger.

We like to think that what F. O. Matthiessen wrote of James's American protagonists in Europe holds true of his governess as well: James endowed them all "with such vitality that they seem to take the plot in their own hands, or rather, to continue to live beyond its exigencies" (39). Indications in her account of a mind that indeed lives beyond the exigencies of plot have prompted generations of readers to fill in the blanks. Each attempt to corral the operations of the narrative perspective and confine it to the language will only dig a deeper hole in the text. James saw to that when he had the governess find herself in the same position as her readers. From the moment she asks, "Was there a 'secret' at Bly—a mystery of Udolpho or an insane, an unmentionable relative kept in unsuspected confinement?" (138)—one knows that James's narrator will be relying on the gothic novel to capture and control what she finds unspeakable. But although the governess draws on fiction to fill in the blanks in the notice of Miles's dismissal, does that mean the boy has not been dismissed for some "dreadful" offense? If we consider the lack of evidence to the contrary insufficient to support her claim that the ghosts of their former caretakers are real, then it follows that we cannot very well assume that the lack of evidence to the contrary provides a basis on which to argue that the ghosts are figures of the governess's unspeakable desires. Assuming the latter, the dominant strain of critical discourse has pursued a symptomatic reading resembling the procedures that Freud famously brought to bear on E. T. A. Hoffman's "The Sandman" in order to demonstrate the basis of literature's uncanny affect. James reverses these procedures.

Rather than send the sophisticated reader in search of more accurate terminology than "love" to name the desire that choreographs the narrator's account as a gothic tale, James has seen to it that another, more sophisticated reading of these missing connections will simply play out at a meta-level the game of connecting the dots that she plays. When she describes the intruder as being "like nobody," for example, the governess invites Mrs. Grose to give this enigmatic figure a local habitation and a name. And when Mrs. Grose echoes her claim with "Nobody" in the interrogative "Nobody?" the governess continues to materialize a male figure from the web of her own associations: "'He gives me a sort of sense of looking like an actor . . . I've never seen one, but so I suppose them. He's tall, active, erect. But never—no, never!—a gentleman.'" Thus, she provides details so vague as to cancel out a host of particularities, leaving only one possibility. As a result, Mrs. Grose responds with another question that the governess takes as confirmation of her suggestion that the man was not a gentlemen: "'A gentleman? . . . A gentleman *he?*'" (146–47). Given the small world to which her acquaintances have been restricted, is it any wonder that Mrs. Grose can think of no one else but the deceased valet, Peter Quint, when she hears that the man is not a gentleman? From this combination of the governess's reading and the limits of the housekeeper's local knowledge, a ghost is born.

A good number of the obstacles that readers have encountered in trying to determine what form of horror the governess confronts arise from the sympathy that seeps through from Douglas's obvious interest in her story to pervade her narrative. James's notebooks from that time find him feeling similarly out of his element as a writer in a European setting. As he put it, "The burden is necessarily greater for an American—for he *must* deal, more or less, even if only by implication, with Europe, whereas no European is obliged to deal in the least with America. No one ever dreams of calling him less complete for not doing so" (Matthiesen 2). The notice she receives from Miles's school reinforces the burden that the gentleman from Harley Street has thrust upon her. That what the school administrators say is true goes without saying, even if their authoritative view contradicts the housekeeper's glowing description of the boy's demeanor. Clearly feeling the limitations imposed on it by custom and communication, the governess quite deliberately exceeds those limitations by means of the only language she has at hand in order to explain events beyond the reach of ordinary language. In revealing the limitations of her literacy, the governess's gothic figuration of her habitat objectifies what are the normally imperceptible points at which the manor house conjoins larger networks of empire (via the parents of Miles and Flora), the city (via their uncle in Harley Street), the supply of itinerate governesses, and the impoverished world from which servants and governesses come to work at the homes of wealthy people and then return to die. Seeing the house and inhabitants at Bly from the peripheral perspective of a provincial woman of no income with a religious upbringing and an imagination fed by novels, James's governess belongs among those protagonists whose very lack of personal life frees them to explore voyeuristically a world in which they'll never be at home.

Whenever the governess reflects on her use of gothic figures, as she does frequently, she dramatizes the operations of a very different form of consciousness than the psychoanalytic subject that was being formulated at that time in Europe: "[Mrs. Grose] had told me, bit by bit, under pressure, a great deal; but a small shifty spot on the wrong side of it all still sometimes brushed my brow like the wing of a bat" (162). Here, her brushstroke of "the wing of a bat" suggests that whenever gothic conventions supply a missing link in relationships at Bly, they inevitably expose another spot of unintelligibility in the carpet—as she puts it, a "small shifty spot on the wrong side of it all" (162). In that the sense of its own limitation is ultimately what prompts the narrator to push ahead, she is not all that different from other James's protagonists and perhaps from James himself, according to Matthiessen. For, like the governess, they also find it impossible to draw a clear line between what they sense and how they understand themselves in the eyes of others. In *The Turn of the Screw*, the narrator thinks her way across a field of sensory information, and what she feels can never be the same as what she formulates in words.

It was Henry's brother William James who developed the concept of "stream of consciousness" to describe the individual self in much the same way—as a process that simultaneously responds to the sensory information it encounters and rushes on before it can capture that sense of its encounter with phenomena linguistically (244). Having explained his intervention in what were then the most influential theories of human consciousness, William James compares the individual consciousness to "a bird's life" consisting of an alternation of flights, or "transitive parts," and perchings, or "substantive parts" (243). As a result, he claims, "The main end of our thinking is at all times the attainment of some other substantive part than the one from which we have just been dislodged" (250).

William James considered the images one glimpses of the operations of his or her own mind not as stable psychic facts but as "transitions, always on the wing, so to speak, and not to be glimpsed except in flight" (253). Recalling brother Henry's figure for such glimpses as "a shifty spot" that "sometimes brushed" one's "brow like the wing of a bat," we might see the purely descriptive theory of human thought that Henry tried out in *The Turn of the Screw* as closer, in strictly formal terms, than either Freud's buried self or George Henry Lewes's embodied polycentric nervous system to William's notion of how consciousness behaves.[10] For purposes of this study of early American fiction, we are especially interested in William's description, in his opus magus, *The Principles of Psychology*, of consciousness as a narrative of "rivalry and conflict of one's different selves." William sees these various selves—empirical, spiritual, emotional, and social—as scattered bits of consciousness that nevertheless cooperate "as a community" to overcome breaks in any one mode of perception. "To regard itself" as a coherent whole, consciousness "can [therefore] consider itself continuous with certain chosen portions of the self" (239).[11] Against this background, it should not come as a surprise that, in promoting "the later James," Matthiessen drew our attention to the many ways in which William's theory of human personality as a stream of consciousness corresponded to the organization of his brother's major novels.[12] Matthiessen's claim that Henry's was precisely the form of subjectivity that his brother William theorized was an argument that could fully realize itself, as Matthiessen admits, not in the novelist's own experience but in certain of the American protagonists whom he transported to Europe. And of all these, perhaps only the perspective of Lambert Strether affords the perfect conjunction of these incompatible perspectives.

If readers remember anything in particular about *The Ambassadors*, it is bound to be the moment where a single image exposes Strether to the social connections that define the fashionable life of Paris as just that. Matthiessen describes the moment when the veil is torn away and the American sees Paris from both perspectives as an anamorphic scene much like a painting: "In the late afternoon, as [Strether] sits at a village café overlooking a reach of the river, his landscape takes on further interest. It becomes a Landscape with Figures, as a boat appears around the bend, a man rowing, a lady with a pink parasol. There, in an instance, was 'the lies in the charming affair.' The skill with which James has held our eyes within his frame has so heightened the significance of every slight detail that such a recognition scene leaps out with the force of the strongest drama" (36). Despite his admiration for James's artistry, the difference in their respective political orientations forced Matthiessen to acknowledge the exclusionary principle of the moves that enabled the novelist to achieve fuller self-realization within an aesthetic framework: "James was not ignorant of what he called 'the huge collective life' going on beyond his charmed circle" but acknowledged "the vast suffering that Paris has suffered . . . in black shadows looming only at the very edge of [his] paintings" (35). This, as Matthiessen suggests throughout his study of what he considered James's "major phase," is where the material of an aesthetic object comes from and into which it is inevitably dispersed. As we said, it does not surprise us that Matthiessen discovers William James's theory of consciousness as the formal principle of Henry James's late novels. What is certainly more unpredictable, though, is the interchangeability of the formal moves producing this model of consciousness and most if not all of the tropes we have culled from American novels written more than a century earlier.

In that these tropes stage events that transform what can be considered real, any perspective to which they grant authority to determine what is real will soon be considered fiction from another point of view. Linked by the principle of anamorphosis, a sequence of descriptions of a society from different positions within that society apparently met that society's complex demands for self-knowledge. As one moves across the historical boundary marked by the establishment of an American literary tradition, however, this continuous network appears to break apart. Rather than forge connections among a multiplicity of incompatible perspectives, the emergence of anamorphic objects in the late novels of Henry James produces a tear or hole in the pattern on the carpet into which narration, or the principle that drives a plot to connect the dots, seems to disappear. James obviously crafted the ghosts in his gothic tale, *The Turn of the Screw*, to disrupt the social network organizing both its setting and the frame tale, subjecting the protagonist and thus her readers to a prisoner's dilemma game, which prevents them, in contrast to the community in *The Asylum*, from pooling information. Establishing an open network of communication in Mitchell's story not only conjoins incompatible class and geographic perspectives in a horizontal network but also installs controls. The governess's story demonstrates, if nothing else, that for lack of information, sharing the network of which the small world is necessarily a part will nevertheless assert a spectral presence within that world. Rather than inner demons, then, we understand the ghosts that appear in the American gothic as the reappearance within a closed community of the weak ties on which it depends for survival in a much larger world.[13]

Chapter 9

Becoming National Literature

Each of the previous five chapters has pursued a different trope from its formulation in the novels of the early republic across the historical line when certain novelists began to write what we still consider great American novels. In doing so, we have repeatedly begged the question: what makes the difference between early American novels that today's scholars read primarily for their historical value and the novels that we consider literary works? Troubled by the politics of Henry James's aestheticism, F. O. Matthiesson's ambivalence toward the very novelist he reclaimed for an American tradition put the question of literary form front and center. By inspiring Matthiessen's ambivalence, Henry James's self-consciously literary style raises what is perhaps a more basic question. We have shown how early American novelists took issue with their British counterparts—in diversely ingenious ways—by mobilizing what we have called democratic writing against the tropes that lay claim to writing as the property of a novelist. In what respect did these early novelists consequently fall short of the literary standard set by later American novelists? The notably high rate of literacy in the early years of the new republic, coupled with the number of printing presses and the quantity of novels published, reprinted, and redacted, unquestionably provided the conditions for exactly the phenomenon that Jacques Ranciére describes as writing "in which the writer is anyone at all and the reader anyone at all" (12). This coincidence made it seem more than reasonable for us to determine if the formal means by which authors and readers began to distinguish literary writing from common literacy were adopted by American novelists as they were in nineteenth-century France. Can this way of thinking about the rise of national literature tell us why—despite all the novels written during the early decades of the United States—literary history has yet to acknowledge a major novelist prior to James Fenimore Cooper?[1]

Rancière identifies democratic writing as the necessary precondition for literary writing in the modern sense of the term, but democratic writing, in his analysis, also hobbled authors with literary ambitions. Writing literature presupposed a readership that could both read and write in the vernacular style common to the narrators of so many of the novels we have discussed. In that democratic writing draws no "boundary between the language of art and that of ordinary life" (13), it was implicitly hostile to any attempt to remove a work from the field of writing and claim it as one's own. To issue from anyone to anyone else within the social field, an author would have to tell himself or herself that "any person standing in my shoes would have to see it my way." Such writing doesn't issue from the person of a writer, then, so much as from the position he or she happens to occupy. By drawing a boundary between the text and the world, literary writing counters the threat that one author could easily be replaced by another. To this end, literary writing establishes a relationship between words and the world specific to a particular piece of writing. It distributes the capacity to read while reserving for itself the capacity to write literature. Much like a story by Poe or James, literature inserts an oblique perspective within the field of vernacular writing that produces a spot of unintelligibility where that field would otherwise appear entirely knowable from one authoritative perspective. Such a change constitutes a change not only in what is perceptible and to whom but also in the community in which novel readers imagine taking part.

We have argued that the novelists of the early national period distinguished themselves from their late eighteenth-century British counterparts by writing in the voice of anyone to anyone. We believe that doing so was the secret of their success in creating links between what were then scattered regional and local readerships. How did the classics of nineteenth-century American fiction hope to distance themselves from this style of writing and still address what James Fenimore Cooper described as "a collection of local communities"? The situation called upon the novelist to portray the nation, in his words, "as a multitude of peculiarities" ("Review" 336). Our readings of Poe, Hawthorne, Melville, Stowe, and James suggest that these writers performed their own signature variations on the very narrative tropes by which their early American predecessors made sense of life in the new United States.

At the same time, as we will argue here, an author like Cooper buried that past and with it the possibility of forming an open network of horizontal affiliations. He did so by means of what Benedict Anderson calls "the biography of nations," a genealogical form designed to suppress the anamorphic linkages that characterize the novels of the early period (*Imagined Communities* 205). Written from the perspective of the present, such an origin story "snatches, against the going mortality rate, exemplary suicides, poignant martyrdoms, assassinations, executions, wars, and holocausts." But, Anderson continues, "to serve the narrative purpose, these violent deaths must be remembered/ forgotten as 'our own'" (*Imagined Communities* 206). As they established the protocols of a distributed network, the first American novels told a different story. Over the course of the nineteenth century, we want to suggest, the great American masterpieces used these tropes to clean house of those horizontal affiliations that violated its boundaries and disfigured the literary lineage that endowed a national community with an identity that can endure over time. The critical tradition that we have traced back to E. M. Forster continues to reinforce this tradition by selecting for educational purposes novels that reproduce this origin story. If, as we have tried to show throughout the past five chapters, the formal moves, tropes, aspects, or protocols developed by the first American novelists continued to do their work in the later novels granted literary status, why have the novels of the early republic all but vanished from the *literary* record? Rather than acknowledge the considerable body of fiction produced during the early republic, literary historians by and large persist in locating the source of our major literature in Puritan New England or American folklore, if not in English and Continental literature—anywhere, it seems, but in the democratic writing on which the literary masterpieces of the nineteenth century arguably depended. We could blame it on the canonizers, as we may appear to do in the case of Leslie Fiedler, who ignores, after all, the ways in which Hawthorne's split resolution of *The Scarlet Letter* acknowledges earlier network novels.

Contrary to literary criticism's habit of casting blame on previous generations of literary criticism for minoritizing certain bodies of American fiction, we shall use one extended example to show how the nineteenth-century novelists whom we consider unquestionably major themselves disavowed their dependency as novelists on the novels of the early republic. Insofar as they found it necessary to distance themselves from democratic writing in order to imagine the nation as a community, however, all major American novelists paradoxically acknowledge their dependence on their early predecessors. They acknowledge this debt, as our previous chapters have argued, by appropriating the narrative tropes of the novels of the early republic for a literary style that is indelibly American. To make this final point, we want to return to the moment when the novel arguably first split off from democratic writing and laid down rules for becoming literature with a brutal clarity that has nevertheless eluded literary criticism authorized by those very readers.

The Literary Origins of the American Novel

By the time he published *The Last of the Mohicans* in 1826, James Fenimore Cooper had already earned a place alongside Washington Irving and William Cullen Bryant as one of the United States' foremost writers and its premier novelist. But while the readership gobbled up Cooper's Indian tale, the critics were sharply divided as to whether *The Last of the Mohicans* displayed the author's mature artistry or pandered to popular taste.[2] We examine how Cooper used indigenous material to persuade his countrymen, diverse and scattered as they were, to think of the former British colonies of North America as their homeland. Hence our question: what was it about this material that made it possible for people who came from elsewhere to imagine they came from North America?[3]

The French and Indian War lasted from 1754 to 1763 and multiplied Britain's national debt to a degree that the victors found it necessary to seek relief by taxing the colonists.[4] The conflict that resulted is no doubt the reason Cooper chose this war as the historical setting for his story of national origins. Any number of historical accounts Cooper might have consulted would surely have repeated the imperialist rhetoric in which supporters of the Stamp Act heralded its passage by Parliament in 1765. David Ramsay's popular account is among those that reported Charles Townshend, Chancellor of the Exchequer, to have argued, "And now will these Americans, children planted by our care, nourished up by our indulgence, till they are grown to a degree of strength and opulence, and protected by our arms, will they grudge to contribute their mite to relieve us from the heavy weight of that burden which we lie under" (Ramsay I:57).

Seizing on the figure of implantation, a dedicated opponent of the Stamp Act, Isaac Barré, famously offered this rebuttal in Parliament:

They planted by your care? No, your oppressions planted them in America. They fled from tyranny to a then uncultivated and inhospitable country, where they exposed themselves to almost all the hardships to which human nature is liable; and among others to the cruelty of a savage foe the most subtle, and I will take upon me to say, the most formidable of any people upon the face of God's earth; and yet, actuated by principles of true English liberty, they met all hardships with pleasure compared with those they suffered in their own country, from the hands of those that should have been their friends. (Ramsay I:57)

Writing a half century after the War of Independence, Cooper launched a similar though certainly more subtle attack on the narrative that had the British "implanting" their own people in North America, as if that would make Great Britain the parents and cultivators of what would otherwise be a barren land. What is more, Cooper drew on the same quasi-mythological narrative as Barré to kick-start a retrospective account of nationhood in which the indigenous American made the crucial difference between Great Britain's claim to govern the colonies and the colonists' assertion of independence. Given that Native Americans weighed in on both sides of the battle between the French and the British, and in view of the fact that the former lost most of their territory in the process, we want to consider how the Native American presence—and not that of the British—was responsible for the fabled maturation of these children of the British empire into subjects capable of self-government. To do so, we look closely at the technical means by which Cooper heralds the transformation of British settlers into Americans.

By situating *The Last of the Mohicans* during the French and Indian War that would eventually determine which European nation claimed sovereignty over much of North America, Cooper turned the contested territory into a space over which sovereignty had been temporarily suspended. He used this space to imagine the United States starting over from scratch, starting, that is, as a heterogeneous assortment of stateless people whose political future was still up in the air. In that moment of indeterminacy, the British encounter with Native Americans reformulated the question of which European power would prevail as a question of what happened as the British colonists acquired mastery of the land on which they had settled.[5] Would this bedraggled group of Europeans reconstitute itself as an extension of Great Britain to the exclusion of other groups similarly struggling to make a home in North America? Or would the new community come to understand itself in relation to those groups with whom it negotiated and against whom it struggled to domesticate colonial territory? Would they, in other words, constitute an alternative community, an exception to the European rule, where the diverse and often hostile peoples of North America might coexist?[6] In practical terms, the colonial situation posed the novelist with the problem of how to formulate a community that was not only British in character but also open to affiliation with many other groups.

That Cooper addressed this seeming contradiction by forecasting marriage between two sentimental characters of British origin is a resolution that has long disappointed Cooper's critics.[7] In this respect, Cooper could not do for the United States what Sir Walter Scott did for England and still establish an American tradition of the novel. But where the English could intermarry with the Scots and cement their claim to Britishness, they could not both do so and include Native Americans. Under those circumstances, the American community would have no claims to Britishness. On the other hand, those critics who simply disapproved of Cooper for excluding Native Americans, along with those of African descent, from his imagined community put themselves in the same position as the early readers of the novel. Some felt relieved when it was clear that Chingachgook's son could not perpetuate the Mohican line through the daughter of a British officer; others expressed disappointment that the possibility of marriage between a colonial woman and a noble savage failed to materialize. Either way, the critic has fallen into Cooper's trap. Like his early reviewers, the contemporary reader will fail to consider what Cooper accomplished by opening up the possibility of a national community based on the principle of interracial romance only in the end to shut it down. We plan to show how this disavowal provided him with a means other than the marriage plot to start up a community and a way other than biological reproduction to ensure the community's future. When we say "way other then biological reproduction," we don't mean to suggest that Cooper came up with an especially progressive alternative, much less a practical one. To the contrary, his alternative was an imagined community that couldn't materialize within the novel, much less in political society, save at an aesthetic remove from daily life. It is nevertheless a fantasy that, for better or worse, Americans have been living with ever since.

It is hardly a secret that the British saw the territory occupied by a less populous and weaker French presence and a variety of Indian clans and tribes as contested territory, and British administrators came up with various strategies for making those inhabitants disappear.[8] Although Cooper can and has been charged with doing much the same thing in his novels, he nevertheless made a point of having his protagonists befriend and learn from Native Americans, who consequently played a decisive role in the war that he chose as the background for his account of the origins of American nationhood. We will insist that his Indian material did so much more than that. As we see it, Cooper used the Indian material for which he is both praised and criticized to carry on a war between two romance traditions. This aesthetic conflict provided the novelist with the terms he needed to organize the debris of warring cultural traditions as a system of relationships that would allow the stateless populations of North America to coexist.

To make this case, we look first to the opening paragraph of *The Last of the Mohicans*, where Cooper maps out the historical materials he will use to wage a literary war within a political war. We turn then to two major digressions Cooper's narrative takes through romance scenarios that openly translate the war for imperial domination into a war for the habitus—a struggle to determine which values, dispositions, and expectations will allow people to imagine living with one another on a daily basis. In the conflict between romance traditions, Cooper used the Native American as a wedge between "the family" and "the community," so that he did not have to imagine the latter in terms of the former. He let "the family" hew to a principle of kinship that maintains consanguinity, while another model of "the community" promotes interracial relations. For Cooper, this move was key to ruling out the possibility of a hybrid lineage while still insisting on the difference between his foundational narrative of national origins and a European romance tradition that sought to broaden the definition of consanguinity to include indigenous peoples.[9] To negotiate what was for the English a notoriously impassible gulf between races, Cooper translated these divergent notions of family and community into alternative literary traditions, pitting the diversity of colonial romance against the exclusivity of Scott's national romances.

In doing so, Cooper developed what would become his signature style of ethnographic description, which would establish resemblances across otherwise proscriptive cultural divides. By opening up this purely aesthetic territory within a world organized around fiercely fought sociopolitical oppositions, Cooper produced a form of imagined community that included hostile groups without obscuring their ethnic and racial differences. He proposed this community as the basis on which any one element of that community—including the British—could maintain exclusionary kinship practices. While forbidding interracial marriage, in other words, the new community made consanguinity an option rather than a requirement for belonging. This is American pluralism. As Ellen Rooney explains, the foundational exclusion that establishes literary critical discourse in the United States is the exclusion of exclusion: "no discourse that takes the process of exclusion to be necessary to the production . . . of community . . . can function within pluralism" (5). This chapter will suggest that the principle of literary pluralism, as she describes it, also provided what Rancière calls the "rules of appropriateness" by means of which the "major" or "great" nineteenth-century American novels distinguished themselves from democratic writing. The novels that now belong to our national literature invite, if not require, what Rooney characterizes as a pluralistic reading.

Native Though British

To appreciate just how carefully Cooper mapped out his strategy for turning the French and Indian War into a literary narrative of national origins, one need look no further than the novel's opening paragraph:

> It was a feature peculiar to the colonial wars of North America, that the toils and dangers of the wilderness were to be encountered before the adverse hosts could meet. A wide and apparently an impervious boundary of forests severed the possessions of the hostile provinces of France and England. The hardy colonist, and the trained European who fought at his side, frequently expended months in struggling against the rapids of the streams, or in effecting the rugged passes of the mountains, in quest of an opportunity to exhibit their courage in a more martial conflict. But, emulating the patience and self-denial of the practiced native warriors, they learned to overcome every difficulty; and it would seem that, in time, there was no recess of the woods so dark, nor any secret place so lovely, that it might claim exemption from the inroads of those who had pledged their blood to satiate their vengeance, or to uphold the cold and selfish policy of the distant monarchs of Europe. (11)

In no more than four sentences, Cooper has reframed the story that the first sentences indicate the novel is about to tell with an entirely different pair of antinomies. The last clause of the first paragraph anticipates the formation of a community that is British American rather than English by contrasting the struggle of British Americans against the wilderness to the "the cold and selfish policy of the distant monarchs of Europe." Between the first and last sentences of this paragraph are the two statements of greatest concern to our argument. In them, Cooper lays out the semiotic negotiations that he will use to transform the history of empire into the story of a pluralistic community.

To have his British Americans throw off British tyranny, Cooper had to find a way to maintain the Britishness of those who anticipated the future citizens of the United States. To do so, he softened the terms of what appears to be an intransigent political contradiction between Britain and the colonies in a first sentence that neglects to name the British as one of the chief combatants of the "colonial wars." Cooper repeated this omission in the last clause of the last sentence by neglecting to name King George as one of "the distant monarchs of Europe." This double omission makes it possible for him to set the experience of the British colonial subjects who insist on their independence in opposition to European sovereignty and not to their British homeland that proved no less autocratic than France. To go by the three sentences leading up to the final clause of the novel's first paragraph, one gathers that Cooper will establish relations of some sort between the colonists and Native Americans that will distinguish the British colonists as truly American.

The statements that suggest how the novel will accomplish this are as vague as they are efficient. The second and third sentences of the paragraph recast the opposition between England and France as a struggle by European colonizers against the American wilderness, which Cooper portrays as "a wide and apparently impervious boundary of forests separating the possessions of the hostile provinces of France and England." The phrasing of the second sentence makes it impossible to decide if Cooper means to say that the wilderness actually severed the possessions of the hostile provinces of England from those of France or whether he is saying that the wilderness cut off the colonies from their European rulers. By setting the Europeans against the American wilderness, the second sentence succeeds in muddying the opposition between warring European nations, thereby opening the way for a quite different argument to develop within his account of a war between the British and the French.

This other opposition begins inauspiciously enough for the colonist as the second sentence formulates the winning combination of American brawn and British brains or, in Cooper's terms, "the hardy colonist and the trained European who fought at his side." He proposes this combination so that the third sentence can diminish the difference between the agents of the British government and colonial subjects, and the fourth sentence then insinuates a different and more definitive contrast. As the third sentence explains, the combined British forces "expended months in struggling against the rapids of the streams, or in effecting the rugged passes of the mountains, in quest of an opportunity to exhibit their courage in a more martial conflict." Their victory ultimately depended less on their courage and skill in "mortal combat" than on what they learned from the struggle itself, which they endured by "emulating the patience and self-denial of the practiced native warriors." This first clause of the paragraph's fourth sentence identifies an acquired "native" quality as the magical supplement that gave the colonists tactical mastery over the American wilderness. By means of this gift from the Indian to the British American, Cooper could do within four sentences what no novelist before him had done—namely, endow the colonists with a character that was still British and yet uniquely American.

Still, something keeps him from turning an account of the French and Indian War into the story of national emergence. Cooper all but names it in the second clause of the last sentence when he indicates that the wilderness is treacherous and unavailable for domestication. The land on which the nation is to be founded must be virgin territory rather than land that is already occupied. Otherwise, it cannot provide the basis on which to establish a home and, by implication, a homeland. Unless that land can be redefined as what John Locke considered "waste," meaning land available to be converted into property, the future community is still a colony established by an act of seizure rather than a nation established by means of cultivation and acculturation.[10] As this second sentence describes the long struggle of the British military through "rapids" and "rugged passes," the land indeed seems resistant to domestication. But once they have acquired the self-denial and patience of "practiced native warriors," qualities necessary to overcoming these natural obstacles, the landscape suddenly takes on a feminine character that presents a greater threat than mortal combat. The fourth sentence takes us onto a terrain colored by the possibility of interracial romance: "there was no recess of the woods so dark, nor any secret place so lovely, that it might claim exemption from the inroads of those who had pledged their blood to satiate their vengeance, or to uphold the cold and selfish policies of the distant monarchs of Europe." Who is tucked away in those recesses and secret places, the Indian or the colonist? In taking on the patience and self-denial of the good Indian, the colonist cannot go native, which would be to behave like the bad, or "vengeful," Indian now lumped together with European sovereignty.

Here is the source of deliberate confusion: the Native American plays both parts; he is not only the treacherous savage who must be driven from the land but also the noble savage whose example teaches the colonists how to wage war and survive in the wilderness. Here, we contend, literary writing goes to work and takes European romance across the line separating it from colonial romance, as Cooper transfers the salient traits of the Native American to the consequently ennobled colonists. This allows him to drag that romance tradition back across the line and lump Native Americans together with the French as if the Indians, too, "uphold the cold and selfish policy of the distant monarchs of Europe." Cooper completes this chiasmus by means of the syntactically tortured fourth sentence that presents the British invasion and seizure of Indian territory as a fairytale rescue of the maiden whose release from captivity enables cultivation of the wasteland. This one final sentence not only steals the Native American's claim to being the first man, or autochthon, but also assigns that identity to the colonist in order to make him the original American. Having done the work of connecting the colonists to the land and separating them from the homeland, this figure of the Indian as mediator disappears.[11]

Although we catch but a glimpse of this double move in the last sentence of the first paragraph, the question remains as to what coupling and uncoupling all these incompatible elements do for the story Cooper is about to tell. The fourth and final sentence of the paragraph makes it rather clear how the novel will use Indian material to produce a habitus that is neither British nor American but the mutually transformative combination of the two characteristic of what Doris Sommer has called "foundational fictions." Although, as Sommer notes, Cooper's story of national origins differs sharply from the pre-Boom Latin American novels that she calls to our attention, it's worthwhile to stress what *The Last of the Mohicans* nevertheless has in common with these novels: the possibility of using an interracial marriage to imagine a community that is both elevated above the old tribal societies and distinct from European sovereignty. The next two sections of this chapter show what Cooper accomplished by raising the possibility of a hybrid or mestizo nation in so many different ways—if all along he intended to eliminate it. We conclude by suggesting how he brought certain rules of literary writing to bear on the democratic writing characteristic of his American predecessors.

Limiting Kinship

Cooper does not begin in earnest to assemble the basis for imagining an alternative community until Chapter 16, when Duncan Heyward, a major from the American South serving in the British army, asks his superior officer for the hand of his daughter in marriage. Can the utterly conventional nature of this request be the reason why Colonel Munro momentarily balks? His response is clearly designed to make us ask why indeed Heyward preferred the insipid Alice, Munro's younger daughter, to Cora, his eldest. Not having heard the story of Munro's two daughters, we have no basis on which to understand his reaction and are left to wonder how Cooper expected to launch a halfway convincing future for a national community from such traditional British stock. That the girls' father himself expresses his astonishment at Heyward's choice of Alice and responds "with a lip that quivered violently" (158) underscores what we already know to be the case: Cora is the more interesting of the two girls and definitely the sister cut from a cloth more befitting an American heroine. To explain "the extraordinary effect produced by a communication which, as it now appeared, was so unexpected" as Heyward's preference for Alice over Cora, Munro offers the contrasting histories of his daughters (158). We take the fact that Heyward must choose one of these women as the partner with whom to form what the novel sees as the precursor of an American family as a clear indication that Cooper was working with two different stories of national origin: one drawn from British romance, and one from colonial romance for which Chateaubriand would be the obvious model.[12]

Though born of a noble Scottish family, Colonel Munro's father lacked the holdings in property to broker a marriage between his son and Alice, his son's first love. In his conversation with young Heyward, the Colonel recalls how his disappointment in love not only prompted him to leave Scotland but also, by making him an officer in the British army stationed in the Caribbean, threw him into the company of women of African descent who "were so basely enslaved to the wants of a luxurious people" (159). His first wife, Cora's mother, is among the offspring of the relationship of colonial occupiers to the people they have colonized and the presumed source of the "native" intelligence that Cora shares with Cooper's good Native Americans. This positions Cora as the progenetrix of a people that synthesizes the diverse populations of North America.

Chapter 16 opens onto a scene with Alice perched on her father's knee, playing with his hair and "pressing her ruby lips fondly on his wrinkled brow" (156). Cora, by contrast, sits in the background, "a calm and amused looker-on; regarding the wayward movements of her more youthful sister, with that species of maternal fondness, which characterized her love for Alice"

(156). Well before the only eligible British male in the novel asks for Alice's hand, this picture has situated Munro's first daughter, Cora, as the figurative mother of Alice, saved by the fact of sisterhood from the incestuous implications of such a role. That picture has also transformed Alice's seductive ministrations into the playfulness of an enchanting child. This family idyll simultaneously opens up and closes down the sordid legacy of the Colonel's colonial love affair and its hybrid offspring, Cora, before that story could be told. But the reader is soon to learn that if Cora were to wed Heyward, their marriage would mix African blood with those descending from her father's British lineage and so appear to legitimate hybridization as the means of transforming those of African as well as Indian descent into Americans. Knowing that Heyward "presumes to the honour of being [the Colonel's] son" (157), we also know that having him marry Cora would simply reproduce the story of the Colonel's colonial romance as the difference between American and British origin stories.

The logic of this double—inclusionary-exclusionary—move consequently shapes the entire memory sequence that unfolds in Chapter 16. Munro has a tendency to mention slavery only to drop it, as he does in his account of marriage to Cora's mother. Similarly, he admits that he expects Heyward to prefer Cora and then proceeds to provide a genealogy likely to confirm this suitor in his choice of Alice. These references to Munro's history in the British colonial army link his family's history to the political history of the conquest of North America. In doing so, however, they destroy that link and separate romance from history. In other words, to include the descendant of a slave in the lineage of its proto-national family would be to contradict the claim implicit in the last sentence of the novel's opening paragraph—that America was unsullied by ownership and available for appropriation, unsullied, that is, by the legacy of colonial violence and slavery that Cora's genealogy recalls. By having Heyward opt for Cora's sister, Cooper opts for another genealogy through which America would fulfill the romance tradition that Munro compromised by marrying a creole woman.

By an interesting twist of narrative logic, Munro's second wife would have been his first had not economic circumstances prevented their union, forcing him to enlist in the British army, which sent him to the Caribbean, where he rose to the rank of lieutenant colonel. It is through Munro's recollection of Alice, the mother of his younger daughter Alice, that we learn that Cora, his elder daughter, was the product of a marriage that disrupted what might have been a classical romance. His first love is one of those ideal women who can remain celibate for twenty-five years until her first and only suitor can return from the colonies a wealthy man and claim her hand in marriage. In thus enduring what appears to be a permanent suspension of the marriage plot, the story of Munro's love for Alice operates within the chronotope of classical romance.[13] Moreover, this romance frames and presumably then contains the colonial romance that had produced the hybrid Cora, a romance that must run its course before Munro can return from the colonies and marry Alice. Insofar as each love affair presupposes and would provide the reproductive mechanism of an entirely different social body—one that remains true to its European origins, the other that records the history of colonial exploitation— the two narratives are incompatible and must occupy different temporal spaces. Nested as they both are within a colonial setting, the aesthetic weight is all on Cora's story.

The novel's pretense that Heyward might well have chosen Cora and that Munro fully expected him to do so seems to put exogamy, or marriage between groups, on an even playing field with endogamy, or marriage within the same group. When Heyward's choice of Alice seems to throw the novel's weight over to the side of endogamy, the Colonel responds with indignation, "You scorn to mingle the blood of the Heywards, with one so degraded—lovely and virtuous enough though she be?" (159). The question to ask at this point is whether Cooper has Munro oppose "blood" to "virtue" and level the charge of racism at Alice's suitor in order to invalidate that charge. Heyward springs the trap set in the chapter's opening scene by admitting that Alice is the irrational choice: "The sweetness, the beauty, the witchery of your youngest daughter, Colonel Munro, might explain my motives, without imposing on me this injustice" (159). Racism, it appears, has nothing to do with his preference for Alice. Curious, is it not, that Cooper defends the British American male, as well as the novel that produces him, against this charge by temporarily endowing the sentimental woman with the power of native "witchery"?

Those who cannot appreciate the extravagant lengths to which the novel must go in order to ensure the purely Scottish heritage of the new American couple should remember that Cooper was writing with keen awareness of the prevailing one-drop rule—which the mention of blood and the possibility of mixing it would surely have been on his readers' minds.[14] Lest we fail to credit him with understanding how endogamous the Heyward-Alice relationship actually is, Cooper made sure that readers understood its limitations not only by occasional nods to the novels of Sir Walter Scott but also by the mother-daughter duo named Alice, each of whom had features of the traditional

British heroine. Despite his insistence that the next generation had to reproduce the European original, Cooper gave Cora more than equal time with
Alice, as well as a much more interesting story. This was necessary for purposes of turning the political conflict between the British and the French into
cultural antinomies that distinguished the future Americans from the "distant
monarchs of Europe," as promised in the final clause of the opening
paragraph.

Her father's recollection of Cora's birth precedes his account of Alice's
birth and constitutes a disruption of British culture as it moves from one side
of the Atlantic to the other, so that before they can make a home in North
America, the colonists will have to struggle against the indigenous people, on
the one hand, and against the British, on the other. But is this really enough
to explain why Cora decisively upstages her half-sister throughout the novel?
By cutting short her participation in the family that will form at some point
in the future, Cooper raises the question of what she—and, through her, the
possibility of colonial romance—is doing there at all. To explain what he
gained by giving Cora so prominent a role in the historical process that will
exclude her, we must turn back to Chapters 11 and 12.

Expansive Family Resemblances

These chapters take place at what was for the British forces the nadir of the
Seven Years' War: the fall of the British Fort William Henry. In keeping with
European practice, the French negotiated a settlement that permitted the
British to leave the captured fort unmolested and make their way to the near-
est British settlement. Largely through incompetence, however, the French
did not force their Native American allies, eager for the booty of victory, to
observe the same rules, and a substantial number of settlers were massacred.
Brought to the fort to join up with other members of the family, daughters
Cora and Alice are caught in this exodus, captured by hostile Indians, and
separated, along with Duncan Heyward, from the group of British refugees
escorted through the wilderness by Hawk-eye and Chingachgook. To take
advantage of this inauspicious moment in colonial history, Cooper drew on
the American captivity narrative to fashion a heroine who could transform
warring traditions of romance into an American origin story.

Confronting a dilemma resembling the one that generates the origin
myth in Claude Lévi-Strauss's analysis of the Oedipus story, Cooper poses

virtually the same question as the anthropologist: is the protagonist attached to the land and native people of America, or is he or she the means of extending a British lineage? As early as the controversy over the Stamp Act, the question of the national narrative to which the colonists belonged had been similarly posed in terms of an opposition between nature and culture. To Charles Townshend's claim that the British had "implanted" their people in North America, Isaac Barré, ardent opponent of the Stamp Act, argued that the colonists had survived on the resources gleaned from the harsh environment where they had, by dint of their natural vigor, taken root.

Cooper's opening paragraph makes the same claim when it declares that the colonists acquired the "patience and self-denial" of the native and became another people as they tamed the American wilderness. In Chapters 11 and 12, the novel performs this crucial step in Cooper's origin story. Here, he exploits the conventional turning point in Indian captivity narratives to consider if Cora will "go native" or maintain her purity and die.[15] Rather than ending in either death or defilement, however, this episode at once rules out interracial romance and indigenizes both heroines of the novel, though in quite different ways. Let us consider what characteristics Cooper strips away from Munro's daughters by putting both his heroines through the trial of captivity and which attributes, as a result, they gain.

Up to the moment when Magua forces Cora to agree to become his squaw or die, she is more than his verbal match. Once Munro's "undaunted daughter" has decisively rebutted Magua's claim that her capture is fitting retribution for the lashing he received from her father, it must come as a surprise, to say the least, to see her suddenly grow passive just as Magua seems intent on carrying out his threat to slaughter not only Cora but Alice and Heyward as well. Indeed, she defers this crucial narrative decision to Heyward and Alice, as if she knows full well that they, being only too conventional, will refuse to consider interracial marriage an option. By putting her fate in the hands of Alice, in other words, Cora as much as chooses death over defilement. By proxy, this decision removes Cora from her mother's narrative tradition so that Munro can proclaim her still "lovely and virtuous" in Chapter 16 and the more eligible of his daughters for Heyward's hand.

Alice, by contrast, remains absolutely true to character, which intensifies exponentially as a result. She does not decide so much as echo Heyward's refusal to consider delivering Cora over to Magua: "Cora! Cora! you jest with our misery! Name not the horrid alternative again; the thought itself is worse than a thousand deaths" (109). Once self-condemned to the fate of a heroine of traditional romance, however, "the delicate and sensitive form of Alice" "shrunk into itself." With arms and head dangling, she was "suspended against the tree, looking like some beautiful emblem of the wounded delicacy of her sex" (110). It is by thus brutalizing the traditional heroine that Cooper transforms Alice's sentimental womanhood into the very emblem of wounded femininity. That Heyward's masculinity proves so inadequate to defend this "beautiful emblem" proclaims the wilderness an unfit place for British culture to take root and thrive.[16]

To understand what Cooper accomplished by putting sentimental womanhood on trial and subjecting it to punishment, we must focus on the now peripheral Cora and her performance in tandem with Alice as a double heroine. Several chapters before Munro recounts his family history, Cora has replaced the colonel's first wife as Alice's missing mother. This positioning tailors both protagonists for a national novel, so that they can bring together the two quite different concepts of relationships collapsed in the single term "family." Though sisters on the father's side, the girls' differences in appearance and behavior to this point have suggested that their inheritance is all on the mother's side—the one fair and stereotypically feminine, the other dark and verbally assertive. Having established their difference, however, Cooper turns right around and makes a sentimental captive of the "undaunted daughter" who argues like Shakespeare's Portia with her captor Magua. Without preparing us for the change, the archfiend simply renders Cora speechless with terror that puts her in a position of supplication more befitting of her sister: "Her voice became choked, and clasping her hands, she looked upward, as if seeking, in her agony, intelligence from a wisdom that was infinite" (109). In this momentary conflation of these two quite different heroines, Cooper offers a preview of how he will resolve the two conflicting traditions of romance that organize the novel.

Carlo Ginzburg offers an instructive model of the strategy we have in mind when he shows how a notion of "family resemblance" that he borrows from Wittgenstein differs from a conventional notion of genealogy that traces family traits genealogically through generations. To think in terms of family resemblances, as Ginzburg explains, we must grasp the synchronic set, or general picture, that forms when any number of individuals—who may or may not be connected by inheritance—share certain qualities. What prompts us to think of various individuals as a family is not a matter of any one feature that appears in all members of a group but of a number of overlapping similarities among those members so that we grasp them as a set. Extrapolating from the difference between these two different models of "family" relations, we can place Alice within a tradition of romance that reproduces and continues the story of her Scottish mother. Both heroines remain faithful to the type until history, in the first instance, accommodates Munro's wish to return from the Caribbean and claim Alice's hand in marriage and, in the second instance, puts Heyward in a position as a British officer to ask Munro for his daughter's hand.

Daughter Alice's relation to daughter Cora, by contrast, is established by a number of formal resemblances that override the differences created by their divergent maternal lines. If Cora grows unpredictably passive in handing her fate over both to her sister and to the poetics of the Puritan captivity narrative, then Alice is caught in the crosshairs of a colonial romance and "wounded" when her golden lock is severed by a tomahawk, just as one nicks Cora's shoulder a few paragraphs before. Belonging to different branches of the tree of literary romance—each of which effectively interrupts the other—the two heroines merge during the ordeal of captivity to form a single figure on the basis of stereotypical behavior that makes their contrasting physical features seem ephemeral.

Ginzburg uses the philosopher's enduring fascination with Francis Galton's composite photographs to turn Wittgenstein's understanding of the concept of family resemblance into a marker of the evolution of his understanding of the pattern that emerged in these images. Influenced by game theory early on in his career, Wittgenstein argued that we don't have to know the game in order to recognize a set of procedures as a game because we recognize the similarities between its procedures and those of other games. Working with this understanding of "family resemblances," he initially proposed that in superimposing different portraits one upon the other, Galton had made the facial pattern of familiar racial or social types perceptible by screening out the individual variations. Insofar as these resemblances could be grounded in the facial structures of his subjects, he reasoned, along with Galton, their images must indicate a common lineage.

At this point in his thinking, the synchronic model of the composite photograph was more or less compatible with the diachronic concept of a family tree. The difference between them did not pose a contradiction, Ginzburg points out, so much as provide different perspectives on the same phenomenon: the one being a history compressed in space and the other a configuration of formal connections drawn out and made continuous in time. Rather than disfigure the object beyond recognition, the fact that the same object is viewed from different viewpoints, in this case, substantiates its identity as such. Cooper takes care that we see his heroines in just these terms when he not only gives them divergent maternal lineages but also links them by a set of resemblances that set them apart from both Europeans and the indigenous population. It is in this respect—in its capacity to hold together contrary cultural perspectives without synthesizing elements from incompatible categories of identity—that "family resemblances" provided Cooper with the means of symbolically resolving the antinomies organizing his novel.[17]

By dramatizing and then screening out the difference between the sisters, the political antagonism that erupts in Chapters 11 and 12 makes it possible for Cooper to imagine two different forms of social relations at once. Understanding full well the threat posed by their Indian captors, Cora "folded Alice to her bosom" and explained the terrible options that they face with "an expression of tenderness, that seemed maternal" (109). As Magua's men move to carry out the threat of massacre, Cora "eluded the grasp of the savage, and reckless of her own safety, threw herself on the bosom of Alice" (112). At the conclusion of the heroic battle between male combatants, Alice rises, "where she had sunk" by the side of Cora, and throws herself once again "on the bosom of the latter," exclaiming, "Cora, my sister, my more than sister, my mother, you too are spared!" (115). Once he has established a clear family resemblance between the two daughters, Cooper can incorporate them in a single family tree that puts the hybrid Cora in the maternal line that produces the thoroughbred Alice. Doing so places Alice within an American tradition of romance originating in America without compromising the purity of her British lineage. Indeed, the composite figure that emerges when femininity remains undaunted under such daunting circumstances is arguably a more interesting and capacious figure than that of heroines of a romance tradition that maintains exclusions based on race.

To conclude this section, we want to stress the fact that race is but one of the factors by means of which Cooper establishes formal connections among his characters. Cora does much more than that. Her withdrawal from a field of action—the wilderness—with whose inhabitants she has demonstrable affinities, initiates Cora's transfiguration from Alice's older sister into something like the mythic Khora, a figure associated with the Magna Mater, as well as with the space outside the Greek city-state classified as neither culture nor nature but as a zone of indistinction in between that both separates and links the two. We are now prepared to address the question of how—given that she cannot marry into the American family tree without nullifying its claim to British descent—does Cora make it possible for Cooper to formulate the symbolic resolution of an irreducible difference that cannot be resolved politically.

To understand why, it is helpful to see how Wittgenstein's notion of "family resemblances" changed over the course of his career. In a 1929 lecture at Cambridge on ethics, he decided that the pattern that emerged from Galton's composite photographs did so because each of the individual portraits he superimposed shared certain features. From this he inferred that although the features had to be already there in the individuals photographed, they would in all likelihood have been imperceptible had Galton not superimposed them. His doing so made the features that appeared in image upon image seem substantial in relation to the individual particularities that flit like ghosts of former selves across the image to form a translucent halo around the composite head at the center of the image. In his *Philosophic Investigations*, Wittgenstein rethought the question of resemblance in terms of the rope used by the British navy. Do we recognize this object, he asked, because of the single red thread that runs its entire length and designates it as belonging to the British navy, or is the characteristic interweaving of many microfibers what allows us to recognize the red thread running through it?

In order to raise the distinctive features of a Jew or African to the abstract level of a type, Galton selected a group of suitable individuals and posed them for the camera in the same position with similar expressions on their faces. It is against the background of a recognizably human face that certain biological features—a nose, jawline, brow ridge, head shape—jump out at us demanding recognition as typical. In his later work, according to Ginzburg, Wittgenstein dropped the question of whether he should hold the subject's face itself or Galton's manipulation of the image responsible for the synecdochal features that triggered the viewers' recognition of a racial type. Rather than look for the typical in Galton's superimposition of images that highlight certain biological features, Wittgenstein found that the uncanny zone of translucency surrounding the composite facial image "opened up new spaces for reflection" (Ginzburg 547).

Pushed into the background by Galton's composite image, this zone preserved the excluded particularities, traces of diverse individuals from various communities who had been artificially removed from their lives and reduced to a single image. This shift from the composite subject to the background from which it emerged caused Wittgenstein "to reformulate 'family resemblances' in terms of a complex crisscross of similarities between members of a given class" (547–48). We are making a similar shift away from the traditional literary critical focus on Cooper's racism, where one finds it equally difficult to get around the fact of racial stereotyping, in order to discover why he, as opposed to Galton, produced what is still considered a literary masterpiece out of such unpropitious material. To lay down the rules for a community that was American and yet not anti-British, he included in his lush descriptions of the wilderness a pattern of formal resemblances among the singular traits that stereotyping screens out but nevertheless preserves, a pattern rather like the halo effect in Galton's stereotypes.

The Aesthetic Common

While it never imagines how a distinctively American family will eventually consolidate itself, *The Last of the Mohicans* goes to great lengths to define the conditions necessary for such a family to emerge. The novel begins at the moment when Fort William Henry has failed to protect British settlers from the French and Indians. What will it take to provide this protection, the novel asks? By refiguring the racially mixed daughter as mother to her purely British sister, Cooper offers the only means by which the British type of domestic woman can be destroyed or, worse, defiled by the strangers she is bound to encounter in the wilderness. As a stand-in for the security that is conspicuously lacking in North America, Cora prefigures the ideological architecture that will eventually enable a heroine borrowed from the British tradition to thrive in the American novel. Chapters 11 and 12 offer a preview of what Cooper is going to offer in terms of such an architecture.

The apotheosis of Alice and Cora as the composite heroine of the novel begins in Chapter 11 with a spectacular display of fallen nature. As the bad Indian Magua flees with his British captives, one of the Narragansett in his party kills a fawn and carries "the more preferable parts of the victim" on his shoulders to the spot designated as their resting place. There ensues a feeding frenzy that offers an ominous preview of the slaughter of the innocents that he will soon threaten to carry out. "Without any aid from the science of cookery," the narrator tells us, the Narragansett began "gorging [themselves] with this digestable sustenance" (100). Seen from the modern side of the Hobbesian divide, the tribal feast is a disgusting disfiguration of what a civilized meal should be. To imagine community emerging out of American soil, then, Cooper has to exorcise the demons that have turned nature into a state of *bellum omnium contra omnes*. By way of indicating that exactly this has happened,

Chapter 12 concludes in the same location but with a very kind of feast. By means of "simple cookery," the Mohicans transform the food left by "the voracious Huron" into a "meal" accompanied by "a draught from that solitary and silent spring"—which, as Cooper tells us in a footnote to the 1831 edition, will become "one of the two principle watering holes in America" (122–23). With this shift from the "raw" to the "cooked," the frenzied behavior of "savages" (119) is replaced by "the silence and diligence of men, who ate in order to enable themselves to endure great and unremitting toil" (122). Cooper's description of the feast bridges the symbolic gulf between primitive and modern political societies.[18] The substitution of the Mohican and the Delaware for the Huron and the Narragansett establishes formal resemblances between tribal law and civil social practices that seem to civilize the one and indigenize the other. In marked contrast with the simplicity of this common meal, Cooper concludes *The Last of the Mohicans* with a lavish ethnographic description of a funeral ritual that achieves two major objectives, both of which depend on his ability to establish aesthetic resemblances between opposing lineages.

The final scene of the novel opens upon "a nation of mourners" that includes "beings of every rank and age, of both sexes, and of all pursuits, [who] had united to form this breathing wall of bodies . . . and were influenced by a single emotion" (340). At first the passage gives no clear indication of the group to whom the mourners belong. There is no mention of race until the narrative fastens its gaze on "six Delaware girls, with their long, dark, flowing tresses." They embellish "the litter of fragrant plants, that, under a pall of Indian robes, supported all that now remained of the ardent, high souled, and generous Cora," at whose "feet was seated the desolate Munro" (340). To read this scene in terms of biological race, signs of which are laced throughout, would require us to screen out all aesthetically active codings and return our focus to the problem of consanguinity. The question of interracial marriage, which deepens as the circle opens to include Uncas in ceremonial attire, would leave us with no way of accounting for Cooper's overwrought description of their common funeral—thus without any explanation as to why he entertained a romance between Cora and Uncas in the first place.

Rather than make Cora the reproductive mechanism of an interracial nation, the novel's conclusion enjoins us to think of their mixed legacy in terms of the politics of an imagined community that can be memorialized in literature but never realized politically. If Chapters 11 and 12 transformed Alice into a living emblem of wounded femininity, confirming her Britishness in this respect, then this final set piece of the novel translates Cora into an emblem of another kind. Separated by death from Alice with whom she was exalted by the ordeal of captivity, Cora can now appear as the heroine of a thwarted colonial romance. Having described in considerable detail her rustic funeral bier, Cooper proceeds to do the same with a spectacle he stages in "the opposite space of the same area": "Seated, as in life, with his form and limbs arranged in grave and decent composure, Uncas appeared, in the most gorgeous ornaments that the wealth of the tribe could furnish" (340). His father, Chingachgook, was placed "directly in front of the corpse" (340). "Clothing their ideas in the most remote and subtle images," the Delaware girls apparently gave voice to the story of interracial love after the ceremony had ended (343). "And why should not such a predilection be encouraged?" (343), we are now licensed to ask along with Cooper's narrator: "That she was of a blood purer and richer than the rest of her nation, any eye might have seen. That she was equal to the danger and daring of a life in the woods, her conduct had proved" (343). On this basis, Cooper's description sets Cora "clothed in remote and subtle images," in contrast to the plainspoken snapshot of "the virgin who wept in the adjacent lodge"; she was, they said, like snow, "liable to melt in the fierce heats of summer, or to congeal in the frosts of winter" (343). In addition to fulfilling the promise of the imagery in the fourth sentence of the novel's opening paragraph, this highly wrought literary description establishes mutually enhancing links between strikingly different "emblems" that, if blended, might easily become ridiculous. Stressing the absolute singularity of each ritual allows him to establish purely formal resemblances between opposing cultures that offer the only way he can substantiate the fantasy of an open and contingent system of social relations. This alternative to what were then legal race-based exclusions from the Anglo-American family not only accommodated cultural differences but also considered them equivalent.

If in writing *The Last of the Mohicans*, Cooper wanted to imagine a new beginning for the United States, then to do so he found it necessary to insert an imaginary space between the "unused" territory for which the European powers were battling and indications of a new national community. To transform what was historically a field crisscrossed by multiple conflicts into a community from which diverse readers could imagine coming, he used aesthetic links to establish common ground among the different, even hostile populations that would necessarily encounter one another there. Their formal arrangement, corresponding details, and the dignity accorded to the sex and race of those commemorated establish a system of resemblances that coalesces as a pattern at least as enduring as the hybrid marriage concluding a colonial

romance. Rather than the political asymmetry of the sexual contract, moreover, the intercultural relationship that Cooper asks us to imagine establishes
a formal equivalence between different cultural rituals, even as the exoticism
of the "indigenous" ceremony exaggerates their differences, allowing those of
British taste to favor Cora's modest bier over Uncas's physical display.

This conclusion subjects the two romance traditions that Cooper faces off
throughout the novel to the same redistribution of sensibility. Until the final
tableau, as we have argued, Cooper shuts down the possibility of forming an
interracial community whenever a colonial romance threatens to redirect his
romance plot. But once he had killed off the best candidates for a biracial
foundational fiction—the most refined of native men and the most indigenous of British women—he was free to exploit the occasion of their funerals
to unleash the alternative origin story that might otherwise materialize: "Years
passed away before the traditional tale of the white maiden, and of the young
warrior of the Mohicans, ceased to beguile the long nights and tedious
marches, or to animate their youthful and brave with a desire for vengeance"
(348). Having relegated this possibility to folklore, Cooper can insert a space
between tribal and political society that contains the twin funerals of Cora
and Uncas, a common space that provides not only the vanishing point of an
interracial heritage but also the point of origin for a national community.
That the vanished set of possibilities is inextricable from the one that will at
some point in the future be able to materialize through Alice and Heyward
also becomes apparent at this moment: we learn from a scout that "the 'open
hand' [of native hospitality] had conveyed the surviving daughter far into the
settlements of the 'pale-faces,' where her tears had, at last, ceased to flow, and
had been succeeded by bright smiles which were better suited to her joyous
nature" (348). Two futures, then: one opening out unto a different America
whose inevitable progress toward nationhood had become the stuff of novels,
including Cooper's own, and the other harking back to a prehistory that has
already passed from wish into oral tradition and from folklore into the record
of collective memory. Rather than end with a consanguineous relationship
that displaces the hybrid couple of colonial romance, then, Cooper offers an
elaborate spectacle to show that one tradition of romance bears only a family
resemblance to the other.

If this were the form of novel we have characterized as democratic writing, the two mutually incompatible perspectives on Cora that the novel
offers—as native heroine and as threat to the claim to British descent—would
simply link mutually incompatible perspectives. Alternatively, if this were

gothic literature, Cora would not melt into Alice but markedly disfigure the heroine of literary tradition. Instead, Cora does indeed emerge from a sequence of captivities that carry out a reversal of the Pygmalion story. This process yields a frozen image of Anglo-American beauty that pushes Alice well into the background—why? How can Cooper's descriptive practice of linking incompatibles perform the aesthetic apotheosis of the hybrid woman? As we saw in the case of the feasts respectively inaugurating Chapter 11 and concluding Chapter 12, Cooper is only too capable of using repetition to displace one view with its positive mirror image and to establish the later feast as the standard for measuring the deviance of the earlier one. The novel's concluding scene, on the other hand, demonstrates that repetition is also capable of leveling and linking cultural differences by establishing resemblances. This use of repetition—as we saw in the gothic texts of Poe and Henry James—tends to yield a common object that identifies itself as artificially bounded. This is what happens, for example, when Poe and James introduce an oblique or external perspective into a country manor house that displaces the central intelligence conventionally presiding over that framework.

The American Origins of Literary Pluralism

It remains for us to consider the implications of a novel that asks us to imagine an open-ended and discontinuous network as a set of social relations complete in itself and yet heterogeneous in terms of what material it contains and the perspectives those elements objectify. To carry off this transformation of what became, during the early decades of the nineteenth century, a form of prose narrative that could circulate across regional and local lines, Cooper obviously felt obliged to remove Cora and Uncas permanently from the social network they might have extended and kept open to diversification. He also felt compelled to reintroduce them in a fantasy that divests them of race in order to weave their cultural features together in a fantasy of inclusive democracy. To advance our understanding of the canonical status accorded to *The Last of the Mohicans* almost as soon as it appeared in print, we have to understand how this writing silenced the voice of colonial romance it appears to celebrate.

In that this novel raised the question of whether Cooper's use of Indian material pandered to popular taste, the first reviewers were asking if there could be some other justification for including this subject matter. Did the novel observe a different set of rules from those responsible for organizing democratic writing to model the very network in which it sought to circulate? To appeal to a literary reader, Cooper had to observe what Jacques Rancière meant by "rules of appropriateness." To establish a literary literacy, these rules would have had to distinguish the novel from democratic writing. These rules could not include Indian material simply to exclude the perspective of Native Americans—although there's no question he accomplished that. Cooper's point, we submit, was to establish the conditions for inclusion in the community of literary readers.

To be received as democratic writing, a novel had to observe an established set of protocols, which could be exercised in any number of ways and still produce a network novel. The number of such novels published during the thirty-year period of the early republic attracted readers in sufficient numbers to warrant several editions of some novels, making it advantageous for publishers to circumvent copyright law and pirate them. When Cooper began to write novels, he consequently entered a field of discourse that had prepared readers to receive and reproduce writing that addressed them in a politely impersonal vernacular and observed a fairly consistent set of narrative protocols. In this way, we have argued, the early novels could establish imaginary social ties among any number of otherwise disconnected communities. It was owing to the repetition of this narrative form, rather than the considerable ingenuity of, say, a Charles Brockden Brown, that a readership recognized and even decided to write novels themselves. The conditions were such, in other words, that neither the voice of the novel nor the tropes it performed were anyone's property in the sense that required readers to subject their own angle on experience to that of an author. If, as Rancière suggests, the dissemination of the network novel was the precondition for becoming literature, then Cooper's rejection of marriage as the means of concluding a biracial romance should tell us that that he was not of a mind to resolve the contention among political factions that organized his narrative. Like his predecessors, he was just not interested in producing a unified point of view.

Cooper, to the contrary, used the machinery of the network novel to break up, disperse, and recombine elements of the very political conflicts that his British counterparts resolved by way of marriage. To represent contending groups, he invented exactly the details that allowed him to transform the active conflict generating a plot so common as the captivity narrative into a mode of description that would come to be recognized as Cooper's own distinctive literary style. It is through description that the novel progresses up a literary ladder from a disgusting account of the savage feast staged by the "bad" Huron and Narragansett to its mirror opposite, the "simple" communal feast of the "good" Delaware and Mohican, and after a number of intermediary steps along the way, arrives at the highly wrought tableau of twin funeral ceremonies performed in a forest clearing. Set in what was formerly a battlefield that would determine who ruled the territory of North America, this final description of the clearing in the forest sweeps away problems the novel could not solve within that space. By elevating conflict from political to cultural differences, in other words, Cooper took the political conflict out of racial difference. He did so, moreover, by including the cultural signs of such difference in a system of equivalences that at once exaggerated and reconciled them. The community assembled there is in no way a unified or comprehensively representative one, but it does imagine that a diverse population can coexist without sacrificing its diversity.

We are not interested in showing more precisely how *The Last of the Mohicans* reconfigures the signs of racial difference that could not coexist without trying to wipe each other out. To address this question, we cannot offer a fulsome description of Cooper's literary techniques, but rather an admittedly reductive account of what his literary description does to the common literacy, or democratic writing, that we have associated with the early American novel. How do the "rules of appropriateness" that Cooper put into practice in *The Last of the Mohicans*, the very rules he mapped out in the novel's opening paragraph, reorganize the network novel? What political inference can we draw from this change in form? First, we must underscore that Cooper's rustic stand-in for the household as the central hub of a future national community presents itself from the perspective of a literary author, thus as both apolitical and one of a kind. This is just another way of saying that the "rules of appropriateness" responsible for turning the novel into literature clearly simulated the conversion of legally unclaimed territory into property.

Owning property—in theory at least—removes the individual from his obligations to the community and secures the habits and heritage that determine the conduct of domestic life. It also qualifies him as a representative individual. By a similar set of moves and with parallel political implications, their "literary" literacy removes the narratives of Poe, Hawthorne, Melville, Stowe, and certainly James from the circulation of writing that could be from anyone to anyone else. These "rules of appropriateness" allow each to manage irreducible differences in a way that objectifies the perspective not of just anyone but of a literary author. Cooper's novel produced something equivalent to the households formulated by the novels of Sir Walter Scott—and for that matter Emily and Charlotte Brontë, Charles Dickens, and George Eliot—households that establish domestic relations of cooperation where there had been internecine political strife. How Cooper defined this apolitical community was not only outrageously political but also recognizably American.

He removed himself from the discursive field where anyone could address anyone else in very much the same written voice. He knew that stepping out of the political arena was a power play in its own right. To read his novel as a work of literature would require readers to privilege the ascent of its description over and above the metonymic movement of its narrative and to perform as an intermediary, or interpreter, between the two. To become a literary text, we are saying, an American novel addressed a reader who was not just anyone but someone willing to collaborate with Cooper in removing his view of the French and Indian War from the field of democratic writing, as defined by the argument between Townshend and Barré. If *The Last of the Mohicans* continues to generate interpretations that approach it from different critical angles, it is because Cooper established the literary ground rules for critical pluralism and, in so doing, inadvertently inaugurated a literary tradition of the American novel.

To read such a novel as literature, we may safely assume that it is trying to figure out a way of managing the problem of diversity without advocating a more equitable distribution of rights or property. *The Last of the Mohicans* rules out any problems that, without the redistribution of rights and property, could not and still cannot be resolved politically. From the opening paragraph to its very last, the novel indeed struggles to formulate a community to which readers can imagine two otherwise contending racial groups belonging without disrupting each other's way of life and cultural practices. This is not something that can be done in the early American novel. When the captivity narrative forcibly conjoins contending racial groups, as it does, for example, in Chapters 11 and 12, it puts such a community beyond the reach of imagination; the persecuted heroine is refigured as an outmoded British stereotype in relation to which Indians will necessarily play the devil. But when they interact as components of a description enriched by literary allusion and fabricated ethnographic detail, these same racialized figures achieve a mutually enhancing relationship that allows them to coexist.

The same condition holds for literary critical readers, so that each may differ from another without disrupting either. To belong to this community, Cooper's reader tacitly agrees to give up the idea of a dominant order of truth.

That reader also agrees that no one "owns" the meaning of a literary text, that all perspectives are potentially valid, and that the resources of the text are sufficient to go around. The assumption is that a diversity of readings not only enriches the critical discourse but testifies to the richness of literature as well. The reader who proceeds on this assumption acquires authority over the object of analysis. To expose the politics of this model of inclusion in turn negates that authority and returns the literary work to the social field from which it sought to remove itself. To politicize the conclusion to *The Last of the Mohicans* would dispel the magic of a form of pluralism that renders internal conflict more or less accidental on grounds that it comes in from outside and disrupts the harmony achieved by emphasizing the features of different groups that allow their practices to converge and become equally intelligible in a single image. A political reading of the conclusion to Cooper's novel would activate the contending interests that it has artfully euthanized and hold open the possibility of continuing the argument.[19]

In view of the fact that the most influential literary histories of the American novel barely mention the considerable number of novels written, published, and circulated in the new United States, it seems only too clear that Cooper succeeded in distancing the literary novel from democratic writing. At the same moment that gave rise to Jacksonian democracy, he imagined a representative community of readers founded on the selective principle of literary pluralism. Such narrowing of the imagined readership responds to a political conflict so basic to the organization of the United States that it has been dividing, destabilizing, demanding, and generating new formulations of an imagined national community ever since.

Notes

INTRODUCTION

1. As we argue elsewhere, Williams sees the "long revolution" in print culture as a delayed effect of Parliament's failure to renew the Licensing Act in 1695. This event was instrumental in the increasing publication of vernacular print a century later, when it produced a shift in the focus of both personal life and government onto the impact of this material on the reading subject (see Armstrong and Tennenhouse, *The Imaginary Puritan* 67).

2. In *We, the People of Europe* 20–21, Étienne Balibar translates the difference between Anderson's "imagined community" and the structures of domination and exploitation that accompany the international expansion of capitalism into a political force in its own right, claiming that "the *nation-form* is not even the ideal type of community, but *the concept of a structure capable of producing determinate 'community effects.'*" It is not simply "an abstraction of the national community" but designates certain "constraints that are exerted together" in order to provide "*a way for economic forces to determine symbolic effects and vice versa.*" This adjustment of Anderson's model tailors it for eighteenth-century European novels, but it requires more adjustment before this model can describe the community effects of novels published in the new United States, which rejected, across the board, the symbolic structure of coordinated constraints that had accommodated the economic forces of British imperialism.

3. Appropriating Anderson's concept of "imagined communities" for nineteenth-century Latin America, Doris Sommer shows how novelists arranged heterosexual marriages to reconfigure the racially differentiated groups of colonialized and colonizer to produce a symbolic basis of internally coherent communities specific to their respective nations. In Chapter 9, we explain how Cooper's *The Last of the Mohicans* formulated a comparable "foundational fiction" for the United States by artfully avoiding interracial marriage.

4. In *The Importance of Feeling English*, Leonard Tennenhouse observes, "Throughout the eighteenth century, as domestic book production grew, American printers devoted their presses to almanacs, sermons (in declining numbers), session law reports, and the like. As a result, colonial booksellers and their customers continued to rely largely on British imports for books on politics and history, belles lettres, and much that was considered useful knowledge" (10). Belles lettres included not only pirated editions but also works of fiction currently popular in England.

5. For a reading of Austen's novels that shows the degree to which they, too, acknowledge the network dependency of the modern nation even in disavowing it, see Armstrong and Tennenhouse, "The Network Novel."

CHAPTER 1

1. Sir Walter Scott published his *Lives of the Novelists* in two volumes between 1821 and 1824. In his *Institutions of the English Novel*, Homer O. Brown identifies the publication of Scott's critical study as being the start of what is a still ongoing process of canonization.

2. In "Rent to Own," Sandra Mcpherson identifies the complex moment in the history of property law that provides the force field in which Austen sets her English country houses. In "The Nineteenth-Century Austen," Armstrong lays out the legal problems afflicting inherited property in Austen's major novels and the banking crisis brought on by waves of inflation, rising debt, and the decision by the Bank of England to go off the gold standard.

3. During the Revolutionary War, British blockades, the disruption of farming, funding for the war, and the interruption of general commerce damaged the economy severely. As Cathy Matson writes, "The short-term costs of the Revolutionary War undoubtedly were steep: incomes fell sharply, citizens and soldiers endured scarcities, planting was disrupted . . . , and farmers' credit recovered only in fits and starts in the interior" ("A House of Many Mansions" 43). Economic historians disagree, however, whether the postwar recovery qualifies as the "transition to capitalism." The economic recovery was uneven and varied according to both region and form of trade (see "A House of Many Mansions" 42–43 for historiographical accounts). At the same time, however, historians do agree that migrations that had been under way before the war began anew following the Treaty of Paris in 1783. Gordon Wood writes, "By the end of the War for Independence the earlier migrations had become a flood. One observer in 1785 thought the movement westward was so great that it seemed 'as if the old states would depopulate, and the inhabitants be transported to the new'" (*Empire of Liberty* 115). See also Matson, "Capitalizing Hope"; Taylor, *Cooper's Town* 89–91; and McCusker and Menard 213–35.

4. It should be noted that *Persuasion*, Austen's last published novel, more or less abandons the idea of reforming the management of hereditary land and formulates its synthesis of love and money by relocating it on board a ship that can travel with the man of property, a captain in the British navy. *Sanditon*, the novel Austen left unfinished at death, deals with land speculation and attempts to formulate social relationships on that shaky foundation.

5. As Samuel Otter points out, rumor's role in *Arthur Mervyn* may well be indebted to Matthew Cary's "A Desultory Account of the Malignant Fever," an account of the 1793 epidemic in Philadelphia that circulated in several editions (32–58).

6. For a discussion of small worlds, see Buchanan 48–60. Buchanan takes the term "small worlds" from the work of Watts and Strogatz.

7. In *The One vs. the Many*, Alex Woloch shows with great care and many examples how "the space of a particular character emerges only vis-à-vis the other characters who crowd him out or potentially revolve around him. It is here," he claims, "that the social dimension of form emerges" (18). We think the competitive dynamic that Woloch traces in British novels is countermanded and indeed overwhelmed in novels of the early republic by a dynamic that subtracts the very features that would distinguish a character as major. Crowding under these circumstances empowers everyone so linked without eliminating their singularity. Without minor characters, there are no major characters, only those with more connections.

8. See the quotation from Foucault that serves as the epigraph to our introduction.

9. Deleuze and Guattari's "Rhizome" informs our notion of narrative style in two key respects. First, it is a system of relations that "connects any point to any other point" in "an acentered, nonhierarchical, nonsignifying system without a General and without an organizing

memory or central automaton, defined solely by a circulation of states" (21). While this sounds emphatically negative, the subtraction of those characteristics comprising taxonomies, trees, and, in our examples, property produces what they describe, borrowing from Gregory Bateson, "a continuous, self-vibrating region of intensities whose development avoids any orientation toward a culminating point or external end" (22). Second, they claim that in the United States, "everything important that has happened or is happening takes the route of the American rhizome. . . . The conception of the book is different" (19). See also Deleuze's conversation with Claire Parnet, "On the Superiority of Anglo-American Literature."

10. On this point, see Rancière's essay, "The Putting to Death of Emma Bovary: Literature, Democracy, and Medicine," *Politics* 49–71.

11. Trish Loughran reminds us that "in 1800, most Americans lived beyond the reach of any printed matter that was not produced by their own local printer or privately sent to them through personal connections" (21). This was a problem that writers such as Royall Tyler and Hugh Henry Brackenridge specifically addressed. See Loughran 21–25.

12. See Tennenhouse, *The Importance* 19–42.

13. In his *Atlas of the European Novel*, Franco Moretti implies as much in describing the geographical limitations of Austen's novels as a pattern "of exclusion, first of all. No Ireland; no Scotland; no Wales; no Cornwall. No 'Celtic Fringe'; . . . a much smaller space than the United Kingdom as a whole. And not even all of England: Lancashire, the North, the industrial revolution—all missing." This literary geography tells us "two things at once: what *could* be in a novel—and what actually *is* there. On the one hand, the industrializing 'Great Britain' of Austen's years; on the other, the small, homogeneous England of Austen's novels" (13–14). For our purposes, it's important that Moretti identifies the latter as "the much older England celebrated by the 'estate poems' of topographical poetry" (13).

14. As Samuel Otter notes, literary critics are generally unsure what to make of the sentimental ending of the novel: "Does Arthur's impending marriage signify patriarchal victory or dependence? A tribute to, or the spoils of, virtue? A sentimental elevation, or a capitulation to the market?" Returning to his own concerns, Otter continues, "Another kind of question to ask might be: what is the relationship between the fever story and the sentimental comedy that follows? Although the yellow fever has subsided in the last part of the book, Arthur's personal fervor has not. Although he insists that he speaks with candor . . . Arthur still does not seem to know his feelings or recognize the consequences of his actions" (68).

CHAPTER 2

1. Gordon Wood contends that "the Lockean notion of the social contract was not generally called upon by Americans in their dispute with Great Britain, for it had little relevance in explaining either the nature of the colonial charters or their relationship to the empire, it became increasingly meaningful in the years after 1776" (*Creation* 283). We disagree. We find that the figure of the Social Contract was dramatically used to think with and provided a conceptual framework in a good number of the colonial documents produced between 1764 and 1776 that protested Parliament's efforts to impose taxes and place restrictions on the colonies. As Middlekauff notes, "Americans were Lockeians by experience as well as general opinion" (123), and they drew upon Locke's notion of property in the *Second Treatise* when they argued against the Stamp Act in 1765–66 (123–23).

2. Alan Taylor makes a key point of contrast. In eighteenth-century colonial America,

"Wealth was necessary but not sufficient for genteel authority. The acquisition of property was the easiest and, usually, the first attainment of the upwardly mobile." Such an individual, however, often lacked "other attributes of gentility: polished manners, urbane tastes, literary knowledge, and legal sophistication." As a result, the man of new wealth had to acquire property in himself in order to serve as representative man: "Colonists of new wealth hastened to complete their portfolios of genteel ways by retraining themselves to speak, walk, gesture, dress, pose, and think like aristocrats. Prestige and high office rewarded those who succeeded" (*Cooper's* 14).

3. In America, there was no need to include this factor; thus, thinking in terms of America provided a convenient way to begin again from scratch, a literary tactic that Defoe used in *Robinson Crusoe* and Malthus corrected a century later.

4. This, as Mike Hill and Warren Montag argue, is why Adam Smith wrote *Theory of Moral Sentiments*. From the first sentence of *Moral Sentiments*, they explain, Smith aligns himself with "those powerful statements of human sociability mobilized in response to Hobbes." "No matter how 'selfish,'" they write, there remains something obvious "that must 'interest' man 'in the fortune of others'" (109).

5. Étienne Balibar reads Locke's claim that "every Man has a Property in his own Person" to argue against C. B. Macpherson that there is "not one possessive individualism" in the *Second Treatise* "but at least two, pushing in two directions" (Balibar, "Possessive Individualism" 301). If we take that phrase to mean that every man derives his rights as a citizen from his property, we limit the concept of "every man" to those few who already own property and exclude the rest of the population from direct political participation. But if we think of property not only as the particular property "constituted" by law but also as property in an abstract and quasi-Spinozan sense as the property "constituent" of every man's capacity to act and thus to own, we end up with an entirely different concept of the rights-bearing citizen. Admittedly stuck within a European tradition of political thinking, Balibar seeks a way out of the contradiction by imagining a subject prior to the exchange of labor for property; see Armstrong, "Just Like a Woman." Admittedly engaged in a struggle with the very tradition in which he writes, Balibar's recent work bears curious resemblance to the argument that shapes the founding documents of the United States.

6. According to Bernard Bailyn, "The ideas and writings of the leading secular thinkers of the European Enlightenment—reformers and social critics like Voltaire, Rousseau, and Beccaria as well as conservative analysts like Montesquieu—were quoted everywhere in the colonies, by everyone who claimed a broad awareness. In pamphlet after pamphlet the American writers cited Locke on natural rights and on the social and governmental contract" (27).

7. Rousseau writes, "This common freedom is a consequence of man's nature. His first law is to attend to his own preservation, his first cares are those he owes himself, and since, as soon as he has reached the age of reason, he is the sole judge of the means proper to preserve himself, he becomes his own master" (I.2.2).

8. "In Rousseau and Contradiction," Fredric Jameson shows that in formulating the Social Contract, Rousseau was self-consciously producing a work of fiction for a government that could not materialize under present historical conditions.

9. Tocqueville expressed dismay at finding no institutions in America for producing an educated populace—he saw this absence leading to the tyranny of the majority. As he contends, "This very equality which makes him independent of each of his fellow men delivers him alone defenseless into the hands of the majority" (501). Indeed, well before Tocqueville, many of the framers of the Constitution were acutely aware of the problem. The belief that a tyranny of the majority was operating at the level of the states under the Articles of Confederation was one motive for calling a Constitutional Convention in 1787. Woody Holton argues, quoting

Madison's letter to Jefferson on October 17, 1788, "In [Madison's] view, the Founders had rescued white Americans from kingly despotism only to subject them to something worse: the
tyranny of 'the major number of the constituents'" (7). See also Sheehan 109–23.

10. We have in mind here the process by which the Constitution was amended. For example, although the document containing seven articles was sent to the state legislatures for ratification in 1787, it was clear that without the addition of a specific set of enumerated rights, the
ratification was likely to fail by as many as three to five states. "The Federal Farmer," one of the
most thoughtful Anti-Federalists, in Jack Rakove's view, felt that "a bill of rights did not create
the rights it declared; a people were entitled to their rights 'not because their ancestors once got
together and enumerated them on paper, but because, by repeated negociations and declarations, all parties are brought to realize them, and of course to believe them to be sacred'" (*Original Meanings* 323–24). Such negotiations, debates, and speeches are, in our view, measures that
convert a form of government into a quite different process of governing.

11. In the documents written to protest Parliament's attempts to impose taxes on the colonies, the colonists regularly insisted that Parliament's actions were in violation of charters and
contracts that colonists insisted should be respected. John Phillip Reid has identified several
justifications that colonists regularly cited to ground their claims that they were not subject to
such parliamentary legislation, including "(1) their rights as Englishmen; (2) natural rights law;
(3) the emigration contract; (4) the original contract; (5) the original American contract; (6) the
emigration purchase; (7) colonial charters" (quoted by Rakove, *Original Meanings* 293). See
Reid, *The Authority of Rights* 65–66.

12. Typical of the documents that insisted on the original charter is Thomas Jefferson's "A
Summary View of the Rights of British America" (1774). From the very outset, Jefferson understands the British monarch as the party who made a charter with each of the colonies. He argues, on the basis of the concept of the original contract, that the king is consequently "no more
than the chief officer of the people, appointed by the laws, and circumscribed with definite
powers, to assist in working the great machine of government, erected for their use, and consequently subject to their superintendence. And in order that these our rights, as well as the inva-
sions of them, may be laid more fully before his majesty, to take a view of them from the origin
and first settlement of these countries" (105).

13. In answer to his question, "So what is an affective fact?" Brian Massumi provides this
explanation: "The mechanism is quite simple: Threat triggers fear. The fear is of disruption. The
fear *is* a disruption." He continues, "The mechanism is a capacity that affect itself has to self-
effect" (8).

14. Landon Carter, the wealthy Virginian planter, wrote that with the Port Act, Parliament
had "declared war against the town of Boston." Thomas Wharton, Quaker merchant from Philadelphia, declared that "this Extensive Continent considers the Port bill of Boston as striking
essentially at the Liberties of all North America." Ebenezer Baldwin, a pastor in Danforth, Connecticut, claimed that "the colonists felt a deeper concern" about the Port Act than they had
about the Stamp Act: "The present Measures tis thought to forbode something more dreadful to
the colonies than that detested Act so pregnant with Mischief" (Slaughter 364). See also Ammerman and Carp.

15. William Warner argues for the unique role that the Boston Committee of Correspondence played in nation making; see also Brown, *Revolutionary Politics*. Ryerson discusses the
importance of the Philadelphia Committee.

16. Although the treaty that concluded the French and Indian War established a western
boundary between the British colonies to the east and the Indian territories to the west, this

demarcation had little effect in preventing settlers from pouring across the mountains and vio-
lating the natural border promised to the Native American nations (see Barr, "Red Continent"
and White 315–65). If one couples that with other internal migrations and the extraordinary increase in immigrants from Europe that led to a population explosion of at least tenfold from
1700 to 1775, it is all but impossible to argue for a representative man.

17. Middlekauff writes, "In every colony ownership of real property was required of voters,
and political leadership, by a tacit agreement, was vested in those who owned" (124). By 1776,
however, newspapers in the North and particularly in Philadelphia were challenging such an
agreement by "appealing for a new political equality that did not depend on the traditional association of political rights and property" (Rakove, *Revolutionaries* 182).

18. Whereas before 1776, the majority of representatives sent to the colonial assemblies
were from the upper classes, following the Revolution, state legislatures included a more economically and socially diverse body of representatives (Main). Wood writes, "In the eyes of the
more established gentlemen . . . these popular upstarts with interests to promote seemed incapable of the kind of disinterested character that republican political leaders were supposed to display" (*Empire* 17).

19. See Bonnie Honig's illuminating discussion of this problem in light of Derrida's argument to the effect that "no signature, promise, performative—no act of foundation—possesses
resources adequate to guarantee itself (106).

20. We perhaps overstress the centrality of the Social Contract in European political
thought, but government by and for men of interests was far from an American invention. In
Europe, too, a similar argument emerged to reformulate the subject of government in light of
industrialization, urbanization, and the impact of investment and speculation on "property."
Jeremy Bentham's principle of utility offered a sweeping reconceptualization of the British people as a fundamentally unmanageable aggregate of self-interested individuals that rendered the
contract ridiculous. Bentham declared, "The time has now come when the utter inaptitude of
the original contract principle in the character of a ground and source of practice in the constitution of government has been placed and stands in a light too clear and strong to be
resistible. . . . The alleged fact of the formation of such a contract is a mere fiction" (*Official
Aptitude Maximized* 347). See Hirschman on what he calls "the promise of an interest-governed
world" (128–35).

21. Zagarri has shown that the larger states argued for a model that gave more weight to
population while smaller states relied on an older model that gave weight in representation to
towns, municipalities, and communities.

22. On factions, Madison wrote in *Federalist* No. 10, "The most common and durable
source of factions has been the various and unequal distribution of property. Those who hold
and those who are without property have ever formed distinct interests in society. Those who are
creditors, and those who are debtors, fall under a like discrimination. A landed interest, a manufacturing interest, a mercantile interest, a moneyed interest, with many lesser interests, grow up
of necessity in civilized nations, and divide them into different classes, actuated by different
sentiments and views. The regulation of these various and interfering interests forms the principal task of modern legislation, and involves the spirit of party and faction in the necessary and
ordinary operations of the government" (Hamilton, Madison, and Jay, *Federalist Papers* 74).

CHAPTER 3

1. Wallace (*Early Cooper* 67–68) and Hastings both make the case for *Persuasion* as Cooper's model. Published anonymously, Cooper encouraged the bookseller, A. T. L. Goodrich, not to deny the rumor that *Precaution* was an English import (Franklin, *James Fenimore Cooper* 265–66). Cowie agrees with the view that the novel was "sure to be taken as the work of an English gentlewoman" (121).

2. See Deleuze on the "impossible object," as one that cannot be held to the principle of noncontradiction (*Logic* 35).

3. It is in much the same terms that Bakhtin explains what happens, for example, to the family novel: "In the family novel and the novel of generations, the idyllic element undergoes a radical reworking and as a result perceptibly pales. Of folkloric time and the ancient matrices only those elements remain that can be reinterpreted and that can survive on the soil of the bourgeois family and family-as-genealogy" ("Forms of Time" 231).

4. Alex Galloway's gloss of Foucault's account of the conflation of information and life sheds light on what we mean here: "Foucault concedes that 'what is discovered by the analysis of [discursive] formations is not the bubbling source of life itself in an as yet uncaptured state,' but rather a form of life that is the *agent* of its vitality, that creates its own vitality through the processes of living" (84).

5. Each in his own way, Jed Esty and John Marx show how modernism's island mentality registered the novelists' sense that the empire was in decline.

6. Homer O. Brown argues that the institutionalization of the novel during the eighteenth century was itself a process of retroactive narration resembling that of British novels themselves.

7. Where Richardson devoted hundreds of pages to laying out the rules for sexual relations, Austen in her minimalist style could simply allude to them, knowing her readers identified them as common sense and with the form of the novel itself. She had little patience with the conduct books and moralism of Hannah More and the sermons of Dr. Gregory. See Armstrong, *Desire and Domestic Fiction* 62–64.

8. Until the 1790s, novels imported from England were cheaper than those reprinted in America, and it was approximately 1850 before the majority of novels read in America were written by Americans and produced in the United States. For an account of English novels read in the early United States, see Tennenhouse, *The Importance of Feeling English* 9–12.

9. Warren Montag explains the biopolitical implications of this kind of Lockean individualism in "The Common Is of No Use," a lecture delivered at a symposium, "The Biological Turn in Literary Studies," Duke University, March 2015.

10. In his lectures titled in English, *"Society Must Be Defended,"* Foucault argues, *pace* Clausewitz, that since the seventeenth century, "politics is war by other means," a condition especially true of national politics. If centuries ago, the bourgeoisie and petit bourgeoisie waged a political war against absolute monarchy, he reasons, their domination did not put an end to it. Understanding its authority as a tactical war against authority, the modern ruling class paradoxically understands its power strategically, as countering power from below that would claim that power for another excluded group. Thus, in Foucault's view, the liberal order displaces absolute power with strategic mobilization of various forms of domination that operate defensively. This means, as he suggests, that the power of the modern nation actually depends on the potential reversibility of such power (45–62).

11. In *Identity and Difference*, Étienne Balibar distinguishes Locke's individual from that of Descartes on grounds that Locke does not presume an individual self a priori to the thinking process by which one knows that one exists. To the contrary, contends Balibar, Locke's individual constitutes its "self" as it articulates "sensation and reflection, word and idea, affect and precept" as "the reverse side of a specific exteriority. . . . A phenomenology of consciousness must always reconstitute or reconquer itself by establishing and conceptualizing its limits" (68–69).

12. While, as Chad Luck observes, "historians have generally made sense of this period of rapid change in property practices by pointing out that, in broader strokes, it reflects a gradual shift from an older idea of property as a 'thing' to an emergent idea of property as a 'bundle of rights,'" he argues that the antebellum novel did no such thing. Focusing chiefly on novels after Cooper, Luck sees American novelists engaging this problematic in very different terms than we do (6–7).

13. Both Hirschman and Bentham (*Principles of Morals and Legislation*) well before him make the point that during the postrevolutionary moment, a number of relatively silenced major thinkers imagined that once "interests" were no longer opposed to "passions," the sole object of government should be to discipline both the unruliness of subjects to be ruled and the abuses of those who ruled. Anticipating socialism as much as capitalism, the promise of an interest-governed world gave rise to many of the biopolitical policies that Foucault attributes to this major shift in European liberalism as the means of managing the precariousness of an interest-governed world. Going by the behavior of its field of characters, the early American novels saw the turbulent period before the scope of "interest" was narrowed down to "commercial interests" as one open to experiments in self-organization.

14. Luck sees the period between the American Revolution and the Civil War as one of "remarkable turmoil in both the theory and the practice of property in America. As a result," he continues, "American writers were awash in a flood of property discourse that gave the incentive and opportunity to rethink thoroughly the nature of the institution" (6). Luck's analysis of the legal discourse of the age makes sense to us, especially because the discourse he identifies was one that engaged not only legal philosophers and historians on both sides of the Atlantic but novelists as well.

15. For an account of the American preference for redacted British novels, see Tennenhouse, *The Importance* 54–64.

16. The U.S. Constitution captured the tension between democratic writing and the concept of writing as the author's property, the basis for the modern notion of authorship, when Article I, Section 8, Clause 8 adapted British law "to promote the Progress of Science and useful Arts, by securing for limited Times to Authors and Inventors the exclusive Right to their respective Writings and Discoveries." After seventy years, the text was to be returned to the public domain. This law displaced the assumption, implicit in democratic writing, that the cultural life of the nation would be promoted if anyone was free to repurpose anyone else's writing, as in the redactions of British novels, with the contrary assumption that individuals would have greater incentive to write if the law guaranteed them ownership of their writing.

CHAPTER 4

1. These allegories come in several forms—predestined westward expansion and "the melting pot" being but two.

2. We are indebted to Khachig Tölölyan for alerting us to the fact that although "flow" is often used to describe the movement of diasporic peoples, the metaphor tends to be misleading; it does not acknowledge the blockages and obstacles that often prevent the regular and continuous flow of electricity, water, and peoples. Nor does it account for the fact that most people are relatively sedentary (654).

3. For an account of the term "diaspora," see Tennenhouse, *The Importance* 9–13.

4. In *Inalienable Possessions*, Annette B. Weiner explains that no matter how much of their culture a group of people gives up, they must hang onto the one thing that "is intrinsic or ineffable" to the identity of the person, family, or tribe if that identity is to remain intact (6–7).

5. As Trish Loughran notes, "Royal Tyler lived in New Hampshire and so published in New Hampshire—with the consequence that readers in Boston . . . who might have wanted a book like Tyler's *Algerine Captive* could not get their hands on it" (21). Joseph Dennie, Tyler's friend and collaborator, explains the problem: "Your novel has been examined by the few and approved. It is however extremely difficult for the Bostonians to supply themselves with a book that slumbers in a stall at Walpole [New Hampshire], supposed by the latest and most accurate advertisements, to be situated 400 miles north of their meridian" (*The Letters of Joseph Dennie* 165, August 30, 1797). See Chavrat 25–26. Lawrence C. Wroth estimates that during the mid-eighteenth century, "books and pamphlets of a literary or political nature ran to 300–500 copies on average" (40). See also Green.

6. As Charlotte Sussman explains, throughout the eighteenth century, "population" usually meant the opposite of "depopulation," which was of greater concern until Malthus shifted the emphasis entirely. We are grateful for the opportunity to have read the manuscript of her book in progress "Peopling the World: Imagining the Population from Milton to Malthus."

7. With the French Revolution undoubtedly at the back of his mind, Malthus argues that even Europe had experienced the apocalyptic consequences "arising from the want of subsistence. . . . Want was the goad that drove the Scythian shepherds from their native haunts, like so many famished wolves in search of prey. Set in motion by the all-powerful cause, clouds of barbarians seemed to collect from all points of the northern hemisphere. Gathering fresh darkness and terror as they rolled on" (28).

8. Malthus objected to industrial labor and believed the nation was better off "if the wealth that supported two hundred thousand men while they were producing silks and laces would have been more usefully employed in supporting them while they were producing the additional quantity of food" (107).

9. For a reading that addresses the frequent use of the figure of the devil, see Hershel Parker's "The Confidence Man's Masquerade" 293–303. Helen P. Trimpi's *Melville's Confidence Men* identifies a contemporary political figure for each character in the novel. In the second volume of his biography of Melville, Parker also offers an account of Melville's desperate economic condition in the 1850s by way of explaining the novelist's loss of confidence in any number of American institutions. In *The Fabrication of American Literature*, Lara Cohen notes, "Critics who have not focused on the characters have nevertheless sought to unify it thematically, reading it as illustrative of a particular principle, such as the hypocrisy of Christianity or the untrustworthiness of language. All of these interpretations present *The Confidence-Man* as a riddle to be solved by the discerning reader who can find a hidden order beneath Melville's baggy disorder" (162–63).

10. In *The Courage of Truth*, Foucault describes the Cynic as the man who speaks the truth by taking on "a dog's life, a life without modesty, shame, or human respect. It is a life that does in public, in front of everyone, what only dogs and animals dare to do, and which men usually hide." It is also "a life which can fight, which barks at enemies, which knows the good from the

bad, the true from the false, and masters from enemies. In that sense," Foucault concludes, it is a "life of discernment which knows how to prove, test, and distinguish" (243).

11. For an account of Poe's use of literary hoax as a narrative strategy, see Cohen 54–64.

12. Based on a study of Victorian novels, Alex Woloch describes the social field of characters as one organized largely by one-on-one into major and minor characters depending on their relative ability to attract readers' attention. *The Confidence-Man* strikes us as a variation on this mode of organization in that Melville's characters exist for us only when and to the degree that his narration elicits their performance.

13. In *Homo Sacer*, Giorgio Agamben borrows the term "bare life" from Walter Benjamin's "Critique of Violence" and uses it in an attempt to displace Michel Foucault's biopolitical lectures at the Collège de France. Agamben describes his project in these terms: "The protagonist of this book is bare life, that is, the life of *homo sacer* (sacred man), *who may be killed and yet not sacrificed*" (12). For an explanation of why the experience of bare life cannot be understood or defined from the position of those who maintain property in themselves, see Agamben, *Remnants of Auschwitz* 15–40.

14. For an account of Malthus's view of slavery, see Emmett. Kant spells out his objection to the slave trade in "The Science of Right" (1790).

15. We base this claim on European intellectuals who, like Kant and Malthus, were troubled by the migration of whole populations as a result of the economic crises of the late eighteenth century. It is important to note that Bentham, writing at the same time, described the "alleged fact of the formation of such a contract [as] a mere fiction" (*Official Aptitude Maximized* 347). Bentham proposed a contrary model of government based on what he called "the principle of utility": "An action then may be said to be conformable to the principle of utility (meaning with respect to the community at large) when the tendency it has to augment the happiness of the community is greater than any it has to diminish it" (*An Introduction to the Principles of Morals and Legislation* 13). In that the principle of utility presupposed a population of self-interested individuals, it was easily as antagonistic to Austen's as Charles Brockden Brown's indiscriminate social network was. In short, the conflict between the two models was an opposition not between two national mentalities but between different sides of a single argument that engaged novelists and intellectuals on both sides of the Atlantic.

16. As Deanna P. Korestsky points out, the eighteenth-century British figure of "the dying slave" exposed the contradiction within liberal theory between the notion of a "self" that can belong only to itself and the notion of a laboring body that can, under laws of slavery, belong to someone else.

CHAPTER 5

1. On the use of minor characters in nineteenth-century British fiction, see Woloch.

2. For an account of the role of eighteenth-century conduct books in defining the new middling classes in Britain, see Armstrong, *Desire and Domestic Fiction* 69–95.

3. We are drawing here on Michel de Certeau's discussion of strategy and tactics.

4. In *Scenes of Subjection*, Hartman memorably argues that sympathy leads "to an obliterating identification of approximation [that] overtakes the proximity to ethical conduct" (35).

5. William Wells Brown was in England when the Fugitive Slave Act was passed in 1850 and understandably stayed to publish his book where he was considered a free man. In the conclusion to the British edition of *Clotel*, he enjoins the British reader to refuse to associate with

"those who traffic in the flesh and bones of those whom God has made of one flesh as yourself" (246). The fact that he addressed British abolitionists in what was, in our view, a distinctively American style probably helped *Clotel* assume the place it now occupies in literary history as one of the first novels published by an African American and set in the United States. Wells Brown also acknowledges in his conclusion to the British edition of *Clotel* that, while he "personally participated" in many of the scenes described, he also lifted generous portions of the text from personal accounts, abolitionist publications, and other sources, which in our view is entirely compatible with the ambiguity of U.S. copyright law as to whether or not published work belonged to the author, an ambiguity reflected in the many pirated and redacted editions published in the United States, as well as the liberties that pirates as well as publishers took with their language. For another view of Wells Brown's use of source material, see Sanborn.

6. Passing operates differently in the population that Brown asks us to imagine, where everyone is mixed. For an account of passing in the nineteenth century, see Hobbs 28–43. See also Fabi 7–43.

7. For a discussion of this kind of gothic element in *Clotel*, see Silyn Roberts 140–63.

8. Sieminski has sought to explain the many reprintings during the 1770s of Mary Rowlandson's account of her captivity and John Williams's *The Redeemed Captive, Returning to Zion* (1707). Haefeli and Sweeney propose a slightly different series of historical readings to explain the considerable number of reprintings of Williams's narrative. Neither of these accounts, however, ventures to explain why so many different captivity narratives that originally appeared in the late seventeenth and early eighteenth centuries were printed and reprinted in the last decade of the eighteenth and first decade of the nineteenth centuries.

9. Between 1817 and 1859, approximately 50,000 copies of Riley's narrative were printed. The publisher claimed to have sold one million copies, but Ratcliffe refutes that claim. The year before the book first appeared, the basic facts of his shipwreck, enslavement, and ransom circulated in newspaper stories along the eastern seaboard. Riley followed up with a letter offering a barebones account of his experience in the *Mercantile Advertiser* (March 1816). Publication of the book inspired numerous reviews that repeated the basic plot and quoted substantial passages. As other members of the crew were rescued, they published their accounts. By 1819, a number of tales had appeared in print that sought to capitalize on Riley's success. Later on, popular anthologies reprinted stories from Riley's account, and later still, excerpts and redacted versions appeared in anthologies marketed for children.

10. To understand the formal principles organizing this imaginary world, we might begin by recalling that during the period from 1790 to 1802, at least 100,000 immigrants entered the United States, and Congress devised four different conditions and procedures for naturalizing them. The Naturalization Act of 1790 enabled an immigrant who was both free and white to become a citizen after just two years of residency. Worried about the number of potential citizens entering the country from revolutionary France and the increase in immigrants fleeing the troubles in Ireland, however, Congress passed the Naturalization Act of 1795 extending minimum residency to five years. To become citizens after that probationary period, residents were required to swear allegiance to the United States, renounce loyalty to their former sovereigns, and give up any and all claims to noble ranks and titles. This act was in turn revised by the Naturalization Act of 1798, which required immigrants to register with a proper agent within forty-eight hours of arriving in the United States, stretched the waiting period for citizenship from five to fourteen years, and prohibited anyone from obtaining citizenship who was a citizen of a state with which the United States was at war. The act of 1798 apparently went too far in thus limiting immigration, and the Naturalization Law of 1802 repealed it. Finding it difficult to distinguish

between guests and enemies, legislators did away with the category of guest by requiring long-term residents to renounce their former homeland.

11. For an accurately subtle reading of the issues at stake in the debate over cosmopolitanism, see Robbins. For a comprehensive investigation of the concept, see Vertovec and Cohen, as well as Appiah.

12. It has become somewhat more common in recent years to recognize *Letters* as a novel. Rice discusses *Letters* "as an early but sophisticated novel" (99–124), Larkin focuses on the novelistic features of *Letters* (52–76), and Ruttenburg characterizes both "*Letters* and *The Memoirs of Stephen Burroughs* as semi-autobiographical fictions" (270). In his introduction to the Penguin edition of *Letters from an American Farmer*, Albert E. Stone tends to read *Letters* as an autobiographical narrative of Crèveceour himself, which becomes especially difficult when he arrives at a sudden change in the narrator's disposition between the cheerful end of Letter XI and the opening of Letter XII: "I wish for a change of place" (200). Rather than consider *Letters* fictional or note that the novels of the period were hardly concerned with maintaining biographical continuity, Stone does some fiction making of his own: "Living for a time on the charity of friends or by occasional surveying jobs, separated from wife and children . . . the once happy farmer suffered in 1779 what we would today all a nervous breakdown" (12).

CHAPTER 6

1. This, of course, was a common charge against Federalists by Anti-Federalists and among the more plebian Anti-Federalists such as Melancthon Smith and William Petrikin against such "aristocratic" or well-born Anti-Federalists as George Mason and Richard Henry Lee. See, for example, Wood, *Radicalism* 258–65.

2. See Badiou 173–77 for his account of what constitutes an event. See also Hallward 114–16.

3. Because the phrase "Great Awakening" is something of a misnomer in this instance, we hesitate to apply it to Whitefield's revival meetings. During the 1760s, 1770s, and 1780s, the term was intended to signify a popular religious enthusiasm that swept through colonial America to challenge clerical authority in the first half of the eighteenth century and had far-reaching secular consequences. Heimert, for example, claims, "The Great Awakening in America was a unique and profound crisis in the history of 'indigenous culture'" (3). Following the Great Awakening, he writes, there were only "*two* parties on the American religious scene," its advocates and its opponents (3). This division lasted well into the nineteenth century, he argues. This view, while still widely held today, must be revised as a result of work by Butler ("Enthusiasm Described"), Conforti, and Lambert (*Inventing*), among others, however. The term was first used by Joseph Tracy in 1841 in his history of revivals that were occurring in the nineteenth century. As Butler explains in *Awash in a Sea of Faith*, the term was neither contemporary nor used by nineteenth-century historians of the revolutionary period. Revivals in New England began "long before 1730," Butler writes, "yet did not appear with force in Virginia until the 1760s. Its supporters questioned only certain kinds of authority, not authority itself, and they usually strengthened rather than weakened denominational and clerical institutions. It missed most colonies, and even in New England its long term effects have been greatly exaggerated" (165). See Guelzo for an extensive historiographical account of the debate on the Great Awakening that suggests something of the persistent popularity for Heimart's thesis despite evidence to the contrary.

4. As Harry S. Stout writes, where people at local revivals in the 1740s were asking, "'What

must I do to be saved?"' their ministers "were repeating the same message in sermon after sermon: you must acknowledge your sin, humble yourself before Christ, and be born again through his Spirit" (202).

5. For a fuller account of the extensive letter writing campaign by his supporters, the advance publicity for his meetings, and the attention paid to cultivating the popular press by Whitefield, see Lambert, *Pedlar in Divinity* 110–30.

6. For an assessment of the French horn, see Dillon's "John Marrant Blows the French Horn."

7. We are indebted to Gregory Brennen for discovering this law and the sources that made it important to the argument of this chapter. Blackstone notes that initially, troving was treated as an action of trespass in which a person "*found* another's goods, and refused to deliver them on demand, but *converted* them to his own use. . . . [Eventually] by a fiction of law actions of *trover* were at length permitted to be brought against any man, who had in his possession by any means whatsoever the personal goods of another, and sold them or used them without the consent of the owner, or refused to deliver them when demanded. The injury lies in the conversion" (151–52). As Plucknett makes clear, trover action is not relevant for cases of theft; the trover action is based on the assumption of "finding." The possession of the chattel is not illegal in itself. It is the use or conversion that constitutes the tort (375).

8. Based on several decades of complex and yet commonsensical theory devoted to the concept of small world networks in the field of mathematics, Buchanan's lay explanation offers us an admirably clear means of tracing the figure of this concept of social relationships in the novels of the new republic and assessing how it operates rhetorically.

9. Alan Taylor begins and ends his revisionary account of the American Revolution with a discussion of "My Kinsman, Major Molineux." To explain why, as a historian, he has relied on Hawthorne's short story to this extent, Taylor claims, "Nothing done since by historian or novelist so concisely conveys the internal essence of the revolution" (*American Revolutions* 2). While we regard the story as a descriptive theory of popular democracy rather than as an allegory of revolution, this story is as key to our understanding of the new republic as it is to Taylor's.

10. Comparing French to British settlements in North America, Scottish philosopher Adam Ferguson, in an *An Essay on the History of Civil Society* (1767), anticipated Tocqueville by several decades in finding it difficult to imagine a unified America because of the British brand of individualism that had taken root and was flourishing there. "One nation lays the refined plan of a settlement on the continent of North America, and trusts little to the conduct of traders and shortsighted men," he claimed with reference to France, while Britain "leaves men to find their own position in a state of freedom, and to think for themselves" (139). By contrast, Tocqueville's familiarity with post-Independence America convinced him that, by freeing men to think for themselves, the British failure to govern the diverse populations of the American colonies had created a power vacuum that would be filled not by Ferguson's sanguine version of Adam Smith's economy but by a dangerous form of popular sovereignty.

11. Tocqueville considered American democracy as its strongest in the New England township: "In the township, where law and government are closer to those governed, the system of representation is not adopted. There is no town council. The body of voters, having appointed the magistrates, directs them in everything other than the pure and simple execution of the laws of the state" (74–75). See also Morgan 255–62.

12. Alkana argues that Hawthorne's readers would have regarded the rebellion that he stages in this story as no joking matter: "The arrival in manufacturing towns and cities of a newly autonomous young man like Robin reflects the conventional fear that a poor, urban

population would not feel bound by traditions of social order. Thus the mob at the end of 'My Kinsman, Major Molineux' offers as its emblem the primary witness: the naïve and innocent young Robin, who may best be understood not merely as a befuddled observer but as a cause of the discord and the riotous mob action with which the tale culminates" (7).

13. Adam Smith considers "both rebels and traitors [as] those unlucky persons, who, when things have come to a certain degree of violence, have the misfortune to be of the weaker party. In a nation distracted by faction, there are, no doubt, always a few, though commonly but very few, who preserve their judgment untainted by the general contagion" (219). Those infected with "the general contagion" mistake independence of mind for "heresy." Their enthusiasm destroys the untainted judgment required for the sympathetic relations or "fellow-feeling" that unifies what Smith regarded as the British ruling class, here represented by Molineux (5).

CHAPTER 7

1. See Simon During, on forms of democracy as an inflection of liberal ethos and neoliberal economics (1–13).

2. In "Headless Capitalism," Dierdra Reber contends that moments of horizontal affiliation on the order that Hawthorne offers up in this story cannot possibly be an alternative to the liberal order so long as they serve to sustain that order by offering the illusion of gratification and empowerment.

3. Galloway writes, "Distributed networks have no central hubs and no radial nodes. Instead, each entity in the distributed network is an autonomous agent" (33).

4. In one key respect, the form of self-organization that takes shape in novels of the new republic resemble Elinor Ostrom's revision of the prisoner's dilemma game in *Governing the Commons*. As she points out, where privatization promotes competition and uneven distribution, centralized administration of those resources leads to hoarding and mismanagement that inevitably exhaust the supply. Both cases replicate the conditions of the prisoner's dilemma game because the participants communicate with a central authority and do not share information with one another. For lack of information as to whether the other prisoner will behave according to his common interests, each prisoner is likely to see that his odds improve if he acts in his own interests and sacrifices the other. Ostrom's study of a fishing village on the coast of Turkey demonstrates what happens when the "participants themselves design their own contracts in light of the information they have in hand" and forgo any higher authority (17). When each fisherman knows what all others know, each feels that he stands to benefit from cooperation.

5. Sansay herself was anything but the proper English lady novelist, and we can perhaps detect in the education of her straight-laced narrator a carefully nuanced understanding of a form of erotic attachment that might provide a clear alternative to both British prudery and colonial promiscuity in a nation that had cast off British authority.

6. Cathy Davidson has noted that more than half of the novels of the early national period were based on seduction stories or had subplots that were seduction stories (215). See also Tennenhouse, *The Importance of Feeling English* 43–55.

7. Buchanan 131.

8. According to Leonore Davidoff, the rituals of the social season were supposed to move each generation of women "out" of the home and into "the best circles," thereby keeping the culture of the community intact, along with its property.

9. See the "Introduction," by Jennifer Desiderio and Angela Vietto, in Hannah Webster Foster, *The Coquette and the Boarding School* 13.

10. See Tennenhouse, "The American Richardson."

11. Newspaper accounts at the time reported the death of "a female stranger" (*Salem Mercury*, July 29, 1788, 2 [94]: 3). Jeremy Belknap, in a letter to Benjamin Rush that was reprinted in Boston's *Independent Chronicle*, wrote, "a woman who died at an inn, of puerperal fever—a stranger, [is] supposed to be from Connecticut" (September 11, 1788), 20:3. The *Massachusetts Centenil* announced, "The public curiosity having been excited respecting a young stranger Lady, who died at the Bell Tavern. . . . It has since been discovered that she was an unmarried lady of a reputable family in Connecticut, of the name of Whitman." Foster, *The Coquette and the Boarding School* 317–19.

12. It is important to note here that married couples don't remove themselves from circulation in Foster's novel. The Richmans remain in social circulation, and even Eliza plans to return after she has given birth.

13. See Armstrong, "Why Daughters Die," for an explanation of this trope in American literature.

14. Ezra Tawil instructively compares *Hobomok* to *A Narrative of the Life of Mrs. Mary Jemison* (108–9).

15. Jemison's narrative was particularly popular throughout the nineteenth century. June Namias writes that the first edition of *A Narrative of the Life of Mrs. Mary Jemison* "was an instant success, selling over one hundred thousand copies in its first year" and subsequently "went through twenty-seven printings and twenty-three editions ranging from 32 to 483 pages" (152).

16. Carl Schmitt writes, "All significant concepts of the modern theory of the state are secularized theological concepts not only because of their historical development—in which they were transferred from theology to the theory of the state . . . but also because of their systematic structure." Whoever decides on the exception—the conditions under which the law can be suspended in the general interest—is sovereign. "The exception in jurisprudence is analogous to the miracle in theology" (36). See also Kahn 25–28.

17. Other examples of Hawthorne's practice can be seen in the genealogy that is generated at the beginning of *House of Seven Gables*, in which daughters are used to legitimize land taken by one family from a rival family, or in such stories as "Rappaccini's Daughter" and "The Birthmark," in which the purification of the woman operates like a form of possession that kills the woman by perfecting her.

CHAPTER 8

1. Where Sacvan Bercovitch sees Pearl in Europe as Hawthorne's way of imagining an un-American space of freedom (152–53), we want to resist the temptation to allegorize. Instead, we suggest that, by shipping her off to England, Hawthorne is saying that the girl has fulfilled her role in the novel; a redeemed Pearl with an inheritance belongs in a sentimental novel, not in the American community that he imagines in *The Scarlet Letter*.

2. See Baltrusaitis for the art historical account of anamorphosis.

3. Ernest Gilman first applied the concept of anamorphosis to literature, arguing that the same thing goes on in Shakespeare's *Richard II* that we see in Holbein's painting: "Two modes of explanation in the same historical event. . . . The play neither endorses nor denies the Tudor myth but builds on its premises to show that the providential theory of the king's double nature

necessarily requires a complex kind of doublethink for which the curious perspective is the visual model" (128).

4. See Greenblatt 23–25 for a discussion of the shifting of perspective required by a polycentric perspective.

5. See Armstrong and Tennenhouse, "The American Origins of the English Novel" 386–410.

6. For a discussion of the veiled lady in American gothic fiction, see Goddu 97–110. Also see Brodhead on veiled ladies in Antebellum entertainment (48–68). Tennenhouse explains how Mitchell's use of the veil in the interpolated tale of Henry Malcomb in Volume II transforms a British trope into an American one (*The Importance* 103–4).

7. See Kadushin 108–34 for a discussion of Stanley Milgram's experiment, which led to the formulation of "six degrees of separation."

8. Foucault, *Abnormal* 109–32, on pathologizing criminaltity.

9. Freud continues a tradition that begins at least as early as Radcliffe when he breaks down his patient's fantasies into "day residue" material and then demonstrates how dreamwork has transformed this material into expressions of fears otherwise inaccessible to rational analysis.

10. For a thought-provoking discussion of Henry James's possible debt in writing *The Turn of the Screw* to his brother's psychological theory, especially William's concern with the varieties of religious experience and his view of delusions as not necessarily indicating pathology, see Halttunen. We are convinced that Henry was dramatizing the questions that his brother's theory raises to eliminate the basis for any authoritative reading of *The Turn of the Screw*.

11. James acknowledges that there often appears "even within the limits of the same self, and between thoughts all of which alike have this same sense of belonging together, a kind of jointing and separateness among the parts." If what is actually a continuous flow of consciousness appears to be a disjointed "chain" of separate segments, it is because of "breaks that are produced by sudden *contrasts in the quality* of the stream of thought" (239).

12. Matthiessen's argument that the kind of self Henry was could only realize itself in the American protagonists whom the novelist transported to Europe led the critic to see Lambert Strether of *The Ambassadors* as the perfect conjunction of these incompatible perspectives (36).

13. Despite his admiration for James's artistry, the difference in their political orientations forced Matthiessen to acknowledge the exclusionary principle enabling the novelist to focus on the aesthetic dimension of sensory experience: "James was not ignorant of what he called 'the huge collective life' going on beyond his charmed circle" but acknowledged "the vast suffering that Paris has suffered . . . in black shadows looming only at the very edge of [his] paintings" (35). This, as Matthiessen suggests throughout his study of what he considered James's "major phase," is where the material of an aesthetic object comes from and into which it inevitably disperses.

CHAPTER 9

1. There is, of course, a difference between such histories of the American novel as Cowie's, which strive for coverage by mentioning as many novels as possible without offering a careful reading or rendering aesthetic judgment, and literary histories shaped by an argument as to the formal properties or political bent distinctive to the American novel. Such literary histories tend to regard Brockden Brown as an anomaly with literary ambitions that died too young to realize them.

2. According to Dekker and McWilliams, early reviewers were divided over Cooper's Indian tales. Some wanted more historical detail and less romance, while others wanted more romance and less history. Still others, notably Lewis Cass condemned "Cooper's Indians to be mere figments of romance, whose language was too figurative, sentiment too elevated," and morality too pure (See Dekker and Williams 8–9).

3. Wayne Franklin reminds us that Cooper said of Brockden Brown's *Edgar Huntley* (1799) that just because it includes "an American, a savage, a wildcat, and a tomahawk" does not make it an American novel (343–44).

4. Recent historians show the origins of the American Revolution to be many and complex. Yet late eighteenth- and early nineteenth-century accounts of the Revolution tend to blame that war on the colonists' response to the Stamp Act—which Parliament saw as a means of paying for that war. Despite their divergent political orientations, David Ramsay's influential *The History of the American Revolution* (1789) and Mercy Otis Warren's *History of the Rise, Progress and Termination of the American Revolution* (1805) agree that that war and its immediate aftermath instigated revolutionary stirrings that led to the break with Britain. It is worth noting, in this regard, that the year prior to publication of *The Last of the Mohicans*, Cooper wrote another novel about the nation's origins, *Lionel Lincoln* (1825), which is set during the Revolution. Critics attribute the failure of that novel not only to its ponderous sermonizing but also to the fact that the events of 1775–76 were all too familiar. See Dekker 37–42.

5. It is important that Cooper set this novel in what was called the Middle Ground. Which nations among the various sovereign Indian nations, as well as contending European powers, could claim control over the disputed territories was very much up in the air. The contest over hunting rights, retaliation for past assaults, and claims to trading and farming rights often led to a mix of uncertain territorial claims and conflicting and uncertain alliances. As Richard White explains, "Although Frenchmen, Shawnees, and Delawares fought side by side, they remained, in a sense, only enemies of a common enemy" (244). For a discussion of the shifting claims and alliances during the French and Indian War, see White 240–48.

6. In taking up these questions, we are tossing our hat in an already crowded ring of provocative critical commentary. Jared Gardner argues that where Cooper's strategy had been to "turn what seem to be conflicts between the races into quarrels between American and European whites" (83), the Indian in *The Last of the Mohicans* functions in more conventional terms, vanishing so that "his claims [to the land] may be rightfully inherited by Americans" (201). Ezra Tawil extends this argument, contending that "it is clear that the 'Indian problem' and the 'slave problem' were intimately and inextricably linked at the level of cultural meanings" so that readers could "think about the problem of slavery in different terms" (6). Our effort will be to explain why Cooper's novel will support any number of critical readings that uncover social elements within his imagined community that were excluded from participation in the political life of the new nation.

7. The list is long of those who have expressed disappointment, dissatisfaction, or disagreement with Cooper's decision to marry Duncan to Alice while killing off Cora and Uncas. D. H. Lawrence set the template when he wrote, "Evidently Cooper—or the artist in him—has decided there can be no blood-mixing of the two races, white and red. He kills 'em off" (58–59). See also Fiedler 204–9; Baym 67–86; Dekker 64–75; Rans 102–30; Axelrad 33–56; Wallace, *Early Cooper* 81–82; Samuels 61–62. Doris Sommer has discussed the response of many Latin American novelists who questioned Cooper's decision not to let Cora marry (52–82).

8. Colonial European maps often ignored or deliberately erased boundaries and sovereign borders that indigenous peoples had negotiated among themselves and respected for centuries

(Barr, "Red Continent"). Modern scholars continue this practice, according to Julianne Barr, when they refer to well-designated Indian geopolitical boundaries as "backlands," "hinterland," or "back country" in describing the movement of colonial settlers into spaces well marked by various Indian treaties (Barr, "Geographies"). Martin Brückner sees the use of maps "in the context of Western expansion serving Americans as a language for instilling, expressing, and enacting the new imperial dynamic of the Eastern states" (14).

9. It is a curious fact that most discussions of the romance element in *The Last of the Mohicans* consider only the one tradition of European romance. By way of contrast, we see as crucial to this novel's form the interaction between a domestic romance that would produce kinship relations among European settlers of British descent (the romance element in Sir Walter Scott's *Waverly* and Leo Tolstoy's *War and Peace* are among the best examples) and the colonial romances that aim at exogamous kinship relations, as in the novella *Atala*, by François-René Chateaubriand, and, later on, in the novels of Latin and South American nationalism.

10. In Chapter 3, Cooper wants us to think of the history of the wilderness as a sequence of violent seizures of the land beginning with Native Americans and followed by European colonists, who learned from their predecessors. As Hawk-eye says to Chingachgook, "Your fathers came from the setting sun, crossed the big river, fought the peoples of the country, and took the land; and mine came from the red sky of the morning, over the salt lake, and did their work much after the fashion that had been set them by yours" (80).

11. Writing less than a decade after the publication of *Last of the Mohicans*, Tocqueville offers a similar account of the disappearance of the Native Americans. Because European settlers drove away the wild game, the native people "lose, almost entirely, the means of subsistence." As they are forced to migrate, he explains, they find their social bonds dissolving: "their homeland has disappeared; soon they will have no people; families will scarcely survive; their common name is lost, their language is forgotten, and the traces of their origins vanish. The nation has ceased to exist. It hardly features in the memories of American antiquaries and is known only to a few European scholars" (379).

12. Dekker and McWilliams indicate that many of Cooper's reviewers, both American and British, called him the American Scott. See also Dekker 20–42. It is worth noting that an anonymous reviewer in the Paris *Globe* found Cooper's *Leather-Stocking Tales* superior to Chateaubriand's *Atala* (Dekker and McWilliams 132–33). For all the reviews of this novel, the question that never gets answered is on what basis Cooper's version of the romance form called to mind both Chateaubriand's romance and Scott's and was, at the same time, distinctively American.

13. In defining the Greek romance, Bakhtin explains, "From the very beginning, the love between the hero and heroine is not subject to doubt; their love remains *absolutely unchanged* throughout the entire novel. Their chastity is also preserved, and their marriage at the end of the novel is *directly conjoined* with their love—that same love that had been ignited at their first meeting at the outset of the novel; it is as if nothing had happened between these two moments, as if the marriage had been consummated on the day after their meeting" ("Forms of Time and the Chronotope in the Novel" 89). In this respect, the Alice-Heyward relationship is organized in much the same way that Munro and Alice's mother's is, that is to say. But another form of romance, which Bakhtin calls "chivalric romance," intervenes in both instances—this other form kicks in when Munro marries Cora's mother, as well as when daughter Alice's story ends, not with her marriage to Heyward but with Cora's and Uncas's funerals. Where Greek romance strives "to reunite the sundered links in the normal course of life's events," according to Bakhtin, chivalric romance subjects the entire world "to 'suddenly,' to the category of miraculous and unexpected chance" (152).

14. Barbara Mann explains that after 1825, two conflicting "rules of race" were competing for social control, "those of recognition and descent. The rule of recognition was the eye test of identity—whoever 'looked white' might pass—whereas the rule of descent, the infamous one drop rule, forbade passing at all times, regardless of generation or appearance" (159).

15. On this trope in captivity narratives, see Armstrong, "Why Daughters Die."

16. Alice's sentimental femininity fulfills anthropologist Annette Weiner's definition of an "inalienable possession" as some quality, trait, or possession that one cannot give away and remain who one is and part of the group to which one belongs. In the case of stolen daughters, such a loss disrupts the continuity of the ethnos of family, tribe, or clan.

17. The double definition of family we have identified in *The Last of the Mohicans* constitutes a major pattern of nineteenth-century thought. Charles Darwin, for example, was prompted by morphological resemblances among the species he observed in South America to formulate an evolutionary narrative. In Cooper's novel, the same models assume the forms, respectively, of consanguineous kinship (Alice) and family resemblances (Cora). Where the one establishes continuity over time on the basis of inheritance and is hostile to differences, the other establishes similarities among natural or culture forms and is enhanced by difference.

18. Here, we have drawn on Arac's reading of *Mohicans* as a confrontation of " 'Nature,' represented by the heroic and unspoiled good Indians," set against " 'civilization,' represented by the British" (9).

19. In *Political Theory and the Displacement of Politics*, Bonnie Honig argues against any convergent form of pluralism and on behalf of what she calls "agonistic democracy" that encourages "dissonance, resistance, conflict or struggle," that is to say, against an expansive, all-inclusive pluralism and on behalf of the divisiveness of the political domain as that which preserves it (2).

Works Cited

Agamben, Giorgio. *Homo Sacer: Sovereign Power and Bare Life.* Trans. Daniel Heller-Roazen. Stanford: Stanford University Press, 1998.

———. *Remnants of Auschwitz: The Witness and the Archive.* Trans. Daniel Heller-Roazen. New York: Zone, 1999.

Alkana, Joseph. "Disorderly History in 'My Kinsman, Major Molineux.'" *English Studies Quarterly* 53 (2007): 1–30.

Althusser, Louis. *Montesquieu, Rousseau, Marx: Politics and History.* Trans. Ben Brewster. London: Verso, 1982.

Ammerman, David. *In the Common Cause: American Response to the Coercive Acts of 1774.* Charlottesville: University of Virginia Press, 1974.

Anderson, Benedict. "Frameworks of Comparison: Benedict Anderson Reflects on His Intellectual Formation." *London Review of Books* 38, no. 2 (21 January 2016): 15–18.

———. *Imagined Communities: Reflection on the Origin and Spread of Nationalism.* Rev. ed. London: Verso, 2006.

Appiah, Anthony Kwame. *Cosmopolitanism: Ethics in a World of Strangers.* New York: Norton, 2006.

Arendt, Hannah. *On Revolution.* New York: Penguin, 2006.

Armstrong, Nancy. *Desire and Domestic Fiction: A Political History of the Novel.* New York: Oxford University Press, 1987.

———. "Just Like a Woman: Balibar on the Politics of Reproduction." *Balibar and the Citizen Subject.* Ed. Warren Montag and Hanan Elsayed. 284–308. Edinburgh: Edinburgh University Press, 2017.

———. "The Nineteenth-Century Austen: A Turn in the History of Fear." *Genre* 23 (1990): 227–46.

———. "Why Daughters Die: The Racial Logic of American Sentimentalism." *Yale Journal of Criticism* 7, no. 2 (1994): 1–24.

Armstrong, Nancy, and Leonard Tennenhouse. "The American Origins of the English Novel." *American Literary History* 4 (Fall 1992): 386–410.

———. *The Imaginary Puritan: Literature, Intellectual Labor, and the Origins of Personal Life.* Berkeley: University of California Press, 1992.

———. "The Network Novel and How it Unsettled Domestic Fiction." *A Companion to the English Novel.* Ed. Stephen Arata, J. Paul Hunter, and Jennifer Wicke. 306–20. New York: Wiley-Blackwell, 2015.

Austen, Jane. *Pride and Prejudice.* London: Penguin, 2003.

Axelrad, Allan M. "*The Last of the Mohicans,* Race Mixing, and America's Destiny."

Works Cited

Leather-Stocking Redux; Or, Old Tales, New Essays. Ed. Jeffrey Walker. 33–56. New York: AMS, 2011.

Badiou, Alain. *Being and Event.* Trans. Oliver Feltham. London: Continuum, 2007.

Baepler, Paul Michel, ed. *White Slaves, African Masters: An Anthology of American Captivity Narratives.* Chicago: University of Chicago Press, 1999.

Bailyn, Bernard. *The Ideological Origins of the American Revolution.* Cambridge, Mass.: Harvard University Press, 1992.

Bakhtin, Mikhail. *The Dialogic Imagination: Four Essays by M. M. Bakhtin.* Ed. Michael Holquist. Trans. Caryl Emerson and Michael Holquist. Austin: University of Texas Press, 1981.

——. "Discourse in the Novel." Bakhtin, *The Dialogic Imagination* 259–422.

——. "Epic and Novel: Toward a Methodology for the Study of the Novel." Bakhtin, *The Dialogic Imagination* 3–40.

——. "Forms of Time and of the Chronotope in the Novel: Notes Toward a Historical Poetics." Bakhtin, *The Dialogic Imagination* 84–258.

——. *Rabelais and His World.* 1941. Trans. Hélène Iswolsky. Bloomington: Indiana University Press, 1993.

Balibar, Étienne. "The Genealogical Scheme: Race or Culture?" *Trans-Scripts: An Interdisciplinary Journal in the Humanities and Social Sciences* 1 (2011): 1–9.

——. *Identity and Difference: John Locke and the Invention of Consciousness.* Trans. Warren Montag. London: Verso, 2013.

——. "'Possessive Individualism' Reversed: From Locke to Derrida." *Constellations* 9, no. 3 (2002): 299–317.

——. *We, the People of Europe: Reflections on Transnational Citizenship.* Trans. James Swenson. Princeton, N.J.: Princeton University Press, 2004.

Baltrusaitis, Jurgis. *Anamorphic Art.* Trans. W. J. Strachan. New York: Abrams, 1977.

Barr, Julianne. "Geographies of Power: Mapping Indian Borders in the 'Borderlands' of the Early Southwest." *William and Mary Quarterly* 68 (Jan. 2011): 5–46.

——. "The Red Continent and the Cant of the Coastline." *William and Mary Quarterly* 69 (July 2012): 521–26.

Baym, Nina. "How Men and Women Wrote Indian Stories." *New Essays on* The Last of the Mohicans. Ed. H. Daniel Peck. 67–86. Cambridge: Cambridge University Press, 1992.

Bentham, Jeremy. *An Introduction to the Principles of Morals and Legislation.* Ed. J. H. Burns and H. L. A. Hart. London: University of London Press, 1970.

——. *Official Aptitude Maximized, Expenses Minimized.* Ed. Philip Schofield. Oxford: Oxford University Press, 1993.

Bercovitch, Sacvan. *The Office of the Scarlet Letter.* Baltimore: Johns Hopkins University Press, 1992.

Bird, Robert Montgomery. *Sheppard Lee, Written by Himself.* New York: New York Review of Books, 2008.

Blackstone, William. *Commentaries on the Laws of England.* 1765. *The Avalon Project: Documents in Law, History and Diplomacy.* Yale Law School. Aug. 23, 2016. <http://avalon.law.yale.edu/subject_menus/blackstone.asp>.

Brackenridge, Hugh Henry. *Modern Chivalry.* Ed. Ed White. Indianapolis, Ind.: Hackett, 2009.

Brodhead, Richard. *Cultures of Letters: Scenes of Reading and Writing in Nineteenth-Century America.* Chicago: University of Chicago Press, 1993.

Brown, Charles Brockden. *Arthur Mervyn or, Memoirs of the Year 1793, with Related Texts.* Ed. Philip Barnard and Stephen Shapiro. Indianapolis, Ind.: Hackett, 2008.

————. *Edgar Huntley; or, Memoirs of a Sleep Walker*. Ed. Philip Barnard and Stephen Shapiro. Indianapolis, Ind.: Hackett, 2006.

————. *Wieland; or the Transformation, An American Tale with Related Texts*. Ed. Philip Barnard and Stephen Shapiro. Indianapolis, Ind.: Hackett, 2009.

Brown, Homer Obed. *Institutions of the English Novel*. Philadelphia: University of Pennsylvania Press, 1997.

Brown, Richard D. *Revolutionary Politics in Massachusetts: The Boston Committee of Correspondence and the Towns, 1672–1774*. Cambridge, Mass.: Harvard University Press, 1970.

Brown, William Wells. *Clotel or the President's Daughter*. Ed. William Edward Farrison. New York: Carol, 1995.

Brückner, Martin. *The Geographic Revolution in Early America: Maps, Literacy & National Identity*. Chapel Hill: University of North Carolina Press, 2006.

Buchanan, Mark. *Nexus: Small Worlds and the Groundbreaking Science of Networks*. New York: Norton, 2002.

Butler, Jon. *Awash in a Sea of Faith: Christianizing the American People*. Cambridge, Mass.: Harvard University Press, 1990.

————. "Enthusiasm Described and Decried: The Great Awakening as Interpretative Fiction." *Journal of American History* 69 (1982): 305–25.

Carp, Benjamin. *Defiance of the Patriots: The Boston Tea Party and the Making of America*. New Haven, Conn.: Yale University Press, 2010.

Cass, Lewis. *North American Review* XXVI (1828). Reprinted in Dekker and McWilliams, 373–76

Certeau, Michel de. *The Practice of Everyday Life*. Trans. Steven Rendall. Berkeley: University of California Press, 1984.

Charvat, William. *Literary Publishing in America, 1790–1850*. Amherst: University of Massachusetts Press, 1959.

Chase, Richard. *The American Novel and Its Tradition*. Baltimore: Johns Hopkins University Press, 1957.

Child, Lydia Maria. *Hobomok and Other Writings on Indians*. Ed. Carolyn E. Karcher. New Brunswick, N.J.: Rutgers University Press, 2011.

Cohen, Lara Langer. *The Fabrication of American Literature: Fraudulence and Antebellum Print Culture*. Philadelphia: University of Pennsylvania Press, 2012.

Conforti, Joseph A. *Jonathan Edwards, Religious Tradition and American Culture*. Chapel Hill: University of North Carolina Press, 1995.

"Constitution of New Hampshire, 1776." *The Avalon Project: Documents in Law, History and Diplomacy*. Yale Law School. Aug. 22, 2016. <http://avalon.law.yale.edu/18th_century /nho9.asp>.

Cooper, James Fenimore. *The Last of the Mohicans*. New York: Penguin, 1986.

————. Review of *A New-England Tale*. *Repository* 4 (May 1822): 336–70.

Cowie, Alexander. *The Rise of the American Novel*. New York: American Book Company, 1951.

Crèvecoeur, J. Hector St. John de. *Letters from an American Farmer and Sketches of Eighteenth-Century America*. Ed. Albert E. Stone. New York: Penguin, 1983.

Davidoff, Leonore. *The Best Circles: Society, Etiquette and the Season*. London: Crescent Library, 1973.

Davidson, Cathy N. *Revolution and the Word: The Rise of the Novel in America*. New York: Oxford University Press, 1986.

"The Declaration of Independence." *The Charters of Freedom*. The U.S. National Archives &

Records Administration. Sept. 29, 2015. <http://www.archives.gov/exhibits/charters/print
  _friendly.html?page=declaration_transcript_content.html&title=NARA%20%7C%20
  The%20Declaration%20of%20Independence%3A%20A%20Transcription>.

Dekker, George. *James Fenimore Cooper, the American Scott.* New York: Barnes & Noble, 1967.

Dekker, George, and John P. McWilliams, eds. *Fenimore Cooper: The Critical Heritage.* Boston:
  Routledge and Kegan Paul, 1973.

Deleuze, Gilles. "Gilles Deleuze on Spinoza's Concept of Affect." *Les Cours de Gilles Deleuze.*
  Trans. Timothy S. Murphy. Aug. 26, 2015. <http://www.webdeleuze.com/php/texte.php?
  cle=14&groupe=Spinoza&langue=2>.

———. *The Logic of Sense.* Trans. Mark Lester with Charles Stivale. Ed. Constantin V. Boundas.
  New York: Columbia University Press, 1990.

Deleuze, Gilles, and Félix Guattari. *A Thousand Plateaus: Capitalism and Schizophrenia.* Trans.
  Brian Massumi. Minneapolis: University of Minnesota Press, 1987.

Deleuze, Gilles, and Claire Parnet. "On the Superiority of Anglo-American Literature." *Dialogues II.* Trans. Hugh Tomlinson. 27–56. London: Continuum, 2006.

Dennie, Joseph. *The Letters of Joseph Dennie 1768–1812.* Ed. Laura G. Pedder. Orono: University
  of Maine Press, 1936.

Dillon, Elizabeth Maddock. "John Marrant Blows the French Horn: Print, Performance, and
  the Making of Publics in Early African American Literature." *Early African American Print
  Culture.* Ed. Lara Langer Cohen and Jordan Alexander Stein. 318–39. Philadelphia: University of Pennsylvania Press, 2012.

———. "The Secret History of the Early American Novel: Leonora Sansay and Revolution in
  Saint Domingue." *Novel: A Forum on Fiction* 40 (2006): 77–103.

Douglas, Ann. *The Feminization of American Culture.* New York: Anchor, 1988.

During, Simon. *Against Democracy: Literary Experience in the Era of Emancipations.* New York:
  Fordham University Press, 2012.

Elmer, Jonathan. *Reading at the Social Limit: Affect, Mass Culture, & Edgar Allan Poe.* Stanford,
  Calif.: Stanford University Press, 1995.

Emmett, Ross B. "Malthus, the Slave Trade, and the Civilizing Effect of the Preventive Checks."
  Michigan State University Property and Environment Research Center (PERC), June 11,
  2014. *SSRN.* Aug. 22, 2016. <http://papers.ssrn.com/sol3/papers.cfm? abstract_id=2449035>.

Esposito, Roberto. *Bios: Biopolitics and Philosophy.* Trans. Timothy Campbell. Minneapolis:
  University of Minnesota Press, 2008.

Esty, Jed. *A Shrinking Island: Modernism and National Culture in England.* Princeton, N.J.:
  Princeton University Press, 2003.

Fabi, M. Giulia. *Passing and the Rise of the African American Novel.* Urbana: University of Illinois
  Press, 2001.

Ferguson, Adam. *An Essay on the History of Civil Society.* Ed. Famoa Oz-Salzberger. Cambridge:
  Cambridge University Press, 2007.

Fiedler, Leslie. *Love and Death in the American Novel.* 1960. New York: Anchor, 1992.

Forster, E. M. *Aspects of the Novel.* New York: Harcourt, Brace & World, 1955.

Foster, Hannah Webster. *The Coquette and the Boarding School.* Ed. Jennifer Desiderio and Angela Vietto. Peterborough, Ontario: Broadview, 2011.

Foucault, Michel. *Abnormal: Lectures at the Collège de France, 1974–1975.* Trans. Graham Burchell.
  New York: Picador, 1999.

———. *The Birth of Biopolitics: Lectures at the Collège de France, 1978–79.* Ed. Michel Senellart.
  Trans. Graham Burchell. New York: Picador, 2008.

——. *The Courage of Truth: The Government of Self and Others II.* Ed. Frédéric Gros. Trans. Graham Burchell. New York: Palgrave-Macmillan, 2011.

——. *Discipline and Punish: The Birth of the Prison.* Trans. Alan Sheridan. New York: Vintage, 1979.

——. "Of Other Spaces: Utopias and Heterotopias." Trans. Jay Miskowiec. 1967. Aug. 22, 2016. <http://web.mit.edu/allanmc/www/foucault>.

——. *Security, Territory, Population: Lectures at the Collège de France, 1977–1978.* Ed. Michel Senellart. Trans. Graham Burchell. New York: Picador, 2007.

——. *"Society Must Be Defended": Lectures at the Collège de France 1975–76.* Trans. David Macey. New York: Picador, 2003.

Franklin, Benjamin. *The Autobiography of Benjamin Franklin.* Ed. Leonard W. Labaree, Ralph L. Ketcham, Helen C. Boatfield, and Helene H. Fineman. New Haven, Conn.: Yale University Press, 1964.

Franklin, Wayne. *James Fenimore Cooper: The Early Years.* New Haven, Conn.: Yale University Press, 2007.

Frierson, William C. "Casual Criticims" [*sic*]. *Sewanee Review* 36 (1928): 376–77.

Gallagher Michael P. *"Aspects of the Novel* by E. M. Forster; *E. M. Forster: The Perils of Humanism* by Frederick C. Crews." *Studies: An Irish Quarterly Review* 53 (1964): 213–16.

Galloway, Alexander R. *Protocol: How Control Exists After Decentralization.* Cambridge, Mass.: MIT Press, 2004.

Gardner, Jared. *Master Plots: Race and the Founding of an American Literature, 1787–1845.* Baltimore: Johns Hopkins University Press, 1998.

Gilman, Ernest. *The Curious Perspective: Literary and Pictorial Wit in the Seventeenth Century.* New Haven, Conn.: Yale University Press, 1978.

Ginzburg, Carlo. "Family Resemblances and Family Trees: Two Cognitive Metaphors." *Critical Inquiry* 30 (2004): 537–56.

Goddu, Teresa A. *Gothic America: Narrative, History, and Nation.* New York: Columbia University Press, 1997.

Goodrich, Samuel Griswold. *Recollections of a Lifetime or Men and Things I Have Seen: In a Series of Letters to a Friend, Historical, Biographical, Anecdotal, and Descriptive.* 2 vols. New York: Miller, Orton, and Mulligan, 1856.

Gould, Philip. *Covenant and Republic: Historical Romance and the Politics of Puritanism.* New York: Cambridge University Press, 1996.

Green, James N. "The Rise of Book Publishing." *A History of the Book in America.* Ed. Robert A. Gross and Mary Kelley. Vol 2. 75–127. Chapel Hill: University of North Carolina Press, 2010.

Greenblatt, Stephen. *Renaissance Self-Fashioning: From More to Shakespeare.* 1980. Chicago: University of Chicago Press, 2005.

Guelzo, Allen C. "God's Designs: The Literature of the Colonial Revivals of Religion, 1735–1760." *New Directions in American Religious History.* Ed. Harry S. Stout and Darryl G. Hart. 141–72. New York: Oxford University Press, 1997.

Hallward, Peter. *Badiou: A Subject to Truth.* Minneapolis: University of Minnesota Press, 2003.

Halttunen, Karen. *Confidence Men and Painted Women: A Study of Middle-Class Culture, 1830–1870.* New Haven, Conn.: Yale University Press, 1982.

——. " 'Through the Cracked and Fragmented Self': William James and *The Turn of the Screw.*" *American Quarterly* 40 (1988): 472–90.

Hamilton, Alexander, James Madison, and John Jay. *The Federalist Papers.* Ed. Clinton Rossiter. New York: Signet, 2003.

Hardt, Michael, and Antonio Negri. *Empire.* Cambridge, Mass.: Harvard University Press, 2001.

Hartman, Saidiya V. *Scenes of Subjection: Terror, Slavery and Self-Making in Nineteenth-Century America.* New York: Oxford University Press, 1997.

Hastings, George E. "How Cooper Became a Novelist." *American Literature* 12 (1940): 20–51.

Hawthorne, Nathaniel. "My Kinsman, Major Molineux." *Nathaniel Hawthorne's Tales.* Ed. James McIntosh. 3–17. New York: Norton, 1987.

———. *The Scarlet Letter and Other Writings.* Ed. Leland S. Person. New York: Norton, 2005.

Heimart, Alan. *Religion and the American Mind: From the Great Awakening to the Revolution.* Cambridge, Mass.: Harvard University Press, 1966.

Hill, Mike, and Warren Montag. *The Other Adam Smith.* Stanford, Calif.: Stanford University Press, 2015.

Hirschman, Albert O. *The Passions and the Interests: Political Arguments for Capitalism Before Its Triumph.* Princeton, N.J.: Princeton University Press, 1997.

Hobbs, Allyson. *A Chosen Exile: A History of Racial Passing.* Cambridge, Mass.: Harvard University Press, 2014.

Hoffman, Daniel. *Form and Fable in American Fiction.* New York: Oxford University Press, 1961.

Holton, Woody. *Unruly Americans and the Origins of the Constitution.* New York: Hill and Wang, 2007.

Honig, Bonnie. *Political Theory and the Displacement of Politics.* Ithaca, N.Y.: Cornell University Press, 1993.

James, Henry. *The Turn of the Screw.* In *The Turn of the Screw and Other Stories.* Ed. T. J. Lustig. 113–236. Oxford: Oxford University Press, 1992.

James, William. *The Principles of Psychology.* Rev. ed. Vol. 1. New York: Dover, 1950.

Jameson, Fredric. "Rousseau and Contradiction." *South Atlantic Quarterly* 104 (2005): 693–706.

Jefferson, Thomas. "A Summary View of the Rights of British America." *Thomas Jefferson: Writings.* Ed. Merrill D. Peterson. 105–22. New York: Library of America, 2011.

Kadushin, Charles. *Understanding Social Networks: Theories, Concepts, and Findings.* New York: Oxford University Press, 2012.

Kahn, Victoria. *The Future of Illusion: Political Theology and Early Modern Texts.* Chicago: University of Chicago Press, 2014.

Kant, Immanuel. "To Perpetual Peace: A Philosophical Sketch." *Perpetual Peace and Other Essays on Politics, History, and Morals.* Trans. Ted Humphrey. 107–43. Indianapolis, Ind.: Hackett, 1983.

———. "The Science of Right." *Marxists Internet Archive.* Trans. W. Hastie. Aug. 22, 2016. <https://www.marxists.org/reference/subject/ethics/kant/morals/cho4.htm>.

Kennedy, J. Gerald. *Strange Nation: Literary Nationalism and Cultural Conflict in the Age of Poe.* New York: Oxford University Press, 2016.

Kittler, Friedrich A. *Discourse Networks 1800/1900.* Trans. Michael Metteer with Chris Cullens. Stanford, Calif.: Stanford University Press, 1990.

Knapp, Lorenzo Samuel. *Extracts from a Journal of Travels in North America Consisting of Accounts of Boston and Its Vicinity.* Boston: Thomas Badger, 1818.

Koretsky, Deana P. "Habeas Corpus and the Politics of Freedom: Slavery and Romantic Suicide." *Essays in Romanticism* 22 (2015): 21–33.

Kramnick, Isaac. "The 'Great National Discussion': The Discourse of Politics in 1787." *William and Mary Quarterly* 45 (1988): 3–32.

Lambert, Frank. *Inventing the "Great Awakening."* Princeton, N.J.: Princeton University Press, 1999.

———. *Pedlar in Divinity: George Whitefield and the Transatlantic Revivals, 1737–1770.* Princeton, N.J.: Princeton University Press, 1994.

Larkin, Edward. "The Cosmopolitan Revolution: Loyalism and the Fiction of an American Nation." *Novel: A Forum on Fiction* 40 (2006): 52–76.

Lawrence, D. H. *Studies in Classic American Literature*. 1923. New York: Viking, 1970.

Leavis, F. R. *The Great Tradition: George Eliot, Henry James, Joseph Conrad*. London: Faber and Faber, 1948.

Lévi-Strauss, Claude. *The Origin of Table Manners*. Trans. John and Doreen Weightman. Chicago: University of Chicago Press, 1990.

———. "The Structural Study of Myth." *Journal of American Folklore* 68 (1955): 428–44.

Lewis, R. W. S. *The American Adam: Innocence and Tragedy in the Nineteenth Century*. Chicago: University of Chicago Press, 1955.

Locke, John. *Two Treatises of Government*. Ed. Peter Laslett. Cambridge: Cambridge University Press, 2015.

Loughran, Trish. *The Republic in Print: Print Culture in the Age of U.S. Nation Building, 1770–1870*. New York: Columbia University Press, 2007.

Luck, Chad. *The Body of Property: Antebellum American Fiction and the Phenomenology of Possession*. New York: Fordham University Press, 2014.

Lukàcs, Georg. *The Historical Novel*. Trans. Hannah Mitchell and Stanley Mitchell. Lincoln: University of Nebraska Press, 1962.

———. "Narrate or Describe?" *Writer and Critic and Other Essays*. Ed. and trans. Arthur D. Kahn. 110–48. New York: Grossett and Dunlap, 1971.

———. *Realism in Our Time: Literature and the Class Struggle*. Trans. John and Necke Mander. New York: Harper & Row, 1971.

———. *The Theory of the Novel*. Trans. Anna Bostock. Cambridge, Mass.: MIT Press, 1971.

Main, Jackson Turner. "Government by the People: The American Revolution and Democratization of the Legislatures." *William and Mary Quarterly* 23 (1966): 391–407.

Malthus, Thomas Robert. *An Essay on the Principle of Population*. Ed. Philip Appleman. New York: Norton, 2004.

Mann, Barbara Alice. "Race Traitor: Cooper, His Critics, and Nineteenth-Century Literary Politics." *A Historical Guide to James Fenimore Cooper*. Ed. Leland S. Person. 155–85. New York: Oxford University Press, 2007.

Markoe, Peter. *The Algerine Spy in Pennsylvania or, Letters Written by a Native of Algiers on the Affairs of the United States in America from the Close of the Year 1783 to the Meeting of the Convention*. Ed. Timothy Marr. Yardley, Pa.: Westholme, 2008.

Marrant, John. "A Narrative of the Lord's Dealings with John Marrant." *American Captivity Narratives*. Ed. Gordon M. Sayre. 203–24. New York: Houghton Mifflin, 2000.

Marx, John. *The Modernist Novel and the Decline of Empire*. Cambridge: Cambridge University Press, 2005.

Marx, Karl. *Capital: A Critique of Political Economy*. Vol I. Trans. Ben Fowkes. New York: Vintage, 1977.

Mason, George. "Draft of a Declaration of Rights Prepared for the Virginia Convention of August 1774." *The Papers of Thomas Jefferson Digital Edition*. Ed. James P. McClure and J. Jefferson Looney. Charlottesville: University of Virginia Press, Rotunda, 2008–2016. Aug. 22, 2016. <http://rotunda.upress.virginia.edu.proxy.lib.duke.edu/founders/TSJN-01-01-02-0089>.

Massumi, Brian. "The Future Birth of the Affective Fact: The Political Ontology of Threat." *The Affect Theory Reader*. Ed. Melissa Gregg and Gregory J. Seigworth. 52–70. Durham, N.C.: Duke University Press, 2010.

Matthiessen, F. O. *Henry James: The Major Phase*. New York: Oxford University Press, 1963.

Matson, Cathy D. "Capitalizing Hope: Economic Thought and the Early National Economy."
    Wages of Independence: Capitalism in the Early American Republic. Ed. Paul A. Gilge. 117–
    36. Lanham, Md.: Rowman and Littlefield, 2006.
———. "A House of Many Mansions: Some Thoughts on the Field of Economic History." *The
    Economy of Early America: Historical Perspectives and New Directions.* Ed. Cathy D. Mat-
    son. 1–70. University Park: Pennsylvania State University Press, 2006.
Matson, Cathy D., and Peter S. Onuf. *A Union of Interests: Political and Economic Thought in
    Revolutionary America.* Lawrence: University Press of Kansas, 1990.
McCusker, John J., and Russell R. Menard. *The Economy of British America, 1607–1789.* Chapel
    Hill: University of North Carolina Press, 1986.
Mcpherson, Sandra. "Rent to Own; or, What's Entailed in *Pride and Prejudice.*" *Representations*
    82, no. 1 (2003): 1–23.
Melville, Herman. *The Confidence-Man: His Masquerade.* Ed. Hershel Parker and Mark Niemeyer.
    New York: Norton, 2006.
Middlekauff, Robert. *The Glorious Cause: The American Revolution, 1763–1789.* New York: Ox-
    ford University Press, 2007.
Miller, D. A. *Jane Austen, or the Secret of Style.* Princeton, N.J.: Princeton University Press, 2003.
Millstein, Roberta L. "Populations as Individuals." *Biological Theory* 4 (2009): 267–73.
Mitchell, Isaac. *The Asylum; or Alonzo and Melissa: An American Tale Founded in Fact.* Ed. Rich-
    ard Pressman. San Antonio, Tex.: Early American Reprints, 2016.
Mitchell, Robert. "Biopolitics and Population Aesthetics." *South Atlantic Quarterly* 115, no. 2
    (Apr. 2016): 367–98.
———. "Population Aesthetics in Romantic and Post-Romantic Literature." *Constellations of a
    Contemporary Romanticism.* Ed. Jacques Khalip and Tres Pyle. 267–89. New York: Ford-
    ham University Press, 2016.
Montag, Warren. "The Common Is of No Use: Property and Life in Locke's *Second Treatise.*" *The
    Biological Turn in Literary Studies.* Symposium. Duke University, Durham, North Caro-
    lina. Feb. 27, 2015. <https://www.youtube.com/watch?v=6c0FtaAPF5k>.
Moretti, Franco. *Atlas of the European Novel: 1800–1900.* London: Verso, 1998.
———. "The Slaughterhouse of Literature." *Modern Language Quarterly* 61, no. 2 (2000):
    207–27.
Morgan, Edmund S. *Inventing the People: The Rise of Popular Sovereignty.* New York: Norton,
    1988.
Namias, June. *White Captives: Gender and Ethnicity on the American Frontier.* Chapel Hill: Uni-
    versity of North Carolina Press, 1993.
Needham, Rodney. "Polythetic Classification: Convergence and Consequences." *Man,* n.s., 10,
    no. 3 (1975): 349–69.
Ostrom, Elinor. *Governing the Commons: The Evolution of Institutions for Collective Action.* Cam-
    bridge: Cambridge University Press, 1990.
Otter, Samuel. *Philadelphia Stories: America's Literature of Race and Freedom.* New York: Oxford
    University Press, 2010.
Panther, Abraham (pseud.). "A surprising account of the Discovery of a Lady who was taken by
    the Indians in the year 1777, and after making her escape, she retired to a lonely Cave
    where she lived nine years." *Women's Captivity Narratives.* Ed. Kathryn Zabelle Derounian-
    Stodola. 86–90. New York: Penguin, 1998.
Parker, Hershel. "The Confidence-Man's Masquerade." *The Confidence-Man: His Masquerade.*
    Ed. Hershel Parker and Mark Niemeyer. 293–303. New York: Norton, 2006.

Plucknett, Theodore F. *A Concise History of the Common Law*. 5th ed. Boston: Little, Brown, 1956.

Poe, Edgar Allan. "The Fall of the House of Usher." *The Complete Tales and Poems of Edgar Allan Poe*. 231–45. New York: Vintage, 1975.

Pratt, Lloyd. *The Strangers Book: The Human of African American Literature*. Philadelphia: University of Pennsylvania Press, 2016.

Rakove, Jack N. *Original Meanings: Politics and Ideas in the Making of the Constitution*. New York: Vintage, 1997.

———. *Revolutionaries: A New History of the Invention of America*. Boston: Houghton Mifflin-Harcourt, 2010.

Ramsay, David. *The History of the American Revolution*. 1789. Ed. Lester H. Cohen. 2 vols. Indianapolis: Liberty Fund, 1990. *Online Library of Liberty*. Aug. 23, 2016. <http://oll.liberty fund.org/titles/1870>.

Rancière, Jacques. *The Politics of Literature*. Trans. Julie Rose. Cambridge: Polity, 2011.

Rans, Geoffrey. *Cooper's Leather-Stocking Novels: A Secular Reading*. Chapel Hill: University of North Carolina Press, 1991.

Ratcliffe, Donald J. "Selling Captain Riley, 1816–1859: How Did This 'Narrative' Become So Well Known?" *Proceedings of the American Antiquarian Society* 117 (2007): 177–209.

Reber, Dierdra. "Headless Capitalism: Affect as Free-Market Episteme." *differences* 23 (2012): 62–100.

Reid, John Phillip. *The Authority of Rights*. Madison: University of Wisconsin Press, 1986.

Reilly, Elizabeth Carroll, and David D. Hall. "Customers and the Market for Books." *The History of the Book in America: The Colonial Book in the Atlantic World*. Ed. Hugh Armory and David D. Hall. 387–99. Cambridge: Cambridge University Press, 2000.

Rice, Grantland. *The Transformation of Authorship in America*. Chicago: University of Chicago Press, 1997.

Robbins, Bruce. "Comparative Cosmopolitanisms." *Cosmopolitics: Thinking and Feeling Beyond the Nation*. Ed. Pheng Cheah and Bruce Robbins. 246–64. Minneapolis: University of Minnesota Press, 1998.

Rooney, Ellen. *Seductive Reasoning: Pluralism as the Problematic of Contemporary Literary Theory*. Ithaca, N.Y.: Cornell University Press, 1989.

Rousseau, Jean-Jacques. *The Social Contract and Other Later Political Writings*. Ed. and trans. Victor Gourevitch. Cambridge: Cambridge University Press, 2014.

Rowlandson, Mary. "The Sovereignty and Goodness of God." *American Captivity Narratives*. Ed. Gordon M. Sayre. 137–76. Boston: Houghton Mifflin, 2000.

Ruttenburg, Nancy. *Democratic Personality: Popular Voice and the Trial of American Authorship*. Stanford, Calif.: Stanford University Press, 1998.

Ryerson, Richard Alan. *The Revolution Is Now Begun: The Radical Committees of Philadelphia, 1765–1776*. Philadelphia: University of Pennsylvania Press, 1978.

Said, Edward W. *Culture and Imperialism*. New York: Knopf, 1994.

Samuels, Shirley. "Women, Blood, and Contract." *American Literary History* 20, nos. 1–2 (2008): 57–75.

Sanborn, Geoffrey. *Plagiarama: William Wells Brown and the Aesthetic of Attraction*. New York: Columbia University Press, 2016.

Sansay, Leonora. *Secret History; or, The Horrors of St. Domingo and Laura*. Ed. Michael J. Drexler. Peterborough, Ontario: Broadview, 2008.

Schmitt, Carl. *Political Theology: Four Chapters on the Concept of Sovereignty*. Trans. George Schwab. Chicago: University of Chicago Press, 2005.

Scott, Sir Walter. "*Emma*: A Novel." *Sir Walter Scott: On Novelists and Fiction*. Ed. Ioan Williams. 225–36. New York: Barnes and Noble, 1968.

Seaver, James A. *A Narrative of the Life of Mrs. Mary Jemison*. Intro. June Namias. Norman: University of Oklahoma Press, 1992.

Sellers, Charles. *The Market Revolution: Jacksonian America, 1815–1846*. New York: Oxford University Press, 1991.

Sheehan, Colleen A. *James Madison and the Spirit of Republican Self-Government*. New York: Cambridge University Press, 2009.

Sieminski, Greg. "The Puritan Captivity Narrative and the Politics of the American Revolution." *American Quarterly* 42 (1990): 35–56.

Silyn Roberts, Siân. *Gothic Subjects: The Transformation of Individualism in American Fiction, 1790–1865*. Philadelphia: University of Pennsylvania Press, 2014.

Slaughter, Thomas P. *Independence: The Tangled Roots of the American Revolution*. New York: Hill and Wang, 2014.

Smith, Adam. *The Theory of Moral Sentiments*. Amherst, Mass.: Prometheus, 2000.

Sommer, Doris. *Foundational Fictions: The National Romances of Latin America*. Berkeley: University of California Press, 1991.

Steinlight, Emily. "Dickens's 'Supernumeraries' and the Biopolitical Imagination of Victorian Fiction." *Novel: A Forum on Fiction* 43 (2010): 227–50.

Stout, Harry S. *The New England Soul: Preaching and Religious Culture in Colonial New England*. New York: Oxford University Press, 1986.

Stowe, Harriet Beecher. *Uncle Tom's Cabin or, Life Among the Lowly*. New York: Penguin, 1986.

Taylor, Alan. *American Revolutions: A Continental History, 1750–1804*. New York: W. W. Norton, 2016.

———. *William Cooper's Town: Power and Persuasion on the Frontier of the Early American Republic*. New York: Vintage, 1996.

Tawil, Ezra. *The Making of Racial Sentiment: Slavery and the Birth of the Frontier Romance*. New York: Cambridge University Press, 2006.

Tennenhouse, Leonard. "The American Richardson." *Yale Journal of Criticism* 12 (1998): 177–96.

———. *The Importance of Feeling English: American Literature and the British Diaspora, 1750–1850*. Princeton, N.J.: Princeton University Press, 2007.

Tocqueville, Alexis de. *Democracy in America and Two Essays on America*. Trans. Gerald E. Bevan. New York: Penguin, 2003.

Tölölyan, Khachig. "The Contemporary Discourse of Diaspora Studies." *Comparative Studies in South Asia, Africa, and the Middle East* 27 (2007): 647–55.

Tracy, Joseph. *The Great Awakening: A History of the Revival of Religion in the Time of Edwards and Whitefield*. Boston: Tappen and Dennet, 1842.

Trimpi, Helen P. *Melville's Confidence Men and American Politics in the 1850s*. Hamden, Conn.: Archon, 1987.

Tyler, Royall. *The Algerine Captive or, The Life and Adventures of Doctor Updike Underhill: Six Years a Captive Among the Algerines*. Ed. Caleb Crain. New York: Modern Library, 2002.

Vertovec, Steven, and Robin Cohen, eds. *Conceiving Cosmopolitanism: Theory, Context, and Practice*. New York: Oxford University Press, 2002.

Wallace, James D. *Early Cooper and His Audience*. New York: Columbia University Press, 1986.

———. "Race and Captivity in Cooper's *Wept of Wish-Ton-Wish*." *American Literary History* 7, no. 2 (1995): 189–209.

Warner, William B. *Protocols of Liberty: Communication Innovation and the American Revolution.* Chicago: University of Chicago Press, 2013.

Warren, Mercy Otis. *History of the Rise, Progress, and Termination of the American Revolution.* Boston: E. Larkin, 1805.

Watt, Ian. *The Rise of the English Novel: Studies in Defoe, Richardson, and Fielding.* Berkeley: University of California Press, 1957.

Watts, Duncan J., and Stephen H. Strogatz. "Collective Dynamics of 'Small World' Networks." *Nature* 393 (1998): 440–42.

Weiner, Annette B. *Inalienable Possessions: The Paradox of Keeping While Giving.* Berkeley: University of California Press, 1992.

White, Richard. *The Middle Ground: Indians, Empires, and Republics in the Great Lakes Region, 1650–1815.* New York: Cambridge University Press, 1991.

Wittgenstein, Ludwig. *The Blue and Brown Books: Preliminary Studies for the "Philosophical Investigations."* New York: Harper & Row, 1960.

Woloch, Alex. *The One vs. the Many: Minor Characters and the Space of the Protagonist in the Novel.* Princeton, N.J.: Princeton University Press, 2003.

Wood, Gordon S. *The Creation of the American Republic, 1776–1787.* Chapel Hill: University of North Carolina Press, 1998.

———. *Empire of Liberty: A History of the Early Republic, 1789–1815.* New York: Oxford University Press, 2009.

———. *The Radicalism of the American Revolution.* New York: Vintage, 1993.

Wroth, Lawrence. *The Book in America.* Ed. Lawrence C. Wroth and Rollo G. Silver. New York: R. R. Bowker, 1951.

Zagarri, Rosemarie. *The Politics of Size: Representation in the United States, 1776–1850.* Ithaca, N.Y.: Cornell University Press, 2010.

Index

affective event, 77, 121, 127, 133, 165, 176
affective fact, 45, 59, 217 n.13
Althusser, Louis, 40
The Ambassadors. See James, Henry
anamorphosis, 14, 159–83, 227–28 nn.2–3
Anderson, Benedict, 15, 77, 185–86, 213 nn.2–3; "Frameworks of Comparison," 3–5; *Imagined Communities*, 3–6, 186
Arendt, Hannah, 49, 73
Aristotle, 66, 140
Arthur Mervyn. See Brown, Charles Brockden
Articles of Confederation, 2, 47, 50, 52, 216 n.9
Austen, Jane, 10, 15, 20, 29–32, 34, 69–70, 103, 213 n.5, 215 n.13, 222 n.15; *Emma*, 18, 125; *Mansfield Park*, 167; *Northanger Abbey*, 69; *Persuasion*, 60, 214 n.4, 219 n.1; *Pride and Prejudice*, 8, 20–26, 30; *Sanditon*, 214 n.4; style, 18–30, 32, 219 n.7

Badiou, Alain, 119
Bakhtin, Mikhail, 63–65, 69; "Discourse in the Novel," 64–65; "Epic and Novel," 64; "Forms of Time and of the Chronotope in the Novel," 64, 219 n.3, 230 n.13
Balibar, Étienne, 75, 213 n.2, 216 n.5, 220 n.11
Balzac, Honorè de, 63
Barnum, P. T., 93
Barrè, Isaac, 187–88, 199, 211
Bentham, Jeremy, 131, 218 n.20, 220 n.13, 222 n.15
Bill of Rights, 57
Bird, Robert Montgomery, *Sheppard Lee*, 91, 109
Blackstone, Sir William, 44, 73, 225 n.4
Bonesana–Beccaria, Cesare, 35, 216 n.6
Boston Committee of Correspondence. *See* committees of correspondence

Boston Tea Party, 45–47
Brackenridge, Hugh Henry, 215 n.11; *Modern Chivalry*, 89
Bronte, Charlotte, 211
Bronte, Emily, 211
Brown, Charles Brockden, 8, 13, 20, 32, 34, 58–59, 71, 78, 109, 166, 171–72, 222 n.15, 228 n.1; *Arthur Mervin*, 23, 32, 77, 81, 88, 91, 108, 114, 128–29, 149, 167, 214 n.5, 215 n.14; *Ormond*, 88–89, 114; style of, 17–19, 23–27, 32, 129; *Wieland*, 114, 126–29, 140–42, 144, 148, 156
Brown, William Hill, *The Power of Sympathy*, 23, 60, 89, 114
Brown, William Wells, *Clotel*, 97–100, 105–9, 116, 121, 222–23 n.5, 223 n.7. *See also* passing
Bryant, William Cullen, 187
Buchanan, Mark, 124–25, 214 n.6, 225 n.8
Burr, Aaron, 143

captivity narratives, 108–9, 115, 167, 198, 209; Barbary captivity narratives, 60, 109–14, 116–17, 168, 223 n.8; Indian captivity narratives, 60, 109–11, 123, 142, 199, 201. *See also* Panther, Abraham; Riley, James; Rowlandson, Mary
Chase, Richard, 70–71
Chateaubriand, François-René, 195, 230 nn. 9, 12
Child, Lydia Maria, *Hobomok*, 148–57, 159–61, 163, 165
Clotel. See Brown, William Hill
Coercive Acts (1773), 44
committees of correspondence, 46, 47, 77
conduction, 103, 105
Conrad, Joseph, 70
Constitution, U.S., 3, 7, 34, 42–43, 50, 54, 56–60, 77–78, 217 n.10, 220 n.16

Acknowledgments

We want to thank Tim Bewes, Edward Dryden, Susan Stanford Friedman, J. Gerald Kennedy, Edward Larkin, Nancy Ruttenberg, Shirley Samuels, and Ezra Tawil for encouraging this project in its early stages. Philip Gould and Lloyd Pratt helped to tame and reference the argument. Warren Montag was invaluable in developing our thinking on Locke and Hobbes. Danuta Fjellestad, David Watson, and the American Studies Program at Uppsala University provided the ideal intellectual milieu for Armstrong to try out an early version of the book's argument, as did Rob Mitchell in organizing the symposium "The Biopolitical Imagination" at Duke University in spring 2015. Tennenhouse wants to thank the English Department at the University of Rochester for the opportunity to present sections of the manuscript on the occasion of the George Ford Memorial Lecture. We drew portions of Chapter 6 from "The Problem of Population and the Form of the American Novel," *American Literary History* 20, no. 4 (2008): 667–85, and portions of Chapter 9 from "Recalling Cora: Family Resemblances in *The Last of the Mohicans*," *American Literary History* (2015): 1–23. Both chapters are consequently indebted to Gordon Hutner's generosity and editorial prowess.

We are beholden to two groups here at Duke University for helping us to think outside the box on questions of novels and their history and theory: a group independent study with graduate students Stefan Waldschmidt, Hannah Rogers, and Gregory Brennen; and the faculty seminar on the contemporary novel, under the auspices of The Novel Project at Duke and funded by the Office of the Deans of the College. Our colleagues in this venture included Erdag Göknar, Roberto Dainotto, Anne Garréta, miriam cooke, Shai Ginsberg, Aarthi Vadde, Anne-Gaëlle Saliot, and Aimee Kwon. Anne Allison read an early version of the introduction.

Along with the completion of the manuscript, we owe its quality of argument to our dear friends Ellen Rooney and Khachig Tölölyan, who magically turned what might have been the toil of two summers' writing into material for wide-ranging, intricate, and often hilarious intellectual suppers. In that few indeed could endure such sustained arguments with either one of us, we feel extremely fortunate not only in these friends but also in each other.